T0180093

Lecture Notes in Computer Science 9756

Commenced Publication in 1973
Founding and Former Series Editors:
Gerhard Goos, Juris Hartmanis, and Jan van Leeuwen

More information about this series at http://www.springer.com/series/7412

Francisco José Perales · Josef Kittler (Eds.)

Articulated Motion and Deformable Objects

9th International Conference, AMDO 2016
Palma de Mallorca, Spain, July 13–15, 2016
Proceedings

 Springer

Editors
Francisco José Perales
UIB-Universitat de les Illes Balears
Palma de Mallorca
Spain

Josef Kittler
University of Surrey
Guildford
UK

ISSN 0302-9743   ISSN 1611-3349   (electronic)
Lecture Notes in Computer Science
ISBN 978-3-319-41777-6   ISBN 978-3-319-41778-3   (eBook)
DOI 10.1007/978-3-319-41778-3

Library of Congress Control Number: 2016943407

LNCS Sublibrary: SL6 – Image Processing, Computer Vision, Pattern Recognition, and Graphics

Printed on acid-free paper

This Springer imprint is published by Springer Nature
The registered company is Springer International Publishing AG Switzerland

Preface

The AMDO 2016 conference took place at the University of Balearic Islands, Palma de Mallorca, during July 13–15, 2016, sponsored by the AERFAI (Spanish Association in Pattern Recognition and Artificial Intelligence) and the Mathematics and Computer Science Department of the UIB. The event was also supported by important commercial and research sponsors, whose contributions are gratefully acknowledged. The main contributors were: VICOM Tech, Hasselt University, EDM (Expertise Cemtrum voor Digitale Media), iMinds, Disney Research, Nvidia Corporation and Juguetrónica S.L.

The subjects of the conference were motion of articulated objects in a sequence of images and models for deformable objects. The research goals in these areas are the understanding and automatic interpretation of the motion of complex objects in real-world image sequences and video. The main topics in these conference proceedings are: Advanced Computer Graphics and Immersive Videogames, Human Modeling and Animation, Human Motion Analysis and Tracking, 3D Human Reconstruction and Recognition, Multimodal User Interaction and Applications, Ubiquitous and Social Computing, Design Tools, Input Technology, Programming User Interfaces, 3D Medical Deformable Models and Visualization, Deep Learning Methods for Computer Vision and Graphics, and Multibiometrics.

The AMDO 2016 conference, a successor of the eight previous editions, has been consolidated as a European reference for symposiums in this research area. The main goal of the conference was to promote interaction and collaboration among researchers working directly in the areas covered by the main tracks of the conference. The focus was on new perceptual user interfaces and technologies emerging to accelerate the impact of the field on human-computer interaction. The new perspective of the AMDO 2016 conference was the strengthening of the relationship between the areas that share, as the key point, the study of the human body using computer technologies as the main tool. The conference included several sessions of oral papers and a tutorial. Moreover, the conference benefited from the contribution of the invited speakers whose talks addressed various aspects of the AMDO research area.

These invited speakers were: Prof. Josef Kittler (University of Surrey, UK), "3D Morphable Face Model and Its Applications"; Prof. Michael Bronstein, (University of Lugano, Switzerland/Intel Perceptual Computing, Israel), "Geometric Deep Learning"; Prof. Miguel Chover (University of Jaume I, Spain), "Democratizing Game Development."

July 2016   F.J. Perales
                                                                          J. Kittler

Organization

AMDO 2016 was organized by the Computer Graphics, Vision and Artificial Intelligence team of the Department of Mathematics and Computer Science, Universitat de les Illes Balears (UIB) in cooperation AERFAI (Spanish Association for Pattern Recognition and Image Analysis).

Executive Committee

General Conference Co-chairs

F.J. Perales	UIB, Spain
J. Kittler	University of Surrey, UK

Organizing Chairs

González M.	UIB, Spain
Mas R.	UIB, Spain
Jaume A.	UIB, Spain
Mascaró Oliver M.	UIB, Spain
Palmer P.	UIB, Spain
Manresa C.	UIB, Spain
Varona X.	UIB, Spain
Buades J.M.	UIB, Spain
Miró M.	UIB, Spain
Fiol G.	UIB, Spain
Moya G.	UIB, Spain
Delgado A.	UIB, Spain
Perales X.	UIB, Spain
Ramis S.	UIB, Spain
Escalera S.	University of Barcelona and Computer Vision Center, Spain

Program Committee

Abasolo, M.	Universidad Nacional de La Plata, Argentina
Aloimonos, Y.	University of Maryland, USA
Arellano, D.	Filmakademie, Germany
Bagdanov, A.D.	University of Florence, Italy
Baldassarri, S.	University of Zaragoza, Spain
Baumela, L.	Technical University of Madrid, Spain
Bowden, R.	University of Surrey, UK
Bronstein, M.	University of Lugano, Switzerland
Campilho, A.	University of Oporto, Portugal
Coll, T.	Universitat de les Illes Balears, Spain

Courty, N.	University of Bretagne Sud, France
Davis, L.S.	University of Maryland, USA
Del Bimbo, A.	University of Florence, Italy
Di Fiore, F.	UHasselt/EDM, Belgium
Dogan, S.	I-Lab, University of Surrey, UK
Dugelay, J.L.	Eurecom, France
Escalera, S.	UB, Spain
Fernández-Caballero, A.	CLM University, Spain
Fisher, B.	University of Edinburgh, UK
Flerackers, E.	LUC/EDM, Belgium
Flores, J.	Mar-USC, Spain
González, J.	CVC-UAB, Spain
González, M.	Universitat de les Illes Balears, Spain
Iñesta, J.M.	University of Alicante, Spain
Jaume, A.	Universitat de les Illes Balears, Spain
Kakadiaris, I.A.	University of Houston, USA
Komura, T.	IPAB-University of Edinburgh, UK
Mahmood, N.	Max Planck Institute, Germany
Manresa, C.	Universitat de les Illes Balears, Spain
Marcialis, G.L.	University of Cagliari, Italy
Mas, R.	Universitat de les Illes Balears, Spain
Matey, L.	CEIT, Spain
Medioni, G.	University of Southern California, USA
Minovic, M.	University of Belgrade, Serbia
Miraut, D.	Universidad Rey Juan Carlos, Spain
Moeslund, T.B.	University of Aalborg, Denmark
Orvalho, V.	University of Porto, Portugal
Pla, F.	Jaume I University, Spain
Radeva, P.	CVC-UB, Spain
Ramos, J.	University of Malaga, Spain
Roca, X.	CVC-UAB, Spain
Qin, H.	Stony Brook University, USA
Salah, A.A.	University of Boğaziçi, Turkey
Seron, F.	University of Zaragoza, Spain
Sigal, L.	Disney Research, USA
Susin, A.	Polytechnic University of Catalunya, Spain
Thalmann, D.	EPFL, Switzerland
Tavares J.M.	University of Porto, Portugal
Terzopoulos, D.	University of New York, USA
Ujaldón, M.	University of Malaga, Spain
Van Reeth, F.	LUC/EDM, Belgium

Sponsoring Institutions

Mathematics and Computer Science Department, Universitat de les Illes Balears (UIB)
Escola Politècnica Superior (UIB) - Universitat de les Illes Balears (UIB)
AERFAI (Spanish Association for Pattern Recognition and Image Analysis)
Ajuntament de Palma
BMN, Banco Mare Nostrum, S.A

Commercial Sponsoring Enterprises

VICOM-Tech S.A., www.vicomtech.es
EDM (Expertise Cemtrum voor Digitale Media), www.uhasselt.be/edm
Disney Research, www.disneyresearch.com
Nvidia Corporation, www.nvidia.es
Juguetrónica, www.juguetronica.com

Contents

Localized Verlet Integration Framework for Facial Models

Ozan Cetinaslan$^{(\boxtimes)}$ and Verónica Orvalho

Instituto de Telecomunicações and Faculdade de Ciências,
Universidade do Porto, Porto, Portugal
ozan.cetinaslan@gmail.com, veronica.orvalho@dcc.fc.up.pt

Abstract. Traditional Verlet integration frameworks have been successful with their robustness and efficiency to simulate deformable bodies
ranging from simple cloth to geometrically complex solids. However, the
existing frameworks deform the models as a whole. We present a Verlet integration framework which provides local surface deformation on
the selected area of the mesh without giving any global deformation
impact to the whole model. The framework is specifically designed for
facial surfaces of the cartoon characters in computer animation. Our
framework provides an interactive selection of the deformation influence
area by using geodesic distance computation based on *heat kernel*. Additionally, the framework exploits the geometric constraints for stretching,
shearing and bending to handle the environmental interactions such as
collision. The proposed framework is robust and easy to implement since
it is based on highly accurate geodesic distance computation and solving the projected geometric constraints. We demonstrate the benefits of
our framework with the results obtained from various facial models to
present its potential in terms of practicability and effectiveness.

Keywords: Facial animation · Physically-based animation · Deformable
bodies · Mesh deformation · Geodesic distance

1 Introduction

Creating appealing surface deformation of rigid and soft bodies has been always
a challenging problem for the area of computer graphics. The major reason is the
increase of the expectations for more realistic effects. In parallel to that theoretical approaches to create these effects have become complicated over many years
for gaining the life-like components. Although there exists sophisticated theories
which define physical laws for animation, the tendency of seeking the efficiency,
easy implementation and robustness is always the main goal during research.
Notable examples are Position-Based Dynamics (PBD) [15] and Nucleus [18],
which define objects as a particle system and particles in the system are related
with each other by geometrical constraints. During the simulations, each constraint is solved iteratively in a non-linear Gauss-Seidel form.

© Springer International Publishing Switzerland 2016
F.J. Perales and J. Kittler (Eds.): AMDO 2016, LNCS 9756, pp. 1–15, 2016.
DOI: 10.1007/978-3-319-41778-3_1

The proposed framework in this paper follows the similar approach as PBD. However, our framework is focused on the facial applications so we use the Verlet integration scheme from [10]. The velocities are stored in an implicit fashion instead of explicit and our main focus is more centered on the direct position manipulation.

Fig. 1. Demonstration of a simple sequence of the proposed framework on a humanoid character. The model includes 6798 vertices. After the collision detection only the assigned area from the heat method (blue painted) is deformed and the rest of the model remains same. (Color figure online)

PBD approaches are quite common for cloth, deformable solids and rigid body simulations. In these particular cases, the dynamic solvers give a global deformation to the object, because the forces or environmental impacts (such as collision) naturally influence the object as a whole. The most important feature of our framework is to create a local deformation area on the model according to the needs instead of running the simulation over the whole model (or object). Therefore, we pre-compute the geodesic distance from a selected center (vertex) to a desired range by using the heat method [6] and set-up a deformable soft area within the defined boundaries. After this operation, the specified deformable area has the geometric constraint properties from PBD and outside of the boundaries the model conserves its rigid behavior (see Fig. 1). This feature gives a significant benefit in terms of flexibility and control for deforming a desired region of a complex model such as face with a minor computational cost.

Our solution provides an expeditious approach for facial surface deformation which combines the projected geometric constraints from PBD and the heat method for the geodesic distance computation. In general, the physically-based facial rigging for deformation is a complicated and highly demanding process which is not the focus of this paper. We address the previously mentioned drawback of global deformation of the complex objects by allowing the determination of the deformable surface arbitrarily on the target model. Similar to the traditional PBD systems, our framework is controllable and retains the simplicity in terms of implementation.

2   Related Work

Almost three decades, physically-based methods have been an active research topic for solid deformations in the field of computer graphics. There exists valuable state of the art reports and courses on this subject such as [2, 16, 21]. Besides,

Bender et al. [3] presented a detailed state of the art report on position-based methods for solid simulations.

Foundation of the proposed framework is based on [10, 15, 18]. Jakobsen [10] presented the main idea behind rigid and soft body simulations in Hitman: Codename 47 game engine. He described Verlet integration scheme and direct position manipulation for deforming the rigid and soft bodies in detail based on constraints for interactive gaming. Müller et al. [15] offered the position based dynamics method which updates the velocities explicitly instead of an implicit velocity calculation and presented a fully general approach for projected constraints. Besides, Stam [18] explained the theory on projection of constraints in Nucleus system similar to position based dynamics method.

The earlier research work on deformable models dating back to the 80's, Terzopoulos [20] introduced the simulation of deformable solids by using the elasticity theory. Provot [17] offered to constrain the length of the spring in a mass-spring cloth simulation for preventing the over-stretching of the springs.

In following years, the research in the field was accelerated, Bridson et al. [5] used projection of constraints with an implicit/explicit time integration scheme and a novel contact collision method. Funck et al. [9] defined shape deformations by divergence free vector fields for realistic looking results with volume conservation and deformations do not include any self-intersections.

The geometric constraint projections have given a notable impact to the research, such as Bergou et al. [4] presented the Tracking process which uses the constraints to enhance the surface deformations with physically simulated details. Kubiak et al. [11] offered a real time thread simulation which computes the stretching, bending, torsion and provides output forces for haptic feedback. Müller et al. [12] proposed to speed up the traditional position based dynamics method with a multi-grid based approach by keeping the origins of constraint projections. Stumpp et al. [19] proposed an adaptive shape matching approach for cloth simulation which uses two different type of clusters for high stretching, shearing and low bending resistance.

In recent years, various techniques have focused on the quality and efficiency, for example, Müller and Chentanez [13] presented the wrinkle meshes for important details in cloth or skin surface of a character by attaching a higher resolution wrinkle mesh to the coarse mesh. Müller and Chentanez [14] proposed a method for rapidly simulate different types of objects by using oriented particles which include the rotation and spin as an additional information for traditional particle approaches. Deul and Bender [7] introduced the multi-layer model for physically-based skinning application by using oriented particles concept incorporating with the position-based constraint projection. Bender et al. [1] offered a simulation method based on continuum mechanics for solid deformation which focuses on physical effects such as elasto-plasticity, anisotropy or lateral contraction. Deul et al. [8] presented a position-based method for rigid bodies by solving the position constraints between rigid bodies.

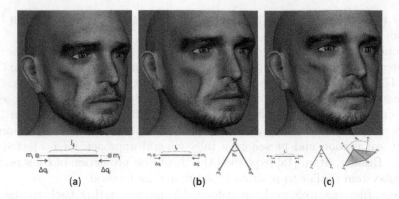

Fig. 2. Illustrations of the constraint projections and the deformations on the model surface: (a) represents only with the stretching constraint, (b) represents the coupling of stretching and shearing constraints, (c) represents the stretching, shearing and bending constraints all together

In the proposed framework, we have taken the advantage of the prior work on geometric constraints for position manipulation with an implicit velocity storage. In contrast to the previous research, we allow the arbitrary selection of the target area on the object for deformation by computing the geodesic distances with the heat kernel [6].

3   Position Verlet Integration

Verlet integration scheme is a refined numerical integration method for defining the equations of motion. Unlike the Euler's method [16], the main idea of this integration model is to exploit the central difference approximation to the second order differential equation shown as in Eq. (1):

$$\frac{\Delta^2 q_n}{\Delta t^2} = \frac{\frac{q_{n+1}-q_n}{\Delta t} - \frac{q_n-q_{n-1}}{\Delta t}}{\Delta t} \tag{1}$$

where Δt is the discrete time step, q_n is the position vector at t_n. Equation (1) is also the definition of acceleration ($a_n = \frac{\Delta^2 q_n}{\Delta t^2}$). According to Störmer-Verlet representation, the position updates are expressed as in Eq. (2):

$$q_{n+1} = 2q_n - q_{n-1} + a_n \Delta t^2 \tag{2}$$

In Eq. (2), right-hand side can be expressed as $q_n + (q_n - q_{n-1}) + a_n \Delta t^2$ which shows for the previous positions, velocities are stored implicitly [10]. We additionally introduce a simple damping parametrization to Eq. (2) to ensure our framework converge to a stable and plausible state. The modified version of Verlet integration in our framework can be written as in Eq. (3):

$$q_{n+1} = q_n + (q_n - q_{n-1})(1 - k_{damp}) + a_n \Delta t^2 \tag{3}$$

where k_{damp} is a damping parameter $k_{damp} \in [0,1]$. This slight modification to the original Verlet integration shown in Eq. (2) is a necessary step which adds an overall aesthetics to our framework. Although damping parameter causes our framework an insignificant payoff, it is important to note that to handle more stability, damping is a required factor for the smooth and pleasing responses in our framework especially during the collision response stage.

4   Description of Deformation Constraints

In this section, we would like to explain the system of interconnected components of the triangulated mesh (input model) which acts like particles in position-based dynamics approach [15]. Accepting the input model as a particle system can be considered as a set points which are connected with each other by links with an arbitrary order. This approach facilitates to operate on each component (such as vertices, edges, faces, etc.) of the input model in the proposed framework.

According to the basics of position-based dynamics [2,3,15], after the predicted positions of the particles are computed in the time integration scheme, these positions are altered by a technique to match up to a group of constraints C_i. The system of constraints is iterated by a Gauss-Siedel form which updates the positions one after another until all constraints are satisfied. During these updates, conservation of linear and angular momentum is a significant matter which is provided implicitly. The displacements of the particles are calculated with the solution of the following Eq. (4):

$$C(q + \Delta q) = 0 \tag{4}$$

where q is the concatenation of vectors which includes particle positions $q = [q_1, q_2, ..., q_n]^T$ and Δq is the correction displacements. Solving the constraint function, a 1st order Taylor-expansion is employed to approximate which is shown in Eq. (5):

$$C(q + \Delta q) \approx C(q) + \nabla_q C(q) \cdot \Delta q = 0 \tag{5}$$

Equation (5) is considered as an undetermined equation. Thus, the directions of the Δq is limited to the directions of the $\nabla_q C(q)$ to conserve both momentums, so with the consideration of the masses (m) of the particles, Δq becomes as in Eq. (6):

$$\Delta q_i = w_i \lambda \nabla_{q_i} C(q) \tag{6}$$

where $w_i = \frac{1}{m_i}$ and λ stands for the Lagrange multiplier which obtained by substituting Eq. (6) in Eq. (5):

$$\lambda = -\frac{C(q)}{\Sigma_j w_j |\nabla_{q_j} C(q)|^2} \tag{7}$$

With the Eqs. (6) and (7), the positions of the particles (or points) are updated after each constraint is computed. In our framework, 3 position constraints are chosen by following [18]: stretching (C_1), shearing (C_2) and bending (C_3) (see Fig. 2). The mathematical expressions of these constraints in the same order listed as follows:

$$C_1(q_{i,j}) = |q_j - q_i| - l_{ij} \tag{8}$$

$$C_2(q_{i,j,k}) = cos^{-1}(M_{ij} \cdot M_{ik}) - \gamma_{ijk} \tag{9}$$

$$C_3(q_{i,j,k,l}) = cos^{-1}(N_{ijk} \cdot N_{ijl}) - \theta_{ijkl} \tag{10}$$

where l_{ij} is the rest length of each edge between the points, γ_{ijk} is the rest angle between edges and θ_{ijkl} is the rest angle between each face primitive. Besides, M and N values are computed as follows:

$$M_{ij} = \frac{q_j - q_i}{|q_j - q_i|}$$
$$M_{ik} = \frac{q_k - q_i}{|q_k - q_i|} \tag{11}$$

$$N_{ijk} = \frac{(q_j - q_i) \times (q_k - q_i)}{|(q_j - q_i) \times (q_k - q_i)|}$$
$$N_{ijl} = \frac{(q_j - q_i) \times (q_l - q_i)}{|(q_j - q_i) \times (q_l - q_i)|} \tag{12}$$

The types of constraints may be increased depending on the requirements. In appendix A, we derive all the constraint from Eqs. (8), (9) and (10) for the gradients, Lagrange multiplier (λ) and the position corrections.

We would like to briefly mention about another constraint which is the easy collision response realization in the proposed framework. Collision handling is a key factor for the demonstration purposes of the position constraint behaviors (see Fig. 3). We have used the advantage of generic collision handling principles in [10,15] because of their stable comportment and smooth adaptation in our framework. Collision constraint is an inequality constraint [15,18] which makes it different from the aforementioned constraints. This unilateral behavior can be expressed as $C(q) \geq 0$. In our particular proposed case, we restricted the collision object as a simple sphere which can be considered as a small ball. According to [15], the constraint function for static collision is defined as $C(q) = (q - s_{col}) \cdot n_{col}$ where s_{col} is the surface penetration (or entry) point and n_{col} is the surface normal. Immediately after the intersection phase, the positions and velocities are updated along the direction of contact point normal at each time frame accordingly. Another interesting point is, the appropriate velocity updates are computed automatically during Verlet integration iterations. In our framework, collision constraint is also computed within the deformation loop of other mentioned position constraints unlike [15].

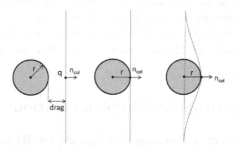

Fig. 3. Illustration of the collision constraint: Left: Before the contact, the straight line represents mesh surface with contact point. Middle: The moment of the contact, after dragging the collision object to the surface. Right: After the contact, the response of the surface with the continuous time.

5   Geodesic Distance Computation

Before applying the operations mentioned in Sects. 3 and 4, our framework allows the selection of the desired area of mesh which is influenced from the deformation. This gives a significant advantage in terms of locality, scalability and control (see Fig. 5). Because the direct position manipulation aspect of PBD approach occurs only inside the boundaries of the selected zone instead of the whole object. In this framework, we have chosen to compute the geodesic distances with the *"Heat Method"* which was presented in [6]. The heat method is an elegant approach to compute the geodesic distances which is based on Varadhan's formula from 1967:

$$d(x,y)^2 = \lim_{t \to 0} [-4t \log k_{t,x}(y)] \tag{13}$$

where $k_{t,x}(y)$ is the heat kernel. This formula basically explains the geodesic distance $(d(x,y))$ can be recovered by the heat transfer from point x to point y in a short time. The basic algorithm to the solution of finding the geodesic distances by using Eq. (13) is summarized as follows: at the beginning user-specified actions can be defined as giving the input as a triangulated facial mesh (M_f) to the framework and selecting any arbitrary vertex on the mesh $(v \in M_f)$.

After the vertex selection, heat method integrates the heat-flow $\dot{u} = \Delta u$ for a fixed time. After that, it evaluates the normalized gradient field $X = -\frac{\nabla u}{|\nabla u|}$. At last, it solves the Poisson equation to find the geodesic distance field (d) in Eq. (13) $\Delta d = \nabla \cdot X$.

Using the heat method for computing the geodesic distances gives some advantages. One advantage, it is highly flexible to be applied on various types of geometric discretization such as point clouds, polygonal surfaces, simplicial mesh, etc. Other advantage, heat method works with sparse linear systems, which can be prefactored once and solved subsequently many times with a notable speed. For further details on the heat method we refer the reader to the article of Crane et al. [6].

6   General Algorithm and Implementation

The proposed framework is specialized to operate on 3D facial models (triangulated mesh) which can be considered as mesh of particles. Each particle (or vertex) on the mesh has been assigned to some physical properties such as mass (m) and position (q). Velocities are omitted because they are already calculated implicitly. The other important data sets are acceleration (a) from the assigned force and time step size (Δt).

Based on the explanations in the previous sections and data sets, the overall procedure which performs the simulation underneath of our framework can be described by Algorithm 1.

Our framework has been implemented as a plugin for Maya 2016 using Python. Third party packages such as Scipy, Numpy and Scikits.sparse have been used for matrix operations. During the implementation, it should be noted that the cotangent computation of the heat method in lines (4)-(5) is performed independent from the cosine calculations in position constraints in lines (22), (24) of Algorithm 1. Another important parameter which we have not discussed yet, is the stiffness (k_{cons}) of the constraint. According to Müller et al. [15], a smooth alternative to apply stiffness parameter is to multiply the displacements by k_{cons}. We have followed the same direction and applied the stiffness parameter only to the bending constraint in line (24) of Algorithm 1. This straightforward calculation has been performed implicitly inside the bending constraint $\Delta q_{be} \leftarrow \Delta q_{be}(1-k_{cons})$ so it has not been reflected in Algorithm 1 just to prevent confusion.

---

input : A triangle mesh $M_f = (V, E, F)$ and a selected vertex $v_i \in V$
output: 2 step output: First, geodesic distances $d(v_i, v_j)$. Second,
      performing the simulation inside the boundaries of the geodesic
      distances

1   $assignBoundaries(v_i, Distance_{min}, Distance_{max})$;
2   **foreach** *face (F) in M_f* **do**
3   **foreach** *edge (E) in F* **do**
4   Compute the cotangent of the angles for Laplacian coordinates
            and areas of the faces by using: $\cot \alpha \leftarrow \frac{E_1 \cdot E_2}{|E_1 \times E_2|}$;
5   **end**
6      $A_i \leftarrow computeFaceArea(\alpha)$;
7 **end**
8 /* integrate the heat flow   */
9 $\dot{u} = \Delta u$;
10 /* evaluate the normalized gradient field   */
11 $X = -\frac{\nabla u}{|\nabla u|}$;
12 /* solve the Poisson equation   */
13 $\Delta d = \nabla \cdot X$;
14 /* simulate points(or vertices) (q) of the mesh inside the
      boundaries of the heat area   */
15 **foreach** $q \in d(v_i, v_j)$ **do**
16      $q_{n+1} \leftarrow q_n + (q_n - q_{n-1})(1 - k) + a_n \Delta t^2$;
17   **foreach** *specifiedIterations* **do**
18          $\Delta q_{col} \leftarrow collisionConstraint(q_{n+1})$;
19          $q_{n+1} \leftarrow q_{n+1} + \Delta q_{col}$;
20          $\Delta q_{st} \leftarrow stretchingConstraint(q_{n+1})$;
21          $q_{n+1} \leftarrow q_{n+1} + \Delta q_{st}$;
22          $\Delta q_{sh} \leftarrow shearingConstraint(q_{n+1})$;
23          $q_{n+1} \leftarrow q_{n+1} + \Delta q_{sh}$;
24          $\Delta q_{be} \leftarrow bendingConstraint(q_{n+1})$;
25          $q_{n+1} \leftarrow q_{n+1} + \Delta q_{be}$;
26   **end**
27      $updateOutputGeometry(q_{n+1})$
28 **end**

Algorithm 1. General Algorithm for the Proposed Verlet Framework

7 Experimental Results and Discussion

The examples in this section were performed on a 4-core Intel i7-2600 3.4 GHz machine with 8 GB of RAM and an nVidia GTX 570 GPU. We tested the proposed framework with different facial models using single threaded CPU implementation for Autodesk Maya 2016. In our experiments, the main purpose was the observation of how the surface responds during collision under different constraint types

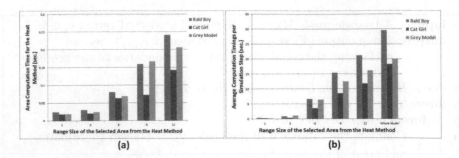

(a)   (b)

Fig. 4. Comparison chart of the heat method (a) and deformation (b) speeds between the example facial models. "Bald Boy" model includes 9562 vertices, "Cat Girl" model includes 6798 vertices and "Grey Model" includes 6720 vertices. (Color figure online)

and to verify the adaptation of the heat method for the developers who already use position-based dynamics.

Figure 4(a) presents the timings to create the soft area on the surface of the mesh. Both complexity of the mesh and the size of the area are the key factors for the run-time. In Fig. 5, the desired size of the area is illustrated in different ranges according to the provided chart in Fig. 4(a). The values clearly show the benefit of exact area selection with the heat method. Therefore in our experiments, we have kept the selection of the target area according to its natural size. Each region of the face is assigned to different size control parameters according to the proportions of the model structure. For example cheek region is slightly wider than chin but narrower than forehead.

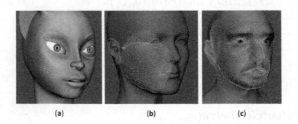

(a)   (b)   (c)

Fig. 5. Example illustration of the selected area by using the heat method with different ranges. (a) shows the area with 1 unit range on the "Cat Girl" (b) shows the area with 6 units range on the "Grey Model". (c) shows the area with 12 units range on the "Bald Boy"

Moreover, the performance of the simulation is strictly dependent on the size of the selected area. Graph from Fig. 4(b) summarizes the average timings according to the range of the selected area. During measuring these timings, we performed 2 iterations to the projected constraints and handled a single collision contact for the same scenario to all three models. An example case can be seen in Fig. 1. For our other experiments, we kept the range of the size control parameter for the selected area $distance_{max} \leq 3$ for better performance. The main advantage of the heat method can be observed clearly from the Fig. 4(b). If the simulation scenario does not require the deformation of the whole mesh, selection of the particular area on the mesh definitely increases the performance of the simulation.

Figure 2 shows the surface response after the collision. Each constraint computation is handled independently but the attachment of these constraints in the simulation loop of Algorithm 1 has increased the quality and smoothness of the surface. In Figs. 1 and 2 the damping parameter from Eq. 3 was kept as 0. However, in Fig. 6 the damping parameter varies between [0.3,0.9]. The relationship between damping value and vertex movements is inverse. Assigning the damping parameter to extreme high values causes the selected surface to react like a rigid body.

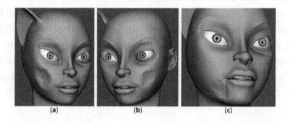

Fig. 6. "Cat Girl" was tested with different damping parameter. (a) $k_{damp} = 0.3$. (b) $k_{damp} = 0.6$. (c) $k_{damp} = 0.9$.

The proposed framework intrinsically operates over the surface of the mesh independent from the prearranged mechanics which lie beneath the model. Figure 7 demonstrates another case with a blendshape model which consists of 40 blendshape targets. We created a sample pose which corresponds to "pain" expression. Our framework performed a collision handling test over the surface of the same model. The existence of the rig elements does not interrupt the computations of the heat method and the position constraints. It is important to note that while the collision object contacts with the model, deformations are limited only inside of the soft area boundaries. Outside of the boundaries, model conserves its rigid behavior.

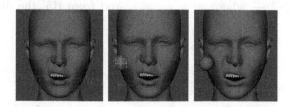

Fig. 7. "Grey Model" consists of 40 blendshape targets. After creating the pose, the interaction test was performed by using the proposed framework.

8   Conclusion

Our Verlet framework allows for the simulation of deformable surfaces on the selected area of the 3D mesh with a desired range. Underneath the framework, we used the recent heat method for the geodesic distance computations and Verlet integration scheme with the position based constraints projections. We have kept the paper as self contained as possible. Therefore, we summarized in detail the foundations of position based dynamics and heat method. We have presented its practical usage with different facial models under several conditions. The proposed framework has been specifically designed for the facial models while nevertheless it is particularly suited for the background characters in 3D animation. Furthermore, it is flexible not only to extend it to other application domains easily, but also it can nicely incorporate with the other existing position based dynamics frameworks.

While our framework is meant to be used to produce soft surfaces in a desired range on the entire mesh, one significant future direction would be the selection of the multiple areas with various ranges and assigning different position constraints on each of these selected areas. Moreover, speed optimization by using GPU or multi-core implementation is an advantageous key factor which we will pursue in future. Finally, we will investigate other techniques to improve our current framework in the direction of physically based skinning [7] for high quality effects.

Acknowledgments. This work is funded by Fundação para a Ciência e Tecnologia/FCT (SFRH/BD/82477/2011), POPH/FSE program, and is a result of the project NanoSTIMA Macro-to-Nano Human Sensing: Towards Integrated Multimodal Health Monitoring and Analytics, NORTE-01-0145-FEDER-000016, supported by Norte Portugal Regional Operational Programme (NORTE 2020), through Portugal 2020 and the European Regional Development Fund. We thank Xenxo Alvarez and Hiroki Itokazu for the models, Thomas Neumann and Timm Wagener for sharing their research material online. We also thank José Serra and Pedro Mendes for their support.

Appendix: Constraint Derivations

The constraint function for **stretching** from Eq. 8 is $C_1(q_{i,j}) = |D| - l_{ij}$ where $D = |q_j - q_i|$. The corresponding gradients are $\nabla_{q_i} C = -n$ and $\nabla_{q_j} C = n$ where $n = \frac{q_j - q_i}{|q_j - q_i|}$. After substituting the gradients to Eq. 7, the Lagrange multiplier becomes $\lambda = \frac{|q_j - q_i| - l}{|w_j + w_i|}$ where $w_i = w_j = 1$, and from [15] the final corrections are:

$$\Delta q_i = -\frac{1}{2}(|q_j - q_i| - l)(\frac{q_j - q_i}{|q_j - q_i|}) \tag{14}$$

$$\Delta q_j = +\frac{1}{2}(|q_j - q_i| - l)(\frac{q_j - q_i}{|q_j - q_i|}) \tag{15}$$

The constraint function for **shearing** from Eq. 9 is defined as $C(q_{i,j,k}) = cos^{-1}(D) - \gamma_{ijk}$, where $D = M_{ij} \cdot M_{ik}$ from Eq. 11. With $\frac{d}{dx}cos^{-1}(x) = -\frac{1}{\sqrt{1-x^2}}$, the corresponding gradients are obtained as follows:

$$\nabla_{q_i} C = -\frac{1}{\sqrt{1 - D^2}} \left(\frac{\partial M_{ij}}{\partial q_i} \cdot M_{ik} + M_{ij} \cdot \frac{\partial M_{ik}}{\partial q_i} \right) \tag{16}$$

$$\nabla_{q_j} C = -\frac{1}{\sqrt{1 - D^2}} \left(\frac{\partial M_{ij}}{\partial q_j} \cdot M_{ik} + M_{ij} \cdot \frac{\partial M_{ik}}{\partial q_j} \right) \tag{17}$$

$$\nabla_{q_k} C = -\frac{1}{\sqrt{1 - D^2}} \left(\frac{\partial M_{ij}}{\partial q_k} \cdot M_{ik} + M_{ij} \cdot \frac{\partial M_{ik}}{\partial q_k} \right) \tag{18}$$

After substituting the gradients to Eq. 7, the Lagrange multiplier becomes:

$$\lambda = -\frac{\cos^{-1}(M_{ij} \cdot M_{ik}) - \gamma_{ijk}}{|\nabla_{q_i} C|^2 + |\nabla_{q_j} C|^2 + |\nabla_{q_k} C|^2} \tag{19}$$

where $w_i = w_j = w_k = 1$. The corrections can be computed easily for the shearing constraint by substituting the gradients and Lagrange multiplier in Eq. 6. We use a middle step to demonstrate the calculations:

$$r_1 = -r_2 - r_3 \qquad r_2 = -\frac{q_i - q_k}{|q_j - q_i||q_k - q_i|} \qquad r_3 = -\frac{q_i - q_j}{|q_j - q_i||q_k - q_i|}$$

The general final correction for shearing constraint is:

$$\Delta q_{i,j,k} = -\frac{(\sqrt{1 - D^2})(\cos^{-1}(D) - \gamma_{ijk})}{|r_1|^2 + |r_2|^2 + |r_3|^2} r_{1,2,3} \tag{20}$$

The constraint function for **bending** from Eq. 10 is defined as $C(q_{i,j,k,l}) = \cos^{-1}(D) - \theta_{ijkl}$, where $D = N_{ijk} \cdot N_{ijl}$ from Eq. 12. According to [15] q_i is set to 0 ($q_i = 0$), with $\frac{d}{dx} \cos^{-1}(x) = -\frac{1}{\sqrt{1-x^2}}$, the corresponding gradients are obtained as follows:

$$\nabla_{q_i} C = -\nabla_{q_j} C - \nabla_{q_k} C - \nabla_{q_l} C \tag{21}$$

$$\nabla_{q_j} C = -\frac{1}{\sqrt{1 - D^2}} \left(\left(\frac{\partial N_{ijk}}{\partial q_j} \right)^T N_{ijl} + \left(\frac{\partial N_{ijl}}{\partial q_j} \right)^T N_{ijk} \right) \tag{22}$$

$$\nabla_{q_k} C = -\frac{1}{\sqrt{1 - D^2}} \left(\left(\frac{\partial N_{ijk}}{\partial q_k} \right)^T N_{ijl} \right) \tag{23}$$

$$\nabla_{q_l} C = -\frac{1}{\sqrt{1 - D^2}} \left(\left(\frac{\partial N_{ijl}}{\partial q_l} \right)^T N_{ijk} \right) \tag{24}$$

After substituting the gradients to Eq. 7, the Lagrange multiplier becomes:

$$\lambda = -\frac{\cos^{-1}(N_{ijk} \cdot N_{ijl}) - \theta_{ijkl}}{|\nabla_{q_i} C|^2 + |\nabla_{q_j} C|^2 + |\nabla_{q_k} C|^2 + |\nabla_{q_l} C|^2} \tag{25}$$

where $w_i = w_j = w_k = w_l = 1$. By following the form mentioned in [15], as a middle step, we take advantage of the following computations before finding the final corrections:

$$r_1 = -r_2 - r_3 - r_4 \tag{26}$$

$$r_2 = -\frac{q_k \times N_{ijl} + (N_{ijk} \times q_k)D}{|q_j \times q_k|} - \frac{q_l \times N_{ijk} + (N_{ijl} \times q_l)D}{|q_j \times q_l|} \tag{27}$$

$$r_3 = \frac{q_j \times N_{ijl} + (N_{ijk} \times q_j)D}{|q_j \times q_k|} \tag{28}$$

$$r_4 = \frac{q_j \times N_{ijk} + (N_{ijl} \times q_j)D}{|q_j \times q_l|} \tag{29}$$

The general final correction for bending constraint is:

$$\Delta q_{i,j,k,l} = -\frac{(\sqrt{1 - D^2})(cos^{-1}(D) - \theta_{ijkl})}{|r_1|^2 + |r_2|^2 + |r_3|^2 + |r_4|^2} r_{1,2,3,4} \tag{30}$$

References

1. Bender, J., Koschier, D., Charrier, P., Weber, D.: Position-based simulation of continuous materials. Comput. Graph. **44**, 1–10 (2014)
2. Bender, J., Müller, M., Macklin, M.: Position-based simulation methods in computer graphics. In: EUROGRAPHICS 2015 Tutorials (2015)
3. Bender, J., Müller, M., Otaduy, M.A., Teschner, M.: Position-based methods for the simulation of solid objects in computer graphics. In: EUROGRAPHICS 2013 State of the Art Reports (2013)
4. Bergou, M., Mathur, S., Wardetzky, M., Grinspun, E.: Tracks: toward directable thin shells. ACM Trans. Graph. **26**(3), 50:1–50:10 (2007)
5. Bridson, R., Marino, S., Fedkiw, R.: Simulation of clothing with folds and wrinkles. In: Proceedings of the 2003 ACM SIGGRAPH/Eurographics Symposium on Computer Animation (2003)
6. Crane, K., Weischedel, C., Wardetzky, M.: Geodesics in heat: a new approach to computing distance based on heat flow. ACM Trans. Graph. **32**(5), 152:1–152:11 (2013)
7. Deul, C., Bender, J.: Physically-based character skinning. In: Virtual Reality Interactions and Physical Simulations (VRIPhys) (2013)
8. Deul, C., Charrier, P., Bender, J.: Position-based rigid body dynamics. In: Computer Animation and Virtual Worlds (2014)
9. von Funck, W., Theisel, H., Seidel, H.P.: Vector field based shape deformations. ACM Trans. Graph. **25**(3), 1118–1125 (2006)
10. Jakobsen, T.: Advanced character physics. In: Proceedings of the Game Developers Conference, pp. 383–401 (2001)
11. Kubiak, B., Pietroni, N., Ganovelli, F., Fratarcangeli, M.: A robust method for real-time thread simulation. In: Proceedings of the 2007 ACM Symposium on Virtual Reality Software and Technology, pp. 85–88 (2007)

12. Müller, M.: Hierarchical position based dynamics. In: Workshop in Virtual Reality Interactions and Physical Simulation "VRIPHYS" (2008)
13. Müller, M., Chentanez, N.: Wrinkle meshes. In: Proceedings of the 2010 ACM SIGGRAPH/Eurographics Symposium on Computer Animation, pp. 85–92 (2010)
14. Müller, M., Chentanez, N.: Solid simulation with oriented particles. ACM Trans. Graph. **30**(4), 1–9 (2011)
15. Müller, M., Heidelberger, B., Hennix, M., Ratcliff, J.: Position based dynamics. J. Vis. Commun. Image Represent. **18**(2), 109–118 (2007)
16. Nealen, A., Müller, M., Keiser, R., Boxerman, E., Carlson, M.: Physically based deformable models in computer graphics. Comput. Graph. Forum **25**(4), 809–836 (2006)
17. Provot, X.: Deformation constraints in a mass-spring model to describe rigid cloth behavior. In: Graphics Interface, pp. 147–154 (1996)
18. Stam, J.: Nucleus: Towards a unified dynamics solver for computer graphics. In: 11th IEEE International Conference on Computer-Aided Design and Computer Graphics, CAD/Graphics 2009, pp. 1–11 (2009)
19. Stumpp, T., Spillmann, J., Becker, M., Teschner, M.: A geometric deformation model for stable cloth simulation. In: Workshop on Virtual Reality Interactions and Physical Simulation "VRIPHYS" (2008)
20. Terzopoulos, D., Platt, J., Barr, A., Fleischer, K.: Elastically deformable models. SIGGRAPH Comput. Graph. **21**(4), 205–214 (1987)
21. Witkin, A., Baraff, D.: Physically based modeling: Principles and practice. In: ACM Siggraph 1997 Course notes (1997)

Robot-Aided Cloth Classification
Using Depth Information and CNNs

Antonio Gabas, Enric Corona, Guillem Alenyà$^{(\boxtimes)}$, and Carme Torras

Institut de Robòtica i Informàtica Industrial CSIC-UPC,
C/Llorens i Artigas 4-6, 08028 Barcelona, Spain
galenya@iri.upc.edu

Abstract. We present a system to deal with the problem of classifying garments from a pile of clothes. This system uses a robot arm to extract a garment and show it to a depth camera. Using only depth images of a partial view of the garment as input, a deep convolutional neural network has been trained to classify different types of garments. The robot can rotate the garment along the vertical axis in order to provide different views of the garment to enlarge the prediction confidence and avoid confusions. In addition to obtaining very high classification scores, compared to previous approaches to cloth classification that match the sensed data against a database, our system provides a fast and occlusion-robust solution to the problem.

Keywords: Garment classification · Deep learning · Depth images

1 Introduction

Manipulation of garments, from a highly wrinkled state when they are on a pile to a completely folded state after proper manipulation, is a very challenging task. To enable such manipulation, complex perceptions are required to determine where to grasp, to recognize the type of garment when lying on a table or hanging from the robot hand, to determine the pose or some preferred grasping points, and later on to remove all the wrinkles and perform the necessary folding operations.

The process of isolation of the cloth piece from a pile was identified as one of the first tasks to be solved for laundry manipulation in a pioneer work by Kakikura et al. [1,3], where the authors separated and identified three different categories (shirt, pants, and towels) using some ad-hoc rules. The problem of grasping a unique garment from a pile has also been tackled by Monso et al. [8]. Where the authors describe the problem of grasping a single garment, as they showed that a naive grasping action executed at the topmost area of a pile can grasp more than one garment at the same time. The authors propose an algorithm where a robot uses a POMDP approach to decide a series of manipulations to increase the probability of grasping only one piece using very simple perceptions.

In this paper, we assume that the robot has already grasped one garment and the objective is to classify it into a category, even if the particular garment has

© Springer International Publishing Switzerland 2016
F.J. Perales and J. Kittler (Eds.): AMDO 2016, LNCS 9756, pp. 16–23, 2016.
DOI: 10.1007/978-3-319-41778-3_2

not been seen before. Similar to our setup, Kita *et al.* have proposed methods to estimate the state of a garment held by a robot. In a seminal work they used monocular views [4], and later they proposed to use depth data obtained using a stereo-rig [5]. Their idea was to pre-compute a database of deformable models and select the best fitting model. Afterwards, they used a second manipulator to change the garment shape and thus increase the recognition accuracy.

More recently, Willimon *et al.* [11] use a stereo rig to classify garments. In their method, the topmost garment of a pile is detected, and grasped using its geometric center. Successive regrasping operations are performed with the end-effector reaching down further until success. Then two images are taken (frontal and side) and the classification process is performed using four basic visual features.

A more elaborated alternative is to use complex feature descriptors. In this direction, Willimon *et al.* [12] explored the use of SIFT and FPFH, and Ramisa *et al.* [10] also compared these descriptors with a new descriptor named FINDDD. This descriptor combines color and depth information to find good candidates for grasping based on a measure of wrinkledness. These works use images of garments lying on a table, and thus are not able to take a second view to disambiguate.

Alternatively, Li *et al.* [6] propose to use a complete 3D model obtained by combining several views using KinectFusion. To obtain this model the robot must grasp and turn completely the garment. Then, 3D features are extracted. Wang *et al.* design specialized features based on coding the distances from the center of the model to its boundaries using cylindrical coordinates. Garments are then identified by matching against a 3-garment database with recognition rates of sweater 85 %, jeans 70 %, and shorts 90 %. Similar to our work, Mariolis *et al.* [7] propose to classify the garments using a Convolutional Neural Network (CNN) as a part of a more general approach. The initial training of the classification CNN is performed in a synthetic dataset and then a real dataset is used for re-training. The authors report an overall success ratio of 89 % over 3 different categories (shirt, pants and towels).

In this paper we propose a method capable of classifying the garment type from the first view, but also able to take advantage of more views in case of confusion by using a robot arm. We propose a Convolutional Neural Network able to perform a fast, robust to occlusions classification and we made the database publicly available. Additionally, we explore the idea of using partial views of the garment. The motivation behind this is that new depth cameras based on ToF sensors are designed to work in closer ranges and some garments, like trousers and unbuttoned shirts, do not fit in the field of view of the camera.

2   Method

The set-up for this system is depicted in Fig. 1, with a pile of clothes placed on a table. We use a Barrett's WAM robot arm for the manipulation of clothing items with a simple gripper, and a Creative Senz3D time of flight (ToF) sensor to capture depth images. ToF cameras (like Kinect ONE, Intel RealSense,

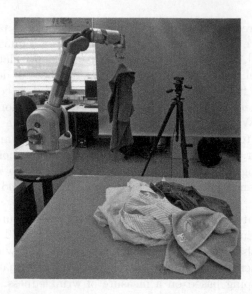

Fig. 1. Setup, including the robot manipulator, the Senz3D ToF camera, and the table where garments are lying.

and Softkinetic DS525/Creative Senz3D) are the new depth sensors that are gradually replacing structured light cameras (like Kinect and Xtion) in robotics applications. The main difference is that usually they are designed for closer distances, where the uncertainty of the depth measurements is lower.

We exploit this fact placing the garment close to the camera, at about 70 cm. The images we obtain reproduce with better definition the wrinkles and other details. However, the complete garment does not fit anymore in the image and thus the depth images acquired correspond to parts of the garment. By using only depth data, our system performs the recognition based on the garment's shape and not the texture. This allows the system to generalize between different clothes of the same category.

2.1 Dataset Generation

One of the main requirements to train a deep neural network is obtaining a big amount of data. In order to automatize the generation of training data, we programmed the WAM robot arm to repeatedly pick up a garment from a pile by random grasping points and place it in front of the depth camera. Once the robot has centered the garment in the camera image, it starts rotating the cloth item while the sensor captures a total of 12 images per revolution.

By continuous repetition of this operation, we generated a dataset containing 4 types of garments: "Shirt", "Trouser", "Towel" and "Polo" (see Fig. 2). We also detected if the garment felt during the scan. When this occurred, we labelled the empty image as "Nothing". This resulting in the final 5 categories, although the empty cases are not taken into account for the result scoring.

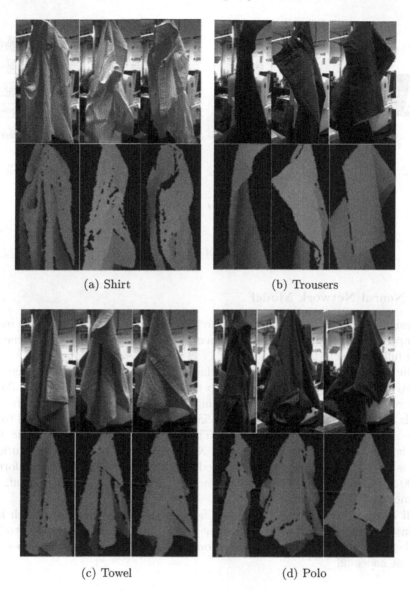

(a) Shirt   (b) Trousers

(c) Towel   (d) Polo

Fig. 2. Examples of color and depth images from the generated database (observe that the entire garment may not be visible). (Color figure online)

A total of 4272 depth images were obtained from the different categories[1]. 80 % of those images were used to train the network and the remaining 20 % to test it.

---

[1] http://www.iri.upc.edu/groups/perception/hangingCloth.

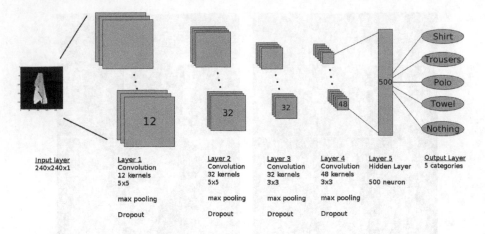

Fig. 3. Architecture of the designed CNN.

2.2   Neural Network Model

We designed a neural network with the architecture depicted in Fig. 3. The model is composed of 5 layers. The first 4 of them are convolutional layers and the last one is fully connected.

The network takes as input a single-channel 240×240 pixel depth image. The first layer consists of a convolution step with 12 kernels of 5×5 pixel followed by a two-fold sub-sampling or max-pooling layer. The second layer consists of 32 kernels of 5×5 pixels plus the max-pooling step. The third layer is equal to the previous one but with kernel size 3×3. The last convolutional layer has 48 3×3 sized kernels and a max-pooling step. Next, the output of the convolutional layer is reshaped as a 1D vector and fed as input to the hidden layer formed by 500 neurons. Finally, the output layer is a softmax layer that outputs the aforementioned 5 classes.

All layers are configured with Rectifier Linear Units (ReLUs), which have proven to be faster than their equivalent tanh units [9]. Also, at the output of each layer, a dropout is performed in order to avoid co-dependences between different nodes [2].

3   Experiments

3.1   Training

The CNN was trained using stochastic gradient descent with a learning rate of 0.05 and a batch size of 30. The initialization of the network weights is sampled randomly from a uniform distribution in the range [-1/fan-in, 1/fan-in], where fan-in is the number of inputs to a hidden unit (taking into account the number of input feature maps and the size of the receptive fields).

For the prevention of over-fitting we use L2 regularization and dropout: L2 Regularization is a very common form of regularization consisting in penalizing the squared magnitude of all parameters directly in the objective. That is, for every weight ω in the network, we add the term $\frac{1}{2}\lambda w^2$ to the objective, where λ is the regularization strength. We set the value of lambda to 0.0001.

We complement the L2 regularization with the Dropout technique. This method deactivates neurons during training with a probability lower than a given threshold. In this application we obtained good results with a value of 0.3. This prevents co-dependencies between different nodes.

3.2   Results

First, we test the network by feeding to it only one example (i.e. one depth image of a single view of the cloth piece). In this experiment, we obtain a 83 % global recognition rate. In the first column of Table 1 we show the recognition rates for all the cloth types in this experiment. As one would expect, the towel is the most distinctive object and thus is the best classified. The trousers, on the contrary, are the most misclassified ones. We also draw a confusion matrix in Fig. 4a to illustrate what elements are prone to be confused. As mentioned, the trousers are the element that causes more confusion. Besides the case where the trousers are involved, the polo-shirt case is the next that causes more confusion (it gets misclassified 2.8 % of the times). There is almost no confusion between polo and shirt because we used unbuttoned shirts that look quite different.

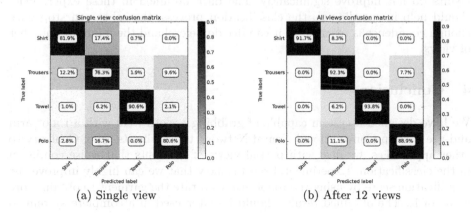

(a) Single view   (b) After 12 views

Fig. 4. Confusion matrices between the different categories.

For the next experiment we take into account all 12 views acquired during the rotation of the garment and select the type with more votes. We assume that similar views will not provide significant new information, so we use the most distant views: for the case of 2 images we use all pairs of opposite views, for the case of 3 images any triplet of equally-rotated and so on. Table 1 shows

Table 1. Recognition rate from 1 to 12 views.

	1	2	3	4	5	6	7	8	9	10	11	12
Shirt	81,9	91	85,4	92,4	87,5	93,8	90,3	95,1	93,8	95,1	91,7	91,7
Trousers	76,3	76,3	77,6	76,9	84,6	82,1	89,1	87,8	90,4	89,1	92,3	92,3
Towel	90,6	91,1	91,1	91,1	91,1	91,7	91,7	93,2	92,7	93,8	93,8	93,8
Polo	80,6	76,9	80,6	78,7	81,5	80,6	86,1	86,1	88,9	88,9	88,9	88,9
All	83	84,7	84,3	85,5	86,8	87,7	89,7	91	91,7	92	92	92

the results of taking into account from 2 to 12 images. As can be seen, the recognition rate is highly improved going from 83 % in the single-view case to a 92 % global score. This big improvement in the recognition is caused by the high recognition increase in the case of the trousers. The trousers are the biggest object in the dataset. Acquiring more views allows the system to disambiguate in complicated cases like partial views of the trousers. The confusion matrix for this scenario is shown in Fig. 4b. As stated, the confusion between items has drastically dropped. The classification in the polo-shirt case has also improved and now we only find misclassifications when the trousers are involved.

The rotation of the garment must be slow in order to avoid oscillation effects. Given that the CNN response is very quick, the cloth movement is the main time-consuming operation. In our tests we obtained up to 12 views of each garment. Other approaches like [7] capture 18 views. We show that after obtaining 9 views results do not improve significantly. The data obtained in these experiments should help in speeding-up the classification process: the robot can stop once enough confidence is reached, or it can decide beforehand the minimum number of views.

4   Conclusions

We have designed a system capable of grabbing a cloth item with a robot arm and use a Deep Convolutional Neural Network to classify its type. Contrary to other approaches, we deal with partial views of garments that cause confusion in the classification. Experimental results show that we can highly improve the classification score by using the robot arm to rotate the garment to obtain more views of it. The obtained results should be later used in a complete system to decide the number of required views and best viewing directions.

As a future work, the designed system can easily be scaled to work with more types of garments with just a few modifications and a bigger dataset. Another interesting topic for future avenues of research is to take the series of captures taken when the robot is rotating the same garment and input them to a Recursive Neural Network. This can help bringing temporal consistency between consecutive individual predictions.

Acknowledgments. This work was partially supported by the EU CHIST-ERA I-DRESS project PCIN-2015-147, by the Spanish Ministry of Economy and Competitiveness under project Robinstruct TIN2014-58178-R, and by the CSIC project TextilRob 201550E028.

References

1. Hamajima, K., Kakikura, M.: Planning strategy for unfolding task of clothes-isolation of clothes from washed mass. In: SICE Annual Conference, pp. 1237–1242 (1996)
2. Hinton, G.E., Srivastava, N., Krizhevsky, A., Sutskever, I., Salakhutdinov, R.R.: Improving neural networks by preventing co-adaptation of feature detectors. arXiv: 1207.0580, pp. 1–18 (2012)
3. Kaneko, M., Kakikura, M.: Planning strategy for putting away laundry-isolating and unfolding task. In: Symposium on Assembly and Task Planning, pp. 429–434 (2001)
4. Kita, Y., Kita, N.: A model-driven method of estimating the state of clothes for manipulating it. In: Workshop on Applications of Computer Vision, pp. 63–69 (2002)
5. Kita, Y., Neo, E.S., Ueshiba, T., Kita, N.: Clothes handling using visual recognition in cooperation with actions. In: International Conferenceon Intelligent Robots and Systems (IROS), pp. 2710–2715 (2010)
6. Li, Y., Wang, Y., Case, M., Chang, S.f., Allen, P.K.: Real-time pose estimation of deformable objects using a volumetric approach. In: International Conference on Intelligent Robots and Systems (IROS), pp. 1046–1052 (2014)
7. Mariolis, I., Peleka, G., Kargakos, A., Malassiotis, S.: Pose and category recognition of highly deformable objects using deep learning. In: International Conference on Advanced Robotics (ICAR), pp. 655–662 (2015)
8. Monsó, P., Alenyà, G., Torras, C.: Pomdp approach to robotized clothes separation. In: International Conference on Intelligent Robots and Systems (IROS), pp. 1324–1329 (2012)
9. Nair, V., Hinton, G.E.: Rectified linear units improve restricted Boltzmann machines. In: International Conference on Machine Learning, pp. 807–814. No. 3 (2010)
10. Ramisa, A., Alenyà, G., Moreno-Noguer, F., Torras, C.: FINDDD: A fast 3D descriptor to characterize textiles for robot manipulation. In: International Conference on Intelligent Robots and Systems (IROS), pp. 824–830 (2013)
11. Willimon, B., Birchfield, S., Walker, I.: Classification of clothing using interactive perception. In: International Conference on Robotics and Automation (ICRA), pp. 1862–1868 (2011)
12. Willimon, B., Walker, I., Birchfield, S.: A new approach to clothing classification using mid-level layers. In: International Conference on Robotics and Automation (ICRA), pp. 4271–4278 (2013)

Head-Pose Estimation In-the-Wild Using a Random Forest

Roberto Valle[1]([⊠]), José Miguel Buenaposada[2], Antonio Valdés[3], and Luis Baumela[1]

[1] Univ. Politécnica Madrid, Madrid, Spain
{rvalle,lbaumela}@fi.upm.es
[2] Univ. Rey Juan Carlos, Móstoles, Spain
josemiguel.buenaposada@urjc.es
[3] Univ. Complutense Madrid, Madrid, Spain
avaldes@ucm.es

Abstract. Human head-pose estimation has attracted a lot of interest because it is the first step of most face analysis tasks. However, many of the existing approaches address this problem in laboratory conditions. In this paper, we present a real-time algorithm that estimates the head-pose from unrestricted 2D gray-scale images. We propose a classification scheme, based on a Random Forest, where patches extracted randomly from the image cast votes for the corresponding discrete head-pose angle. In the experiments, the algorithm performs similar and better than the state-of-the-art in controlled and in-the-wild databases respectively.

Keywords: Head-pose estimation · Random forest · Real-time · In-the-wild

1 Introduction

Head-pose estimation is an essential preprocessing step for accurately inferring many facial attributes, such as age, gender, race, identity or facial expression. Additionally, head-pose is also used in other contexts, such as identifying social interactions [9,14], focus of attention [1,17], or gaze estimation [19].

By estimating the head-pose, we mean predicting the relative orientation between the viewer and the target head. It is usually parametrized by the head's yaw, pitch and roll angles [15]. Yaw and pitch rotations are the most informative for interpersonal communication and cause the largest appearance changes in the expressive parts of the face. For this reason, most approaches only estimate one of them or both. In this paper, we consider the problem of inferring the discretized yaw angle from a face image.

Facial pose estimation methods may be broadly organized into four groups. *Subspace* approaches assume that facial appearance changes, originated by pose variations, lie on a low-dimensional manifold embedded in a high-dimensional feature space [2,3,18]. Approaches based on *flexible models* fit a face deformable

© Springer International Publishing Switzerland 2016
F.J. Perales and J. Kittler (Eds.): AMDO 2016, LNCS 9756, pp. 24–33, 2016.
DOI: 10.1007/978-3-319-41778-3_3

model and estimate pose from the location of a set of landmarks [21]. Methods based on *classification* discretize the range of poses in a group of classes and solve the problem using a classification algorithm [20]. *Regression* approaches estimate a continuous function that maps facial features to the space of poses [8, 10,12,13,16].

Depending on the input data, methods may also be grouped into those using 2D images [2,3,10,12,13,16,18,20,21] or 3D range data [8]. Range data images provide direct shape information which facilitates head-pose estimation. On the other hand, RGB or gray-scale 2D images are more ubiquitous, but make pose estimation harder because of the lack of texture in some facial regions.

Traditionally, pose estimation algorithms have been evaluated in laboratory conditions, using databases such as Pointing-04 or CMU Multi-PIE [10–13,16]. Nowadays, the interest has shifted towards evaluations involving more realistic and challenging situations using databases such as AFLW or AFW with images acquired "in-the-wild" [18,21].

In this paper, we present a classification approach to estimate head-pose in-the-wild, based from 2D images, on a regression forest. Our algorithm obtains discrete orientation data from the predictions of a Random Forest. It achieves results close to the state-of-the-art in laboratory conditions evaluated using the Pointing-04 database, and better than Zhu and Ramanan [21] and Sundararajan and Woodard [18] on the challenging AFLW and AFW databases. Additionally, it performs in real-time at 80 FPS.

2   Head-Pose Classification Based on a Random Forest

We propose Random Forest in order to obtain a discrete head-pose estimation. The Random Forest is a well-known machine learning algorithm formed by an ensemble of T decision trees, whose prediction is determined by combining the outputs from all the trees. This technique has been successfully used in a variety of computer vision problems, such as classification, regression and probability density estimation [5]. Moreover, it is a widely used machine learning algorithm because it may be trained with a moderately low amount of information and the resultant ensemble can perform in real-time.

2.1   Patch-Based Channel Features

We use visual features as Dantone *et al.* [6]:

- From each training image, we randomly choose a set of square patches, $\mathcal{P}_i = \{(\mathcal{I}_i, h_i)\}$, where h_i is the pose and $\mathcal{I}_i$ is the appearance of the patch, described by a set of channels $\mathcal{I}_i = (\mathtt{I}^1, \dots, \mathtt{I}^k)$ [7]. $\mathtt{I}^\alpha$ are the values of channel α in image 1. The channels are gray-scale values, Sobel borders and 35 Gabor filters, some of which are shown in Fig. 1.
- Our features are the difference between the average values in two rectangles, R_1 and R_2, in a channel. We describe each of them with the pair of rectangle

coordinates within the patch boundaries in channel α, $\theta = (R_1, R_2, \alpha)$. So, given patch p and parameters θ, the feature value is:

$$f(p, \theta) = \frac{1}{|R_1|} \sum_{\mathbf{q} \in R_1} \mathbf{I}^\alpha(\mathbf{q}) - \frac{1}{|R_2|} \sum_{\mathbf{q} \in R_2} \mathbf{I}^\alpha(\mathbf{q}), \tag{1}$$

where $\mathbf{q} \in \mathbb{R}^2$ are pixel coordinates.

The splitting nodes (weak learners) of the decision trees in the Random Forest use these features to select the best channels and face subregions to regress the head-pose. Since we address the problem of head-pose in-the-wild, this kind of local feature will be more robust than an holistic approach.

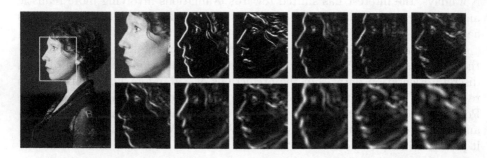

Fig. 1. Sample channels used in our approach.

2.2 Training Regression Forest

Following the standard Random Forest approach [4], we train each decision tree using a randomly selected set of patches from a random subset of the training faces. We optimize each weak learner by selecting the $\theta = (R_1, R_2, \alpha)$, from a random pool of candidates $\phi = (\theta, \tau)$, that maximizes the information gain

$$IG(\phi) = \mathcal{H}(\mathcal{P}) - \sum_{S \in \{L, R\}} \frac{|\mathcal{P}_S(\phi)|}{|\mathcal{P}|} \mathcal{H}(\mathcal{P}_S(\phi)), \tag{2}$$

where τ details the threshold over the feature value, $\mathcal{P}_L(\phi) = \{\mathcal{P}|f(P, \theta) < \tau\}$, $\mathcal{P}_R(\phi) = \mathcal{P} \backslash \mathcal{P}_L(\phi)$, and $\mathcal{H}(\mathcal{P}_S(\phi))$ is the class uncertainty measure. In our case, $\mathcal{H}(\mathcal{P}) = log(\sigma\sqrt{2\pi e})$ is the Gaussian differential entropy of the continuous patch labels.

2.3 Pose Estimation

Once we have trained the Random Forest for image patches, and given an input image I, we estimate the head-pose orientation as follows:

1. Detect face bounding box in I.
2. Resize bounding box to $W \times H$ pixels, denoted $\mathtt{I}_r$.
3. Compute α channels from $\mathtt{I}_r$.
4. Extract from $\mathtt{I}_r$ patches of size $N \times N$ with a stride of S pixels, denoted $\mathcal{P}$, the set of input patches.
5. For each patch $p_i \in \mathcal{P}$:
   5.1. For each tree t_j in the Forest (see Fig. 2):
      5.1.1. Input p_i to t_j.
      5.1.2. The leaf node of t_j reached by p_i provides a discrete distribution of the face orientation, $p(yaw|p_i, t_j)$.
   5.2. Compute the patch face pose distribution, $p(yaw|p_i) = \sum_j p(yaw|p_i, t_j)$.
6. Compute the final face pose distribution, $p(yaw|\mathtt{I}_r) = \sum_i p(yaw|p_i)$.
7. The final classification is the most probable discrete orientation in $p(yaw|\mathtt{I}_r)$ (see Fig. 3).

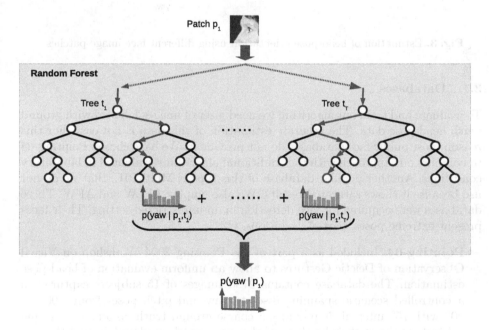

Fig. 2. Random Forest classification of an individual image patch. The result is a discrete probability distribution of the yaw angle.

3   Experiments

In this section, we compare different state-of-the-art approaches with our method on both controlled and in-the-wild databases.

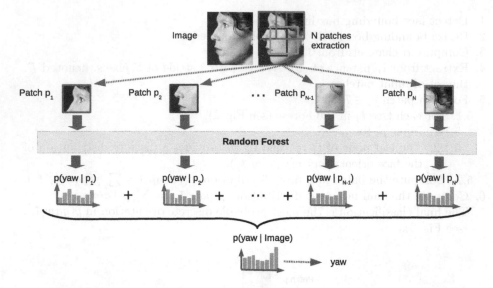

Fig. 3. Estimation of head-pose orientation using different face image patches.

3.1 Databases

To evaluate and train our algorithm we need a set of images labelled with ground truth head-pose data. The accurate estimation of this data is not easy. For this reason most public face databases do not provide it. We have chosen Pointing-04 to compare our approach with the traditional algorithms evaluated in laboratory conditions. Another popular database of this type is Multi-PIE, that we do not use because it shows saturated results. We also employ AFLW and AFW. These databases were acquired for face detection in an unrestricted setting. Their faces present extreme poses, partial occlusions, etc.

- **Pointing-04**. Included as a part of the Pointing 2004 Workshop on Visual Observation of Deictic Gestures to allow an uniform evaluation of head-pose estimation. The database contains 2790 images of 15 subjects captured in a controlled scenario spanning discrete yaw and pitch poses from $-90°$ to $90°$ with $15°$ interval. It provides a coarse ground truth obtained by asking subjects to direct their heads toward a set of markers placed around them in a room.
- **AFLW**. Provides an extensive collection of 25993 in-the-wild faces, with 21 facial landmarks annotated depending on their visibility. To the best of our knowledge, this is the largest public database providing face pose labels in an uncontrolled scenario. AFLW uses manually annotated landmarks positions to approximate face bounding box and coarse yaw, pitch and roll angles by fitting a mean 3D face using the POSIT algorithm.
- **AFW**. Consist of 250 images with 468 challenging in-the-wild faces. It is commonly used as a test set because of the low number of images. It provides

large variations in scales and discrete poses annotated for angular yaw from $-90°$ to $90°$ with $15°$ interval plus facial bounding box.

3.2 Evaluation

As in related work, we employ the mean absolute error (MAE) metric in order to evaluate and compare the algorithms. In addition, we also display results using a cumulative error distribution, representing the percentage of test faces with absolute error lower than some degrees of tolerance. Finally, since our approach provides discrete classification results, we also show the confusion matrix. In our implementation we discretize angular yaw in steps of $15°$ $\{-90°, -75°, -60°, -45°, -30°, -15°, 0°, +15°, +30°, +45°, +60°, +75°, +90°\}$, which let us to compare our results with other state-of-the-art approaches.

We follow a $90\%/10\%$ hold-out evaluation scheme to deduce the performance on Pointing-04 and AFLW databases. Given the small size of AFW, we only use it for testing. In this case we train the algorithm with a balanced data set from AFLW with 700 images per class.

3.3 Configuration of Random Forest Parameters

We use the same configuration of parameters for our algorithm in all experiments. We resize the face bounding box provided by each database to 105×125 pixels and assume the head to be the prominent object in the rectangle. The forest has $T = 20$ trees each of them trained from a randomly selected set of images equally distributed by yaw angle (9100 for AFLW and 2457 for Pointing-04). From each bounding box we randomly extract 20 patches of 61×61 pixels. The performance of the algorithm is quite sensitive to this parameter. A smaller patch would not capture enough information to predict the poses. On the other hand, a larger patch would provide an implementation more sensitive to occlusions.

Tree growing stops when the depth reaches 15, or if there are less than 20 patches in a leaf. We train each tree node by selecting the best parameters from a pool of $\phi = 50000$ samples obtained from $\theta = 2000$ different combinations of $[\alpha, R1, R2]$ and $\tau = 25$ thresholds. The maximum random size of the subpatches defining the asymmetric areas R1 and R2 is set to be lower than a 75% of the patch size.

For efficiency and accuracy reasons, we also filter out leaves with a maximum variance threshold set to 400. This limits the impact in the final prediction of non-informative leaves. A pair of crucial test-time parameters are the number of trees in the forest and the stride controlling the sampling of patches. We process only 1 out of 10 possible patches. Test values can be empirically tuned to find the desired trade-off between accuracy and temporal efficiency of the estimation process, making the algorithm adaptive to the constraints of different applications.

In Fig. 4 we show a set of sample results. Green and blue lines represent the estimated angular yaw and the ground truth respectively.

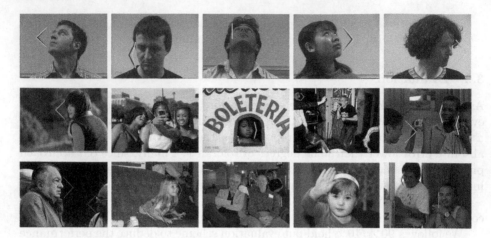

Fig. 4. Sample results for Pointing-04 (top), AFLW (middle) and AFW (bottom) databases. Green and blue lines indicate respectively pose estimation and ground truth yaw angle. (Color figure online)

3.4   Results

In the first experiment, we evaluate the performance of the proposed algorithm in Pointing-04, a database acquired in laboratory conditions. The results in Table 1 show that our proposal has a MAE close to the state-of-the-art in this database. Also, our classification accuracy, i.e. specific discrete head-pose angle properly labelled with the correct class, is behind the best. Nevertheless, in a 93.54 % of the cases the error in our approach is lower than 15°. All three approaches with better results use holistic HOG-based face features [10,12,13]. In this constrained context, this global feature is slightly more informative for estimating face pose than the set of local patches that we use in our approach. However, as we show in the sequel, local representations will have better performance in unconstrained situations.

Table 1. Head-pose estimation results in a constrained database.

Method	Pointing-04	
	MAE	Accuracy (0°)
Stiefelhagen [16]	9.5°	52.0 %
Haj *et al.* [12]	6.56°	67.36 %
Hara and Chellappa [13]	5.29°	-
Geng and Xia [10]	4.24°	73.30 %
Our method	**7.84°**	**55.19 %**

Table 2. Head-pose estimation results for in-the-wild databases.

Method	AFLW		AFW	
	MAE	Accuracy ($\leq 15°$)	MAE	Accuracy ($\leq 15°$)
Haj *et al.* [12]	-	-	-	78.7%
Zhu and Ramanan [21]	-	-	-	81.0%
Sundararajan and Woodard [18]	17.48°	58.05%	17.20°	58.33%
Our method	**12.26°**	**72.57%**	**12.50°**	**83.54%**

In the second experiment, we consider the unconstrained situations appearing in real-world situations. In Table 2 we present the results for AFLW and AFW databases. Here our approach achieves the best performance, both in terms of MAE and classification accuracy with an error less than 15°. These results proves the powerful representational ability of local features with a nonlinear regression algorithm. This approach can deal with challenging in-the-wild conditions, such as the presence of occlusions, illumination changes or facial expressions.

Our algorithm also outperforms its competitors in terms of computational requirements. It submits a frame rate of 80 FPS (12 ms per image) on an Intel Core i7 CPU processor at 3.60 GHz with 8 cores multi-threaded, 300 times faster than the second best approach, Zhu and Ramanan [21]. Sundararajan and Woodard [18] provides similar runtime performance, but with a clearly worse head-pose accuracy.

Finally, in Figs. 5 and 6 we compare the cumulative head-pose error of our approach against Sundararajan and Woodard [18]. We also present the confusion matrix of the yaw classification label. The colour intensity in it represent the percentage of success for each class (see bar on the right side). As can be seen, most incorrect predictions are adjacent to the proper ground truth angle. The largest errors are between ±90° and ±45° classes. This is reasonable, given the lower appearance variation between them.

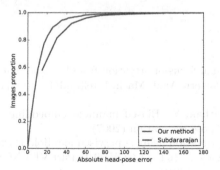 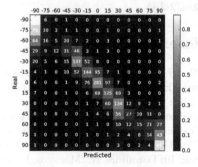

Fig. 5. Cumulative head-pose error distribution and confusion matrix for AFLW. (Color figure online)

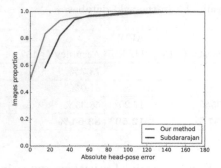 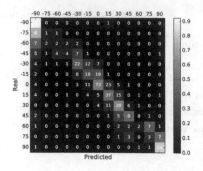

Fig. 6. Cumulative head-pose error distribution and confusion matrix for AFW. (Color figure online)

We developed our own open-source code of the previously described Random Forest classifier algorithm. All implementations could be made publicly available after submission.

4   Conclusions

In this paper, we have presented an algorithm to estimate head-pose yaw angle in unrestricted situations. To this end, we learn a regression forest from random face patches. We obtain the optimal splitting in each tree node according to the entropy computed from continuous yaw angle. The experimental evaluation shows that our algorithm performs best in the tests on unrestricted databases, proving the superior robustness of this local representation with the presence of occlusions, illumination changes, motion blur and exaggerated facial expressions.

Acknowledgements. The authors gratefully acknowledge funding from the Spanish Ministry of Economy and Competitiveness under project SPACES-UPM (TIN2013-47630-C2-2R).

References

1. Ba, S.O., Odobez, J.M.: Multiperson visual focus of attention from head pose and meeting contextual cues. IEEE Trans. Pattern Anal. Mach. Intell. **33**(1), 101–116 (2011)
2. Balasubramanian, V., Ye, J., Panchanathan, S.: Biased manifold embedding: a framework for person-independent head pose estimation (2007)
3. BenAbdelkader, C.: Robust head pose estimation using supervised manifold learning. In: Daniilidis, K., Maragos, P., Paragios, N. (eds.) ECCV 2010, Part VI. LNCS, vol. 6316, pp. 518–531. Springer, Heidelberg (2010)
4. Breiman, L.: Random forests. Mach. Learn. **45**(1), 5–32 (2001)
5. Criminisi, A., Shotton, J., Konukoglu, E.: Decision forests for classification, regression, density estimation, manifold learning and semi-supervised learning. Tech. Rep. MSR-TR-2011-114, Microsoft Research (2011)

6. Dantone, M., Gall, J., Fanelli, G., Gool, L.V.: Real-time facial feature detection using conditional regression forests. In: Proceedings of Conference on Computer Vision and Pattern Recognition (CVPR) (2012)
7. Dollar, P., Tu, Z., Perona, P., Belongie, S.: Integral channel features. In: Proceedings on British Machine Vision Conference (BMVC) (2009)
8. Fanelli, G., Dantone, M., Gall, J., Fossati, A., Van Gool, L.: Random forests for real time 3D face analysis. Int. J. Comput. Vis. 101(3), 437–458 (2013)
9. Gaschler, A., Jentzsch, S., Giuliani, M., Huth, K., de Ruiter, J., Knoll, A.: Social behavior recognition using body posture and head pose for human-robot interaction. In: Proceedings of the International Conference on Intelligent Robots and Systems (IROS) (2012)
10. Geng, X., Xia, Y.: Head pose estimation based on multivariate label distribution. In: Proceedings of the Conference on Computer Vision and Pattern Recognition (CVPR) (2014)
11. Gross, R., Matthews, I., Cohn, J., Kanade, T., Baker, S.: Multi-PIE (2008)
12. Haj, M.A., González, J., Davis, L.S.: On partial least squares in head pose estimation: how to simultaneously deal with misalignment. In: Proceedings of Conference on Computer Vision and Pattern Recognition (CVPR) (2012)
13. Hara, K., Chellappa, R.: Growing regression forests by classification: applications to object pose estimation. In: Fleet, D., Pajdla, T., Schiele, B., Tuytelaars, T. (eds.) ECCV 2014, Part II. LNCS, vol. 8690, pp. 552–567. Springer, Heidelberg (2014)
14. Marín-Jiménez, M.J., Ferrari, V., Zisserman, A.: Here's looking at you, kid: detecting people looking at each other in videos. In: Proceedings on British Machine Vision Conference (BMVC) (2011)
15. Murphy-Chutorian, E., Trivedi, M.M.: Head pose estimation in computer vision: a survey. IEEE Trans. Pattern Anal. Mach. Intell. 31(4), 607–626 (2009)
16. Stiefelhagen, R.: Estimating head pose with neural networks. In: Proceedings of International Conference on Pattern Recognition Workshops (ICPRW) (2004)
17. Subramanian, R., Yan, R.Y., Staiano, J., Lanz, O., Sebe, N.: On the relationship between head pose, social attention and personality prediction for unstructured and dynamic group interactions. In: Proceedings of International Conference on Multimodal Interaction (2013)
18. Sundararajan, K., Woodard, D.L.: Head pose estimation in the wild using approximate view manifolds. In: Proceedings of Conference on Computer Vision and Pattern Recognition Workshops (CVPRW) (2015)
19. Valenti, R., Sebe, N., Gevers, T.: Combining head pose and eye location information for gaze estimation. IEEE Trans. Image Process. 21(2), 802–815 (2012)
20. Wu, J., Trivedi, M.M.: A two-stage head pose estimation framework and evaluation. Pattern Recognit. 41(3), 1138–1158 (2008)
21. Zhu, X., Ramanan, D.: Face detection, pose estimation, and landmark localization in the wild. In: Proceedings of Conference on Computer Vision and Pattern Recognition (CVPR) (2012)

Spatiotemporal Facial Super-Pixels for Pain Detection

Dennis H. Lundtoft$^{(\boxtimes)}$, Kamal Nasrollahi,
Thomas B. Moeslund, and Sergio Escalera

Aalborg University, Aalborg, Denmark
dlundt10@gmail.com

Abstract. Pain detection using facial images is of critical importance in many Health applications. Since pain is a spatiotemporal process, recent works on this topic employ facial spatiotemporal features to detect pain. These systems extract such features from the entire area of the face. In this paper, we show that by employing super-pixels we can divide the face into three regions, in a way that only one of these regions (about one third of the face) contributes to the pain estimation and the other two regions can be discarded. The experimental results on the UNBC-McMaster database show that the proposed system using this single region outperforms state-of-the-art systems in detecting no-pain scenarios, while it reaches comparable results in detecting weak and severe pain scenarios.

Keywords: Facial images · Super-pixels · Spatiotemporal filters · Pain detection

1 Introduction

Remote monitoring of e.g. chronically ill patients is an increasing courtesy of physicians, as it improves quality of life of patients rather than staying at a hospital. However, remote extraction of data can be limited, as several measurements rely on direct contact, one such example is pain measurement using facial images.

Pain, which is a sensation of the body expressing itself to be damaged or in danger, is rather important for doctors to monitor. In long-durations it can heavily impact the quality of the life. A popular technique for measuring pain is patient self-report, however, for babies and for people in some illnesses, such as dementia, there are cases where the patient is unable to express their pain. To deal with such scenarios, automatic detection of pain using imaging techniques is of growing interest. The focus of this paper is therefore to develop a pain detection system using deformable facial images.

The rest of this paper is organized as follows: the related work in the literature on pain detection is reviewed in the next section in which the contributions of this work are also highlighted. Then, in Sect. 3 the proposed system is explained. The obtained experimental results are reported then in Sect. 4. Finally, the paper is concluded in Sect. 5.

© Springer International Publishing Switzerland 2016
F.J. Perales and J. Kittler (Eds.): AMDO 2016, LNCS 9756, pp. 34–43, 2016.
DOI: 10.1007/978-3-319-41778-3_4

2   Related Work

The current systems on pain detection can be divided into two groups: the first group only decides if a given image is of a painful case or not, while the second group besides clarifying the pain presence determines its level as well.

In the first group, the work of [3,14] use a Support Vector Machine (SVM) classifier that works with eigenfaces to see if there is any sign of pain in a given face of an infant or not. The work of [3] was then extended by [6], using a Relevance Vector Machine (RVM) instead of SVM as it introduces a degree of uncertainty to the estimated pain depending on the posterior probability score. The work of [11] utilized automatized facial expression analysis, using Gabor filters on eight different orientations and nine different spatial frequencies, to find facial Action Units (AU) to distinguish between faked and genuine pain. Then, these AUs were used to see if the pain was genuine of faked. AUs have also been used in [4] for defining a rule-based system for detecting the pain/no-pain case. Active Appearance Models (AAM) have been used in [2] to decouple shape and appearance parameters from digitized facial images, while in [15] Multiple Instance Learning (MIL) has been used to handle training data by putting it into bags, which are labeled as either positive, if the bag contains a positive instance, or negative, if no positive instances exist in the bag. Then, a Bag of Words (BoW) approach is used for determining whether a set of frames contains pain or not.

In the second group, where the focus is on determining the level of the pain, the work of [13], which is an extension of [2], uses facial expression analysis and 3D head pose to find the level of the pain. In [10], three feature sets of Facial landmarks (PTS), Discrete Cosine Transform coefficients (DCT) and Local Binary Patterns (LBP) are extracted from the facial images, and are then fed to a Relevance Vector Regression (RVR) to estimate the pain intensity. In [7] canonical appearance of the face using AAM are passed through a set of log-normal filters to get a discriminative energy-based representation of the facial expression which is then used to estimate the pain level. Inspired by this work, in [8] another energy-based system has been developed for pain estimation which uses spatiotemporal filters.

The proposed system in this paper is inspired by and based on the work of [8]. The current work treats pain as a spatiotemporal process and hence uses steerable filters to extract energy released from the face during the pain process. The main contributions of this paper can be summarized as below:

- As opposed to the work of [8] which uses facial landmarks to divide the face into three regions, we define our facial regions using super-pixels.
- It is shown in the experimental results that such a division of the face, results in three regions, similar to [8]. However, from these three regions, only one of them contributes properly to the pain estimation, as opposed to [8] which uses all the three regions. The proposed system therefore uses only this single facial region and the other two regions are discarded.
- Though the proposed system's performance in determining the level of the weak and severe pain is on average about 6 % lower than the performance of

[8], its performance in determining the no-pain scenarios is about 15 % better than the performance of [8]. These are further explained in the experimental results sections.

3   The Proposed System

The block diagram of the proposed system is shown in Fig. 1. Having an input video sequence, for each frame, first, the face region will be detected and segmented from the background. Then, using Procrustes analysis, warping, and image registration the facial images found in the video sequence are aligned. Then, super-pixels are formed for each face image. These super-pixels are used to define the region of interest from which spatiotemporal released energies are found and used for detecting pain. These steps are explained in the following sub-sections.

Fig. 1. The block diagram of the proposed system

3.1   Face Detection

Since the database employed in the experimental results, UNBC-MacMaster [12], already provides the positions of 66 facial landmarks in each frame, these landmark positions are used to detect the face. To do so, a Delauney triangulation is applied to the positions of the landmarks Fig. 2(a), which spans a facial mask as seen in Fig. 2(b). This mask is used to segment the face from the rest of the image Fig. 2(c).

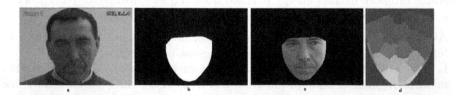

Fig. 2. Segmenting the face area and obtaining super-pixels: (a) Delauney triangulation of facial landmarks, (b) the spanned mask by the triangulation, (c) the segmented face, (d) and its SLIC super-pixel labels.

3.2   Facial Image Alignment

The segmented facial regions from the previous step, need to be aligned as they might have been displaced due to other sources of motion that are not directly related to pain, such as eye blinking and speaking motions. To do so, following [8], we utilize Procrustes analysis on the facial landmarks, followed by a piece-wise affine warping, and an inpainting step.

3.3   Super-Pixel Regions

Having aligned the facial images, for each face, we form a set of super-pixels. The super-pixels are determined using the spatial proximity and the color similarity between pixels. We use SLIC super-pixel algorithm of [1] for this purpose. SLIC super-pixels are clustered in a five-dimensional $[labxy]$ space, where $[lab]$ is a color vector in CIELAB color space and $[xy]$ is the pixel position. The SLIC algorithm uses two parameters: the first, the desired number of approximately equally sized super-pixels in the image K, meaning the approximate size of each super-pixels in an image with N pixels is $\frac{N}{K}$ pixels, the second, cluster centers at every grid interval $S = \sqrt{\frac{N}{K}}$. The onset super-pixel centers $C_k = [l_k a_k b_k x_k y_x]^T$ is initially set at the regular grid intervals S. Since the spatial extent of a super-pixel is S^2, it is assumed that pixels associated with a cluster center lie within a $2S \times 2S$ area of the center on the xy plane, which is the spatial search area of pixels associated to the cluster center. We use the same distance measure of [1] to calculate the distance between the pixels and centers of the clusters.

In order to locating center of a super-pixel on the edge of the super-pixel, and to reduce the chance of choosing a noisy pixel as the center, a gradient descent algorithm in a 3×3 neighborhood is performed from the initial position of the centers. The gradient of the image is calculated using both the color and intensity information as:

$$G(x,y) = \|I(x+1,y) - I(x-1,y)\|^2 + \|I(x,y+1) - I(x,y-1)\|^2 \quad (1)$$

where $I(x,y)$ is the lab vector at pixel position (x,y) and $\|,\|$ is the L_2 norm. The search radius around a cluster center is $2S \times 2S$. Pixels are initially associated with the nearest cluster center, and then a new cluster center is calculated using the average $labxy$ vector of all pixels belonging to the cluster. This is performed iteratively until a convergence is met. Lastly, connectivity is ensured by relabeling unconnected labels to largest neighboring cluster. The resulted super-pixels by the SLIC algorithm applied a detected face from Fig. 2(c) can be seen in Fig. 2(d).

Having found the super pixels, the next step is to use them to form some facial regions and use only those super-pixels/regions that are contributing to the pain detection and estimation. The state-of-the-art works of [8,9] use facial landmarks positions to divide facial area into three regions: region (1) eyes and eyebrows, region (2) nose and the cheeks, and region (3) mouth and lower part

Fig. 3. The three different regions formed on the facial image, Left: region 1 consisting of eyes and upper face. Middle: region 2 consisting of nasal area and cheeks. Right: region 3 consisting of mouth and lower face.

of the face (Fig. 3). The super-pixels are therefore grouped in a way that three such regions are formed.

Though three regions have been formed, as discussed in Sect. 4, when looking at the calculated spatiotemporal energy released from the different regions (discussed in the following subsection) it could be seen that region 2 was by far the most dominant and stable region when it came to pain detection, and that the other two regions often contributed a large amount of noise compared to the pain responses coming from them, hence it was decided to only use the second region, i.e., the nasal and cheek region, as a singular region of interest.

3.4 Spatiotemporal Features

Having detected the facial region of interest, we need to extract the features by which we detect the presence or absence of the pain and estimate its intensity. For this purpose, following [8,9] we use spatiotemporal energy released by the pixels. These are extracted by steerable filters. A steerable filter is an orientation-selective convolution kernel, which can be expressed by a linear combination of a set of rotated versions of itself. Such an oriented filter can be synthesized at any given angle, which is called steering. The steerable and separable filters are separated into basis filter banks, splitting them up into several sub-filters of lower complexity (i.e. separable). Once they are split up, the filters are multiplied by a set of gain maps, which adaptively control the orientation of the filters (i.e. steerable).

These filters have been proposed for extraction of spatiotemporal data in [5] in which the second derivative Gaussian filter G_2 and the Hilbert transform H_2 of the second derivative Gaussian are used. It is applied to a sequence of 2D images, utilizing the spatial domain x and y as well as the temporal domain t. The formulas for a two dimensional Gaussian $G(x, y)$ and its second derivative with regard to x is as:

$$G(x, y) = e^{-(x^2+y^2)} \quad G_2(x, y) = \frac{\partial^2 G}{\partial x^2} = (4x^2 - 2)e^{-(x^2+y^2)} \tag{2}$$

The Hilbert transform of the second derivative Gaussian is defined as:

$$H_2(x, y) = (-2.254x + x^3)e^{-(x^2+y^2)} \tag{3}$$

The second derivative Gaussian and Hilbert transform functions are then separated into basis functions, splitting the complexity of the functions up into fewer dimensions. For the second derivative Gaussian function six basis functions are needed for its separable set, as it has a 2nd order polynomial. The Hilbert transform requires 10 basis functions, as its polynomial is of 3rd order. The amount of basis functions required in the basis set is $M \geq \frac{(N+1)(N+2)}{2}$ where N is the order of the polynomial.

Next step is then to filter the image sequence $I(x, y, t)$ by G_2 and H_2 at the orientations $(\alpha, \beta, \gamma)_i$, which are found using the spherical coordinate orientation $(\theta, \phi = \frac{\pi}{2}, \rho = 1)$:

$$\alpha = cos(\theta)sin(\phi), \beta = sin(\theta)sin(\phi), \gamma = cos(\phi) \qquad (4)$$

In this work θ takes the value of the four main directions $\theta = [0, 90, 180, 270]$. Filtering the image sequences at these orientations with the G_2 and H_2 filters provides a local energy measure as:

$$E(x, y, t, \theta) = [G_2(\theta) * I(x, y, t)]^2 + [H_2(\theta) * I(x, y, t)]^2 \qquad (5)$$

which is normalized by the sum of the consort response, by:

$$\hat{E}(x, y, t, \theta) = \frac{E(x, y, t, \theta)}{\sum_j E(x, y, t, \theta_j) + \epsilon} \qquad (6)$$

where θ_j is all directions and ϵ is a bias constant to prevent numerical instability at small energy levels. Finally, the measured energy is filtered from too small values to remove likely noise, by:

$$\dot{E}(x, y, t, \theta) = \hat{E}(x, y, t, \theta) \cdot z(x, y, t, \theta) \qquad (7)$$

where Z_θ is a constant to threshold low energy values and equals to one if $\hat{E}(x, y, t, \theta) > Z_\theta$, otherwise it is zero.

The measured energy is the spatiotemporal features of the images, which can be used to determine the pain index. The calculated pixel-based energy is then collected in oriented histograms over the region of interest, using:

$$H(t, \theta_j) = \sum E(x, y, t, \theta_j) \qquad (8)$$

where H is the histogram of each respective direction θ_j which accumulates all the released energy.

Since muscles always move back to their resting position after exertion, the complimentary orientation histograms are combined. This means that histograms represent vertical or horizontal energy instead of a direction, by merging the histograms from complementary orientations together. We have observed that the the vertical motion is more active during pain expression while the horizontal motion of muscles were fairly docile. This indicates that horizontal motion is weak at determining pain, thus this work will only utilizes the histogram representing vertical motions.

3.5 Pain Intensity Estimation

Since in this work we only utilize one facial region (compared to [8] which uses all the three facial regions), and since we consider only vertical muscle (compared to [8] which considers both vertical and horizontal motion), the pain index is calculated as:

$$PI = \sum_{t=1}^{n} UD_t \tag{9}$$

where n is the number of frames and UD_t is the histogram of the vertical muscle motion. Several post-processing steps are then used on the pain index, this includes smoothing it using a moving average filter and normalizing it to the ground truth. Furthermore, the estimated pain index using Eq. 9 often has issues with negative values before and after a pain episode, resulting in lower values overall in the pain episode as it often starts from a negative value. In order to compensate for this discrepancy, we simply "lift" the pain episode by the most negative number before the pain episode, ensuring that it starts at 0 when the pain index starts ascending.

4   Experimental Results

In this section we first give the details of the employed database, then, we show why keeping only region 2 of Fig. 3 is enough for detecting the pain. Finally, we represent the obtained results and compare them against state-of-the-art similar systems.

4.1 The Employed Database

The proposed system, which has been implemented in MATLAB 2014b, has been tested on the UNBC-MacMaster shoulder pain database [12]. This public benchmark database consists of 25 different subjects, with varying gender and age, having shoulder pain performing both active and passive movements while being filmed. It consists of in total 200 video sequences, each with ground truth pain intensity values and positions of facial landmarks for each frame of the video sequences. From the 200 video sequences 79 consisted of sequences containing pain according to the ground truth. Therefore, only these 79 pain sequences were used when testing the system. The ground truth pain intensity values were calculated using the Facial Action Coding System (FACS) metric, which considers the severity of movement of key facial action units, from which a pain intensity is calculated on a scale of 0–16.

4.2 Why only Region 2?

When looking at the calculated spatiotemporal energy released from the different regions, it could be seen that region 2 is by far the most dominant and stable

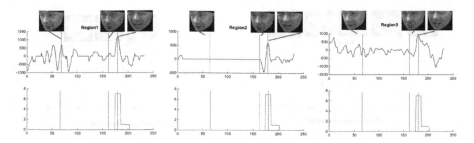

Fig. 4. The results of the proposed system from the three different facial regions (top) against the ground truth (bottom) for a pain sequence. The x and y axises of the plots show the time and the pain index, respectively.

region when it comes to pain detection, and that the other two regions often contributed a large amount of noise compared to the pain responses coming from them. Figure 4 shows an example where the first and third regions contained large amounts of noise along with the relevant frames, while the second region had less noise and mainly contained energy at the relevant frames indicated by the red lines. First frame is an example of where a frame results in noise due to non-pain related eye movement. Second frame is a "neutral" face and last showcased frame displays the subject's facial expression during pain. The drawback of only using region 2 is that people are vastly different, which also meant that the pain expression vary throughout the subjects. While some subjects mainly used cheeks/nasal area others expressed their pain by tightly closing their eyes or widely opening their mouth. This work chose to focus more on being autonomous, thus not requiring manual interaction to determine which region should be used which meant only the most stable region of interest is used, while this has been done manually in [8]. Hence, it was decided to only use the second region, i.e., the nasal and chin region, as a singular region of interest.

4.3 Results

Figure 5 shows the pain indexes obtained by the proposed system against the ground truth provided in the database for a simple (right) and a challenging (left) pain sequence. It can be seen from these figures that there are generally good agreement between the results of the proposed system and the ground truth.

The results of the proposed system are compared against two state-of-the-art pain detection systems of [7,8]. Following these two works, the obtained pain index of Sect. 3.5, is classified into three different categories of no pain (if the pain index is zero), weak pain (if the pain index is either 1 or 2), severe pain (if the pain index is larger than or equal three). The results using the UNBC-McMaster database is shown in Table 1. It can be seen from this table, that our system is not as good as [8] (on average about 6 % lower) in detecting the weak

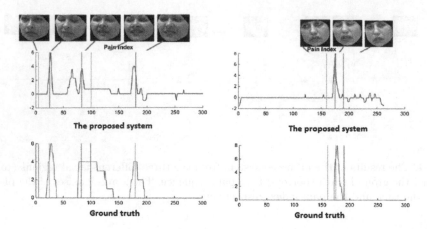

Fig. 5. The results of the proposed system against the ground truth for a simple (right) and a challenging (left) pain sequence.

and severe pain, but it is much better this system in detecting no-pain cases (about 15 % better on average).

Table 1. The results of the proposed system against two systems of [7,8] using the UNBC-McMaster database.

System	No pain [%]	Weak pain [%]	Severe pain [%]
The proposed system	**91.70**	55.75	63.4
[7]	65	36	70
[8]	77	**62**	**70**

5   Conclusion

This paper proposed a spatiotemporal approach for detecting pain from facial images using steerable filters. To discard parts of the face which contribute negatively to the pain estimation process, we divided the face into three regions using super-pixels. Then, only of the region that contributes properly to the pain estimation has been kept and used. The experimental results on public benchmark database of UNBC-McMaster show that the proposed system outperforms state-of-the-art similar systems in detecting no-pain scenarios, while it produces comparable results in detecting weak and severe pains.

References

1. Achanta, R., Shaji, A., Smith, K., Lucchi, A., Fua, P., Susstrunk, S.: Slic superpixels compared to state-of-the-art superpixel methods. IEEE Trans. Pattern Anal. Mach. Intell. **34**(11), 2274–2282 (2012)

2. Ashraf, A.B., Lucey, S., Cohn, J.F., Chen, T., Ambadar, Z., Prkachin, K.M., Solomon, P.E.: The painful face âĂŞ pain expression recognition using active appearance models. Image Vis. Comput. **27**(12), 1788–1796 (2009). visual and multimodal analysis of human spontaneous behaviour
3. Brahnam, S., Chuang, C.F., Shih, F.Y., Slack, M.R.: Machine recognition and representation of neonatal facial displays of acute pain. Artif. Intell. Med. **36**(3), 211–222 (2006)
4. Chen, Z., Ansari, R., Wilkie, D.J.: Automated detection of pain from facial expressions: a rule-based approach using aam. In: SPIE Medical Imaging, p. 831430. International Society for Optics and Photonics (2012)
5. Derpanis, K., Gryn, J.: Three-dimensional nth derivative of gaussian separable steerable filters. In: IEEE International Conference on Image Processing, 2005, ICIP 2005, vol. 3, pp. III-553–III-556, September 2005
6. Gholami, B., Haddad, W.M., Tannenbaum, A.R.: Agitation and pain assessment using digital imaging. In: Annual International Conference of the IEEE Engineering in Medicine and Biology Society 2009, EMBC 2009, pp. 2176–2179. IEEE (2009)
7. Hammal, Z., Cohn, J.F.: Automatic detection of pain intensity. In: Proceedings of the 14th ACM International Conference on Multimodal Interaction. pp. 47–52. ACM (2012)
8. Irani, R., Nasrollahi, K., Moeslund, T.B.: Pain recognition using spatiotemporal oriented energy of facial muscles. In: 2015 IEEE Conference on Computer Vision and Pattern Recognition Workshop, pp. 679–692 (2015)
9. Irani, R., Nasrollahi, K., Simon, M.O., Corneanu, C.A., Escalera, S., Bahnsen, C., Lundtoft, D.H., Moeslund, T.B., Pedersen, T.L., Klitgaard, M.L., et al.: Spatiotemporal analysis of RGB-DT facial images for multimodal pain level recognition (2015)
10. Kaltwang, S., Rudovic, O., Pantic, M.: Continuous pain intensity estimation from facial expressions. In: Bebis, G., Boyle, R., Parvin, B., Koracin, D., Fowlkes, C., Wang, S., Choi, M.-H., Mantler, S., Schulze, J., Acevedo, D., Mueller, K., Papka, M. (eds.) ISVC 2012, Part II. LNCS, vol. 7432, pp. 368–377. Springer, Heidelberg (2012)
11. Littlewort, G.C., Bartlett, M.S., Lee, K.: Automatic coding of facial expressions displayed during posed and genuine pain. Image Vis. Comput. **27**(12), 1797–1803 (2009)
12. Lucey, P., Cohn, J.F., Prkachin, K.M., Solomon, P.E., Chew, S., Matthews, I.: The UNBC-McMaster Shoulder Pain Expression Archive Database (2011). link to UNBC-MacMaster Shoulder Pain Database
13. Lucey, P., Cohn, J.F., Prkachin, K.M., Solomon, P.E., Chew, S., Matthews, I.: Painful monitoring: automatic pain monitoring using the unbc-mcmaster shoulder pain expression archive database. Image Vis. Comput. **30**(3), 197–205 (2012)
14. Monwar, M., Rezaei, S.: Appearance-based pain recognition from video sequences. In: International Joint Conference on Neural Networks, 2006, IJCNN 2006, pp. 2429–2434 (2006)
15. Sikka, K., Dhall, A., Bartlett, M.: Weakly supervised pain localization using multiple instance learning. In: 2013 10th IEEE International Conference and Workshops on Automatic Face and Gesture Recognition (FG), pp 1–8. IEEE (2013)

Type P63 Digitized Color Images Performs Better Identification than Other Stains for Ovarian Tissue Analysis

T.M. Shahriar Sazzad[1(✉)], L.J. Armstrong[1], and A.K. Tripathy[1,2]

[1] Edith Cowan University, Joondalup, WA, Australia
{t.sazzad,l.armstrong}@ecu.edu.au, amiya@dbit.in
[2] Don Bosco Institute of Technology, Mumbai, India

Abstract. Ovarian reproductive tissues are responsible for human reproduction. It is important for the pathology experts to perform routine examination for ovarian reproductive tissues to prescribe necessary treatments for women who face conceiving complications. Manual microscopic analysis is considered the best analysis approach for experts in the laboratory as existing scanning modalities do not provide satisfactory results for identification. Due to longer processing time and observation variability between experts computer based approaches have become popular as it can reduce time and can identify the reproductive tissue accurately. In this paper a new modified approach is presented and comparative analysis were performed using existing computer based approaches on three different types of digitized images acquired from microscopic biopsy slides. Proposed new modified approach indicates acceptable accuracy rate in comparison to manual identification approach to analyze ovarian reproductive tissues.

Keywords: Histopathology · Color digitized microscopic image · Image artifacts · Mean shift · Region fusion · Cluster · Ovarian reproductive tissues

1 Introduction

Women can face conceiving complication at any age however; most women who want to conceive their first child after the age of 35 face complications. Medical experts are unable to provide necessary treatments unless they know the ovarian reproductive tissue condition accurately. Pathology experts perform reproductive tissue analysis in the laboratory and provide detailed report to medical experts. Electronic scanning devices especially ultrasound scanner requires to visualize larger size tissue and expert interpretation is essential [1]. At present there is no suitable approach established to analyze ovarian reproductive tissue using ultrasound scanner for pathology experts. As an alternative option microscopic approach is considered as a viable option. Microscopic analysis is called the "gold standard" method [2] however; this process requires longer processing time, effort and has intra observation variability between experts [3]. Computer assisted approaches can reduce processing time and can be useful to experts in terms of accuracy rate [3, 4].

© Springer International Publishing Switzerland 2016
F.J. Perales and J. Kittler (Eds.): AMDO 2016, LNCS 9756, pp. 44–54, 2016.
DOI: 10.1007/978-3-319-41778-3_5

All tissues inside the ovary are colorless [5]. Experts use dyes or color chemicals to separate the tissues from one another and for easy analysis using microscopes [5]. From all different types of pathology microscopic biopsy slides type H&E (haematoxylin and eosin) is considered as most commonly used slide by experts [6]. Due to intensity variation issues associated with type H&E [7] ovarian reproductive tissue digitized images acquired from H&E biopsy slides are hard analyze [8, 9]. To overcome the problem with type H&E study by [6] mentioned type PCNA is a better choice. Additionally, it is possible to analyze digitized images of type PCNA which performs better than type H&E [6]. Research work of [10] also mentioned that type PCNA is a better stain than type H&E and type P63 could be another viable choice. Study of [11–13] incorporated type P63 for their work which also supports that type P63 is a better option than type H&E.

2 Related Work

Using type H&E and type PCNA most related research works were carried out for cancer cell, blood vessel or lymphatic vessels rather than ovarian reproductive tissue analysis. Only a few research works has been carried out to analyze ovarian reproductive tissues among which mostly are based on animal reproductive tissue analysis [1, 3, 6, 14, 15]. Human reproductive tissue analysis were carried out by [10] using type PCNA and by [11–13, 16] using type P63. All exiting above mentioned related research works using type PCNA and type P63 claimed automated approaches as no processing of calibration parameters are required for new test dataset. Only exception is the work of [10] which requires new calibration parameters for a new data set.

Although some research works already been carried out using type PCNA and type P63 and the results indicates that type PCNA and type P63 performs better than type H&E but no comparative analysis has been mentioned in compare to type H&E.

An example of 100× magnification for type H&E, type PCNA, type P63 non-counter-stained and counter-stained digitized images acquired from microscopic biopsy slides are shown in Fig. 1.

Cancer cells, blood vessels, lymphatic vessels and animal ovarian reproductive tissue are different in comparison to human reproductive tissues therefore; an approach developed for a specific type of tissue analysis is not appropriate for analyzing other tissue types or diseases [17].

Use of a filter during pre-processing stage, segmenting the regions using a segmentation approach and identify the regions of interest using appropriate features are considered as the basic medical image processing steps. Most related works considered grayscale threshold based segmentation approaches where type H&E and type PCNA digitized images were tested. For type P63 instead of grayscale threshold based segmentation approaches color image segmentation approaches were incorporated with correcting image artifacts issues [11–13, 16].

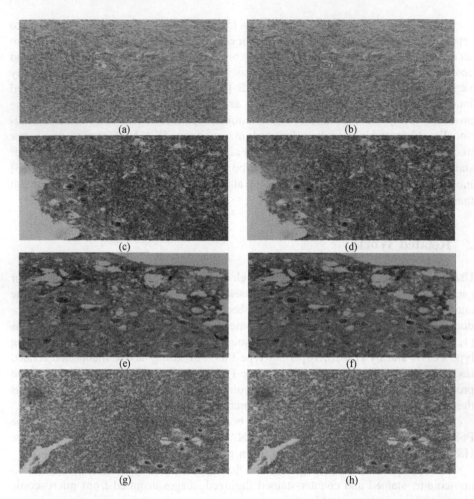

Fig. 1. (a) indicates type H&E, (b) indicates annotated image of (a), (c) indicates type PCNA, (d) indicates annotated image of (c), (e) indicates type P63 non-counter stained image, (f) indicates annotated image of (e), (g) indicates P63 counter stained image, (h) indicates annotated image of (g). Red marked regions are confirmed nucleus identified by 2 experts and blue marked regions are confirmed by at-least 1 expert. (Color figure online)

3 Proposed Method

This research study has proposed a new modified automated approach where type H&E, type PCNA and type P63 (non-counter and counter stained) digitized color images were used as research test images. A detailed flowchart of the proposed method for this study is shown in Fig. 2.

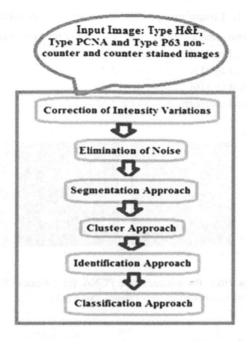

Fig. 2. Block diagram for automated identification process

3.1 Correcting Image Artifacts

Study of [11] reported that image artifact issues can be corrected using different methods but their proposed approach provides satisfactory results in comparison to other methods. Modification is made in this research study where instead of cell diameter, cell radius, microscopic eye piece magnification (10× according to expert) and image magnification were considered for morphological operation which indicates similar improved results proposed by [16] but saves almost half of the time for correcting image artifact issues shown in Fig. 3. Table 1 indicates processing time for all existing approaches.

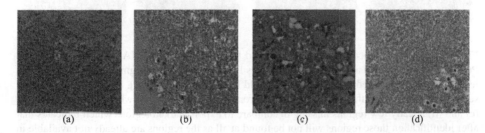

(a)   (b)   (c)   (d)

Fig. 3. (a) Indicates type H&E, (b) indicates type PCNA, (c) indicates P63 non-counter stained and (d) indicates P63 counter-stained corrected images using this study proposed modified approach

Table 1. Comparative processing to correct image artifacts

Correcting image artifact issue	Processing time (seconds)
Proposed by [11]	3.31
Proposed by [12]	3.22
Proposed by [16]	3.13
Proposed approach	1.51

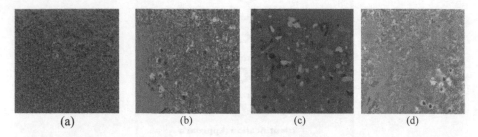

Fig. 4. (a) Indicates type H&E, (b) indicates type PCNA, (c) indicates P63 non-counter stained and (d) indicates P63 counter-stained filtered images using [11]

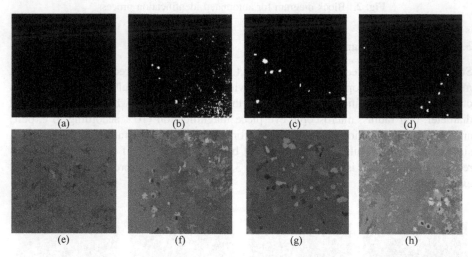

Fig. 5. (a) and (e) Indicates type H&E, (b) and (f) indicates type PCNA, (c) and (g) indicates P63 non-counter stained and (d) and (h) indicates P63 counter-stained segmented images. (a), (b), (c) and (d) are segmented images using threshold based approach of [10]. (e), (f), (g) and (h) are segmented image using this study proposed approach. For (a) there is no white region and for (b), (c) and (d) already few regions missing in compare to expert marked regions which indicates that after identification those regions will not be found at all as the regions are already not available in the image.

3.2   Filter Operation

Research study by [11] proposed mean-shift pixel based filter due to the fact that most used median filter for ovarian reproductive tissue analysis do not provide satisfactory results. Study of [11–13, 16] incorporated the approach of [11]. This research study also incorporated the approach of [11]. The results are shown in Fig. 4.

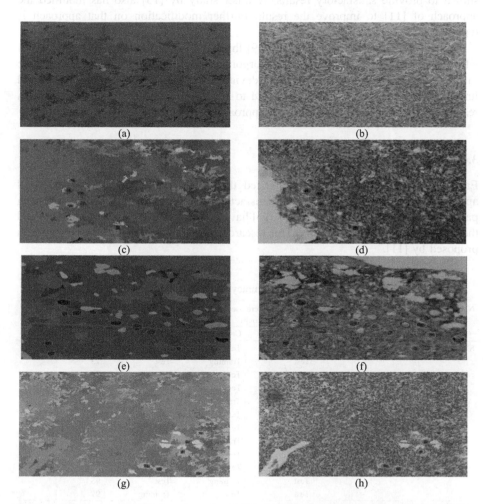

(a)   (b)

(c)   (d)

(e)   (f)

(g)   (h)

Fig. 6. (a) Indicates identified regions for H&E, (c) indicates identified regions for PCNA, (e) indicates identified regions for P63 non-counter stained and (g) indicates identified region for P63 counter stained image using this study proposed approach. (b) is an annotated result from experts for (a), (d) in an annotated image for (c), (f) is an annotated image for (e) and (h) is an annotated image for (g). Except H&E (1 region missed) for all other images this study was able to identify all the regions correctly without identifying any false regions.

3.3 Color Segmentation

Segmentation using threshold based approaches are generally suitable for gray-scale images but not suitable for color images [16]. As one of the automated approach proposed by [10] incorporated threshold based segmentation approach this research study tested with the same approach. Unfortunately the results were not satisfactory due to the fact that too many expert marked regions were missed after segmentation shown in Fig. 5. Study of [11] proposed a modified region fusion approach of [18] which had shown to provide satisfactory results. Another study by [13] also has modified the approach of [11] to improve the result. Further modification on that approach is reported in this research study.

Instead of using HSV color model [19] this study incorporated RGB color model where a median filter operation was incorporated on 3 different channel to preserve image edges. Minimization of standard deviation equation was used from [11] and finally region merging test was performed to get the segmented result. Segmentation results of this study proposed modified approach is shown in Fig. 5.

3.4 Cluster Approach

Early research study by [11] incorporated their modified mean-shift cluster based approach which was shown to provide satisfactory results without using any processing parameter. Research works by [11–13, 16] have incorporated the approach of [11] and their results were also satisfactory. This research study incorporated the same approach proposed by [11].

Table 2. Classification accuracy test using SVM classifier

Name	Stain type	150 images were used (50 in each group)			Classification accuracy %	
		Group 1	Group 2	Group 3		
SVM	H&E	Training	Test	Test	77	76
		Test	Training	Test	73	
		Test	Test	Training	78	
	PCNA	Training	Test	Test	90	90
		Test	Training	Test	89	
		Test	Test	Training	91	
	P63 (non-counter)	Training	Test	Test	95	95
		Test	Training	Test	97	
		Test	Test	Training	93	
	P63 (counter)	Training	Test	Test	96	97
		Test	Training	Test	98	
		Test	Test	Training	97	

Table 3. Comparative result for all automated approaches

Number of test images PCNA (403), P63 non-counter (493), P63 counter (475)	Image type	Avg. processing time (sec)	Precision	Recall
Proposed method	PCNA	24.37	0.91	0.90
	H&E	24.10	0.78	0.80
	P63 (non-counter stain)	**20.43**	0.95	0.96
	P63 (counter stain)	22.21	**0.96**	**0.97**
Automated approach [12]	PCNA	24.73	0.89	0.90
	H&E	24.40	0.75	0.78
	P63 (non-counter stain)	22.30	0.95	0.955
	P63 (counter stain)	22.83	0.96	0.965
Automated approach [11]	PCNA	24.55	0.90	0.89
	H&E	24.33	0.77	0.73
	P63 (non-counter stain)	22.57	0.96	0.95
	P63 (counter stain)	23.02	0.955	0.965
Automated approach [10]	PCNA	26.80	0.79	0.74
	H&E	25.11	0.61	0.64
	P63 (non-counter stain)	24.10	0.75	0.73
	P63 (counter stain)	24.46	0.76	0.77
Automated approach [13]	PCNA	24.37	0.875	0.91
	H&E	23.36	0.73	0.78
	P63 (non-counter stain)	22.12	0.945	0.96
	P63 (counter stain)	22.60	0.96	0.96

3.5 Identify Ovarian Nucleus

Studies by [10–13, 16] incorporated same features information for identification and have achieved satisfactory results. This research study also used the same feature information to identify the reproductive tissues. Study test image results are shown in Fig. 6.

3.6 Classify Identified Regions to Improve Accuracy

During identification some false regions were found which may or may not be reproductive tissues due to the fact that experts provided results are not always accurate as they have observation variability issues. Study of [13] used 3 most popular classification approaches among which SVM classifier was able to perform most accurate results. For this research study SVM classifier was incorporated to test the false regions. Table 2 indicates classification accuracy of false regions for this research study test images.

4 Experimental Results

This research study's proposed modified approach was able to identify ovarian reproductive tissues with an accuracy of 79 % for type H&E, 90 % for type PCNA, over 95 % for both type P63 non-counter and counter stained images. Among all existing approaches this study proposed approach was able identify more regions for type H&E although accuracy rate is less than 80 %. Table 3 indicates that type P63 is a better choice in compare to other types. Additionally, the study proposed approach requires less processing time in comparison to all other existing approaches.

5 Discussion and Conclusion

Automated approaches to analyze ovarian reproductive tissue were tested with the proposed modified approach in this study. After analyzing 4 different types of digitized images the result indicates that type H&E is not suitable as it does not maintain the "gold standard" criteria. Even using a classification approach the accuracy rate was not found satisfactory for type H&E. Type PCNA was able to maintain the "gold standard" criteria however type P63 counter and non-counter stained images have more accuracy rate than type PCNA. From Table 3 it is possible to say that type P63 performs better identification than other stains.

This study is novel due to the fact that this is the first published study where type H&E, type PCNA and type P63 digitized images were analyzed. Additionally classification test was performed to increase the accuracy rate. Three new modifications were proposed in this study which includes modification of intensity variation correction approach, modified segmentation approach and classification of identified false regions in comparison with [11–13, 16].

This study analyzed 12 different batches (300 images) of H&E images, 16 different batches (403 images) of type PCNA and 16 different batches (493 images) of type P63 non-counter and (475 images) counter stained images. This study proposed modified approach is fully automated as for new set of image batches calibration or processing parameter is not required. In future this research study will review and analyze other stains such as type Ki67 and type NIH if the images can be collected from the experts.

Acknowledgement. The authors would like to thank Assistant Professor and head of the department (Pathology) and domain expert Doctor Sadequel Islam Talukder (MBBS, M.Phil (Pathology), Shaheed Sayed Nazrul Islam Medical College, Kishoreganj, Bangladesh) for providing the test images, annotated images and necessary feature information.

References

1. Skodras, A., Giannarou, S., Fenwick, M., Franks, S., Stark, J., Hardy, K.: Object recognition in the ovary: quantification of oocytes from microscopic images. In: 2009 16th International Conference on Digital Signal Processing, pp. 1–6 (2009)
2. Kiruthika, V., Ramya, M.: Automatic segmentation of ovarian follicle using K-means clustering. In: 2014 Fifth International Conference on Signal and Image Processing (ICSIP), pp. 137–141 (2014)
3. Muskhelishvili, L., Wingard, S.K., Latendresse, J.R.: Proliferating cell nuclear antigen—a marker for ovarian follicle counts. Toxicol. Pathol. 33, 365–368 (2005)
4. Lamprecht, M.R., Sabatini, D.M., Carpenter, A.E.: CellProfiler™: free, versatile software for automated biological image analysis. Biotechniques 42, 71 (2007)
5. Magee, D., Treanor, D., Crellin, D., Shires, M., Smith, K., Mohee, K., et al.: Colour normalisation in digital histopathology images (2009)
6. Picut, C.A., Swanson, C.L., Scully, K.L., Roseman, V.C., Parker, R.F., Remick, A.K.: Ovarian follicle counts using proliferating cell nuclear antigen (PCNA) and semi-automated image analysis in rats. Toxicol. Pathol. 36, 674–679 (2008)
7. Mouroutis, T., Roberts, S.J., Bharath, A.A.: Robust cell nuclei segmentation using statistical modelling. Bioimaging 6, 79–91 (1998)
8. Bucci, T.J., Bolon, B., Warbritton, A.R., Chen, J.J., Heindel, J.J.: Influence of sampling on the reproducibility of ovarian follicle counts in mouse toxicity studies. Reprod. Toxicol. 11, 689–696 (1997)
9. Bolon, B., Bucci, T.J., Warbritton, A.R., Chen, J.J., Mattison, D.R., Heindel, J.J.: Differential follicle counts as a screen for chemically induced ovarian toxicity in mice: results from continuous breeding bioassays. Toxicol. Sci. 39, 1–10 (1997)
10. Kelsey, T.W., Caserta, B., Castillo, L., Wallace, W.H.B., Gonzálvez, F.C.: Proliferating cell nuclear antigen (PCNA) allows the automatic identification of follicles in microscopic images of human ovarian tissue. arXiv preprint arXiv:1008.3798 (2010)
11. Sazzad, T., Armstrong, L., Tripathy, A.: An automated detection process to detect ovarian tissues using type P63 digitized color images. In: 2015 IEEE 27th International Conference on Tools with Artificial Intelligence (ICTAI), pp. 278–285 (2015)
12. Sazzad, T., Armstrong, L., Tripathy, A.: An automated approach to detect human ovarian tissues using type P63 counter stained histopathology digitized color images. In: IEEE-EMBS International Conference on Biomedical and Health Informatics (BHI), pp. 25–28 (2016)
13. Sazzad, T., Armstrong, L., Tripathy, A.: A comparative study of computerized approaches for type P63 ovarian tissues using histopathology digitized color images. In: 10th International Conference on Computer Graphics, Visualization, Computer Vision and Image Processing (CGVCVIP 2016), Portugal (2016)
14. Sertel, O., Catalyurek, U.V., Shimada, H., Guican, M.: Computer-aided prognosis of neuroblastoma: detection of mitosis and karyorrhexis cells in digitized histological images. In: Engineering in Medicine and Biology Society 2009, EMBC 2009, pp. 1433–1436. Annual International Conference of the IEEE (2009)

15. Azevedo, L., Faustino, A.M., Tavares, J.M.R.: Segmentation and 3D reconstruction of animal tissues in histological images. In: Tavares, J.M.R.S., Natal Jorge, R.M. (eds.) Computational and Experimental Biomedical Sciences: Methods and Applications, pp. 193–207. Springer, Switzerland (2015)
16. Sazzad, T., Armstrong, L., Tripathy, A.: Type P63 non-counter stained digitized color images performs better identification than other stains for ovarian tissue analysis. In: 2016 20th International Conference on Information Visualisation (2016)
17. Matthews, J., Altman, D.G., Campbell, M., Royston, P.: Analysis of serial measurements in medical research. BMJ: Br. Med. J. **300**, 230 (1990)
18. Nock, R., Nielsen, F.: Statistical region merging. IEEE Trans. Pattern Anal. Mach. Intell. **26**, 1452–1458 (2004)
19. Sazzad, T.S., Islam, S., Mamun, M.M.R.K., Hasan, M.Z.: Establishment of an efficient color model from existing models for better gamma encoding in image processing. Int. J. Image Process. (IJIP) **7**(90), 90–100 (2013)

Interactive Acquisition of Apparel
for Garment Modeling

Fabian Di Fiore$^{(\boxtimes)}$, Steven Maesen, and Frank Van Reeth

Expertise Centre for Digital Media, Hasselt University - tUL - iMinds,
Wetenschapspark 2, 3590 Diepenbeek, Belgium
{fabian.difiore,steven.maesen,frank.vanreeth}@uhasselt.be
http://www.edm.uhasselt.be

Abstract. In this paper we set out to find a new technical and commercial solution to easily acquire garment models. The idea is to allow
the creation of new stylized versions of garments just by applying a new
print design. To this end we introduce a technique for model acquisition
of new apparel collection that makes use of a sparse set of guidelines
in combination with an intuitive graphical user interface allowing the
user to obtain and refine a 2D mesh representation of the garment. To
achieve a 3D-ish look of the virtual garment we employ structured light
scanning to automatically obtain a shadow map. We believe our system allows online clothes shops to bring new visual art into bespoke
clothing to make apparel products more valuable compared to other garments on the market. Furthermore it helps artists and designers in virtual
prototyping and visualizing garments with new print designs.

Keywords: Fashion · Garments · Creative fashion · Fabric rendering ·
Artist

1 Introduction

Motivation. The creative industry, fashion industry, and clothing and textile
branches in particular are undergoing meaningful changes as the clothing industry in the EU is in crisis — the production index is only 88.9 % of its value from
2010. Revival of the sector should arise from research and innovative solutions.
Besides clothes shops, designers are also affected by the crisis and have difficulties in supporting oneself from their artistic activity. One of the main reasons
for this situation is the lack of means to exploit their work effectively on the
market.

Our ambition is to support the clothing and textile industry and visual artists
by providing a new technical and commercial solution which enables easy acquisition of garments allowing to create new stylized versions as is illustrated in the
inset (Fig. 1).

© Springer International Publishing Switzerland 2016
F.J. Perales and J. Kittler (Eds.): AMDO 2016, LNCS 9756, pp. 55–65, 2016.
DOI: 10.1007/978-3-319-41778-3_6

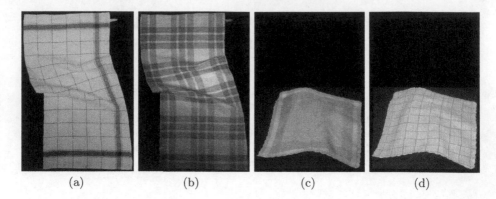

(a)   (b)   (c)   (d)

Fig. 1. (a) Picture of a real towel. (b) Stylized version now depicting a folk-checkered cotton kitchen towel. (c) Picture of a real handkerchief. (d) Virtual handkerchief rendered using a gold linen fabric.

Contribution. In this paper we present a system to capture apparel products and create new stylized versions by applying a new print design to the acquired garment models.

Our method allows online clothes shops to bring new visual art into bespoke clothing to make apparel products more valuable compared to other garments on the market. Furthermore it helps artists and designers in virtual prototyping and visualizing garments with new print designs.

Approach. In Sect. 2 existing techniques for model acquisition of apparel will be analyzed. We will also look at common CAD & Design tools and their limitations. In Sect. 3 we propose our new acquisition approach. Regarding model acquisition of new apparel collection we will pursue the use of a sparse set of guidelines in combination with an intuitive graphical user interface allowing the user to obtain and refine a 2D mesh representation of the garment. To aid the user in achieving a 3D-ish look of our 2D virtual garment, structured light scanning is employed to automatically obtain a shadow map. In Sect. 4 we look at the results of our implementation. Finally, Sect. 5 is our concluding section in which we also set the context for future work.

2   Related Work

In this section we discuss different methods for creating or acquiring garment models.

CAD and Design Tools. During recent years CAD and Design tools have been widely adopted in the fashion creative industry. These can be broken down into two categories: B2B (Business-to-Business) and B2C (Business-to-Consumer) tools.

B2B tools, mainly provided through CAD-CAM solutions, offer an improvement into "offline" design activities like virtual prototyping, draping and rendering fabrics. Most known CAD suppliers are Browzwear, Optitex, Assyst, Lectra, Gerber technology, Grafis and Dassault System. These tools are only intended to support designers working for branded manufacturers in order to express and formalize their creativity during product conceptualization and formalization.

B2C tools, mainly provided through e-commerce companies, offer consumers a made-to-order/made-to-measure configuration tool. Consumer needs are met by decomposing apparel items in style options (collar, cuff, etc.), functional options (type of material, e.g. cotton, wool, breathable materials, etc.) and size options, according to which the consumers can customize their garment. These proprietary tools, however, have specifically been developed for bespoke fashion. Examples of bespoke fashion companies are Tailorstore, Youtailor and Bivolino.

Model Acquisition of Apparel. Existing cloth modeling [1,2] involves a very expensive process in terms of computational cost due to the flexible nature of the cloth objects. One of the first attempts was made in the 1992 Disney feature animation movie Aladdin [3] for creating the Magic Carpet. Initially, a CGI model was about to be employed, however, as it looked too computerish [4] a hybrid (2D and 3D) approach was followed. That is, the magic carpet animation was entirely drawn on paper by a traditional animator after which a 3D model artist carefully laid out a geometric computer model over the drawn carpet.

A less labor-intensive approach is to make use of particle-based cloth simulation. Here, cloth is treated like a grid work of particles connected to each other by springs. Whereas for the geometric approach one has to take care manually for simulating the inherent stretch of a woven material, the particle-based technique inherently accounts for stretch (tension), stiffness, and weight by means of physical laws [5]. The resulting meshes, however, are very coarse making them less suitable for realistic texturing as self-shadowing effects and subtle wrinkles are often missing.

Specialized approaches (such as offered by Vidya [6] and Second Sight [7]) combine cloth simulation with 3D body scanning and CAD assistance in order to achieve a true 3D model. Others make (re)use of real photographs of humans and redress those digitally using painting tools (e.g., Lafayette recolors garments [8]) and post-production techniques (H&M draws or digitally pastes clothes on the models [9]). This demands a sophisticated setup and many (human) resources making it not feasible for SMEs or artists to implement.

Shape from texture is a computer vision technique where a 3D object is reconstructed from a 2D image [10]. Like human perception it is capable to realize patterns, estimate depth and recognize objects in an image by using texture as a cue [11].

Ebert et al. [12] use colour-coded cloth textures for retexturing virtual clothing. Together with range scans of the garment a parametrization of the mesh is obtained. The authors use a color code which has a limited size of codewords so that the pattern is repeated over the whole fabric. In this method the color code is only used for the parametrization of the surface.

Hilsmann and Eisert [13] employ optical-flow tracking to replace a textured region on a shirt by a virtual one. Their method uses a-priori knowledge of the color (i.e. green) of the shirt and the knowledge that there is a rectangular highly textured region an the shirt. A shading map is derived from the intensity of the uniform colored shirt after removal of the texture. These assumptions, however, make it impracticable for our case in which we deal with non-uniform colored and all-over textured garments.

The work by Guskov et al. [14] and Scholz et al. [15] is closest to our work. They use color-coded quad markers for the acquisition of non-rigid surfaces. Results for different surface types, including a T-shirt are presented.

3   Approach

In order to acquire new apparel collection coping with (subtle) wrinkles and shadows we want to employ a sparse set of guidelines giving the user intuitive control over obtaining and refining a mesh representation of how the piece of garment has been deformed. Users can identify these guidelines by means of an non-technical intuitive graphical user interface.

In a first step (as illustrated in Fig. 2(b)), lines (already present or specifically printed) on the undeformed cloth need to be identified. This can be easily accomplished by the user by drawing straight guidelines on top of these lines. The guidelines are then sampled (according to a user-defined measure) by our tool in order to create a 2D base mesh corresponding to the undeformed cloth (Fig. 2(c)). Using subdivision techniques a smoother mesh can be obtained (Fig. 2(d)) without the need for extra guidelines.

In a second step (as illustrated in Fig. 2(e–h), a deformed version of the base mesh is created in a similar way. As the initially parallel lines now are deformed, the user has to identify them by means of curved guidelines (in our case subdivision curves) instead of straight lines. The identification of the guidelines itself needs to happen in the same order as in the first step in order to end up with a one-to-one correspondence between the deformed and undeformed guidelines. When overlapping areas of fabric are involved such as permanent and stubborn creases users can also indicate extra features. For instance, a user explicitly could mark the start and end of a crease (for the undeformed as well as the deformed garment) indicating that the absolute distance between the marks needs to be preserved. This would prevent the final texture (in a later step) from unwanted stretching/squeezing behavior.

As in both steps the number of guidelines, order of identification and number of samples are the same, the base and deformed mesh will have the same topology. Consequently texture coordinates calculated for the base mesh can be transferred to the deformed mesh resulting in a visually realistic simulation of the deformed garment when applying a texture pattern on the virtual model (Fig. 2(i)).

Finally, to achieve a 3D-ish look of our 2D virtual garment, a shadow map and mask are applied yielding a realistic result (Fig. 2(j–l)).

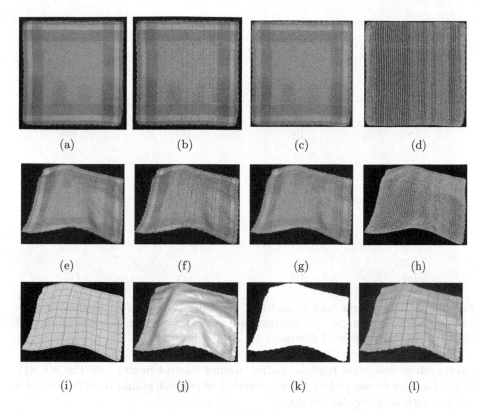

Fig. 2. Overview of our approach. (a–b) Original (ironed) handkerchief without/with user imposed guidelines. (c) 2D base mesh. (d) Base mesh after two subdivision steps. (e–f) Target wrinkled handkerchief without/with user imposed guidelines. (g) Target handkerchief with initial base mesh. (h) Target mesh after two subdivision steps. (i) Rendering of virtual handkerchief using a cotton-like fabric. (j–k) Shadow map and mask automatically derived using structured light scanning. (l) Final rendering of virtual handkerchief.

3.1 Guideline Creation

Concerning the identification of the deformed guidelines we employ subdivision curves (see Fig. 3) in combination with an intuitive graphical user interface. The idea is that you start by placing a simple polyline (by means of control points) on top of the deformed line which will act as a control curve (Fig. 3(a)). Then, by repeatedly refining (i.e. subdividing) this control curve a new and more smooth curve is created (see Fig. 3(b–d)). To this end, we employ the Chaikin scheme [16] in which each old vertex gives rise to two new vertices. When this process is repeated several times a very good approximation of the uniform quadratic B-spline curve defined by the original set of vertices is obtained.

Furthermore, in order to allow the user to further refine the curved guideline we extended the subdivision curves with an additional support of normal

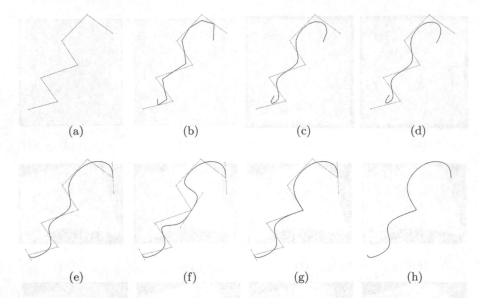

(a)   (b)   (c)   (d)

(e)   (f)   (g)   (h)

Fig. 3. Subdivision curve used as guideline. (a) Control curve. (b–d) Subdivided (consecutive subdivision steps). (e) Interpolating vs approximating. (f) Tension control (flatten). (g) Tension control (sharpen). (h) Resulting curve.

interpolation and local tension control around control points (see Fig. 3(e–g)). This allows us to use only a limited number of control points to fully control a subject with an irregular outline.

3.2   Shadow Map Generation

To achieve a 3D-ish look of our 2D virtual garment, a shadow map texture needs to be created which can be rendered on top of the current result. The idea is to generate this shadow map using a structured light scanning approach which involves projecting a known pattern of light onto a scene, and recovering scene geometry by analyzing distortions of the pattern [17].

Our setup consists of one projector and four cameras as shown in Fig. 4(top row). Starting from our target garment shape, reconstruction is accomplished by projecting structured light patterns which in turn are captured by our camera system. These patterns allow each projector pixel to be identified and triangulated resulting in a large point cloud (Fig. 4(a)). Next, a mesh of the object's surface is reconstructed using standard meshing techniques (Fig. 4(b)). Note that the reconstructed mesh approximates only the visual surface of the object rather than the whole object meaning it cannot be textured directly as missing depth information (e.g., wrinkles) will stretch/squeeze the texture nor can it be viewed from multiple angles. Since we are only interested in generating a shadow map, this poses no problem as the mesh still can be rendered from a light's perspective. The resulting depth buffer is then captured in a texture which will be used as a shadow map (Fig. 4(c)).

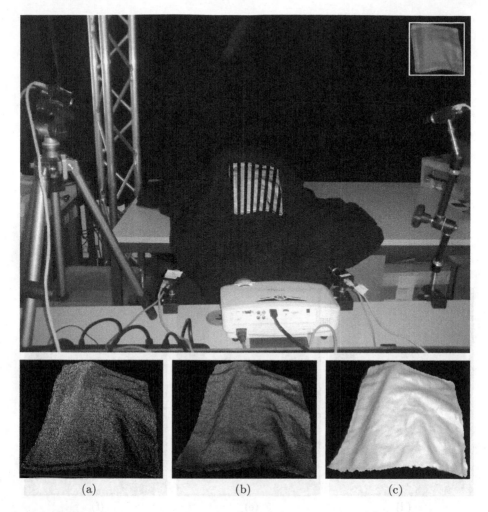

Fig. 4. Shadow map generation of a handkerchief (original is shown in the inset). Top row: Structured light scanning in action. Bottom row: (a) Identified 3D point cloud. (b) Reconstructed mesh of the visual surface. (c) Captured depth/shadow map as rendered from the light's perspective.

4   Results

In this section we look at some of the virtual garments created using our technique.

Figure 5 illustrates the acquisition process of a kitchen towel (being used in our institute's kitchen). Figures 5(a–b) depict the towel with user imposed guide lines respectively put flat on a table and naturally folded. Only 9 guidelines have been used and the existing striped pattern has been used as a visual guidance for laying out these guidelines. Figure 5(c) shows the employed shadow map and

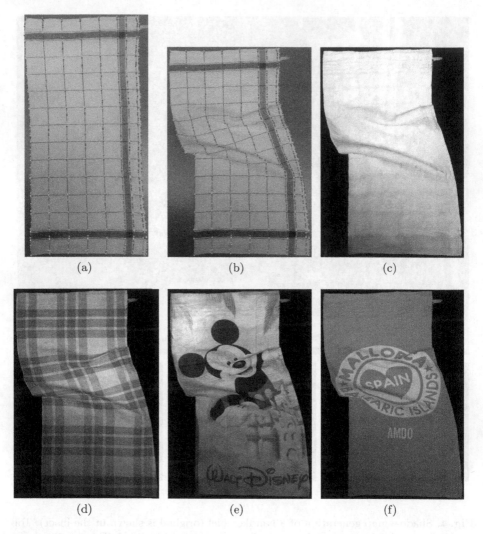

Fig. 5. Towel. (a) Original kitchen towel with user imposed guidelines. (b) Target folded towel with user adjusted guidelines. (c) Shadow map and mask (combined into one image) derived using standard image-processing algorithms. (d–f) Renderings using different textures: (d) folk-checkered cotton kitchen towel, (e) kids' bath towel ©Disney Enterprises, (f) AMDO beach towel.

mask combined into one image. By employing assorted textures various kinds of towels can be created: (d) a folk-checkered cotton kitchen towel, (e) a kids' bath towel, and (f) an AMDO beach towel.

Figure 6 illustrates the acquisition process of a handkerchief. Figure 6(a–b) respectively depict an ironed handkerchief as well as a wrinkled version together with user imposed guidelines. In this case 18 guidelines have been laid out on the existing striped fabric. Figure 6(c) shows the automatically derived shadow

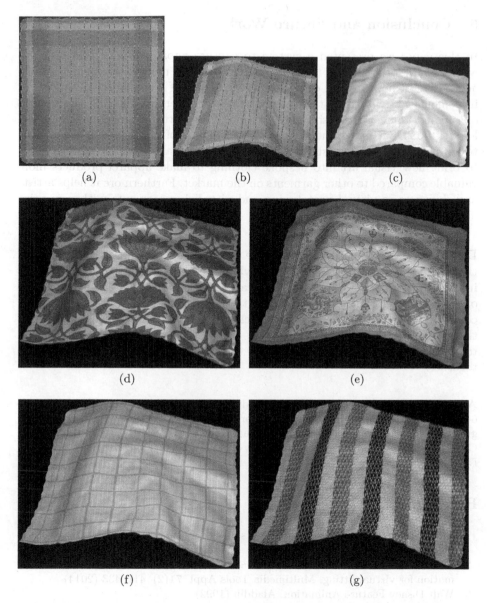

Fig. 6. Handkerchief. (a) Original ironed handkerchief with user imposed guidelines. (b) Target wrinkled handkerchief with user adjusted guidelines. (c) Shadow map and mask (combined into one image) automatically derived using our structured light scanner. (d–g) Renderings using different fabrics: (d) cotton, (e) French silk, (f) gold linen, (g) crochet yarn.

map and mask. New stylized handkerchiefs are depicted using different sorts of fabrics illustrating the robustness of our method: (d) cotton, (e) French silk, (f) gold linen, and (g) crochet yarn.

5   Conclusion and Future Work

In this paper we presented a system to capture apparel products in order to apply a new print design to the acquired garment models. Regarding model acquisition of new apparel collection we made use of a sparse set of guidelines in combination with an intuitive graphical user interface allowing the user to obtain and refine a 2D mesh representation of the garment. To achieve a 3D-ish look of the 2D virtual garment, we proposed the use of structured light scanning to automatically obtain a shadow map. Our method allows online clothes shops to bring new visual art into bespoke clothing to make apparel products more valuable compared to other garments on the market. Furthermore it helps artists and designers in virtual prototyping and visualizing garments with new print designs.

Discussion and Future Work. One of the main difficulties of the tool is the manual identification of guidelines when heavy distortions are involved. For instance, a scarf with a knot in which case large parts of the guidelines will be obscured. Therefor, instead of acquiring the garment model at once, the garment could be captured in several phases each corresponding to a piece of garment that is more convenient to handle. For the scarf case, it would narrow down to capturing three pieces (the knot and the two loose ends) and merging these together.

Acknowledgements. This study was conducted in view of the research project iArt–644625 financed by the EU programme Horizon 2020. We also gratefully express our gratitude to the European Fund for Regional Development (ERDF) and the Flemish Government, which are kindly funding part of the research at the Expertise centre for Digital Media.

References

1. Bridson, R., Zhang, D.: Advanced topics on clothing simulation and animation. In: SIGGRAPH Course Notes 6 (2005)
2. Liu, L., Wang, R., Zhuo, S., Luo, X., Gao, C.: Mesh-based anisotropic cloth deformation for virtual fitting. Multimedia Tools Appl. **71**(2), 411–433 (2014)
3. Walt Disney Feature Animation. Aladdin (1992)
4. Walt Disney Home Video: Diamond in the Rough: the Making of Aladdin. Aladdin Platinum Edition, Disc 2. DVD (2004)
5. Lander, J.: Devil in the blue faceted dress: Real time cloth animation. World Wide Web. http://www.gamasutra.com/view/feature/131851/devil_in_the_blue_faceted_dress_.php
6. Vidya. World Wide Web. http://www.human-solutions.com/vidya/
7. Second Sight. World Wide Web. http://medialab.hva.nl/blog/project/3d-fashion/
8. Lafayatte. World Wide Web. http://www.lafayettebyme.com/
9. H&M. H&M puts real model heads on fake bodies. World Wide Web. http://jezebel.com/5865114/hm-puts-real-model-heads-on-fake-bodies

10. Lobay, A., Forsyth, D.A.: Shape from texture without boundaries. Int. J. Comput. Vis. **67**(1), 71–91 (2006)
11. Zhou, B., Chen, X., Fu, Q., Guo, K., Tan, P.: Garment modeling from a single image. Comput. Graph. Forum **32**(7), 85–91 (2013)
12. Ebert, A., Schädlich, J., Disch, A.: Innovative retexturing using cooperative patterns. In: IASTED International Conference on Visualization, Imaging and Image Processing, pp. 432–437 (2003)
13. Hilsmann, A., Eisert, P.: Tracking and retexturing cloth for real-time virtual clothing applications. In: Gagalowicz, A., Philips, W. (eds.) MIRAGE 2009. LNCS, vol. 5496, pp. 94–105. Springer, Heidelberg (2009)
14. Guskov, I., Klibanov, S., Bryant, B.: Trackable surfaces. In: Proceedings of the 2003 ACM SIGGRAPH/Eurographics Symposium on Computer Animation, SCA 2003, pp. 251–257 (2003)
15. Scholz, V., Stich, T., Magnor, M., Keckeisen, M., Wacker, M.: Garment motion capture using color-coded patterns. In: ACM SIGGRAPH 2005 Sketches, SIGGRAPH 2005 (2005)
16. Chaikin, G.M.: An algorithm for high-speed curve generation. Comput. Graph. Image Process. **3**(4), 346–349 (1974)
17. Scharstein, D., Szeliski, R.: High-accuracy stereo depth maps using structured light. In: Proceedings of 2003 IEEE Computer Society Conference on Computer Vision and Pattern Recognition, 2003, vol. 1, p. I-195 (2003)

Realistic Crowds via Motion Capture
and Cell Marking

Seth Brunner[1], Brian Ricks[2], and Parris K. Egbert[1(✉)]

[1] Brigham Young University, Provo, UT, USA
seth.brunner@gmail.com, egbert@cs.byu.edu
[2] University of Nebraska at Omaha, Omaha, NE, USA
bricks@unomaha.edu

Abstract. Ever since the first use of crowds in films and video games there has been an interest in larger, more efficient and more realistic simulations of crowds. Most crowd simulation algorithms are able to satisfy the viewer from a distance but when inspected from close up the flaws in the individual agent's movements become noticeable. One of the bigger challenges faced in crowd simulation is finding a solution that models the actual movement of an individual in a crowd. This paper simulates a more realistic crowd by using individual motion capture data as well as traditional crowd control techniques. By augmenting traditional crowd control algorithms with the use of motion capture data for individual agents, we can simulate crowds that mimic more realistic crowd motion, while maintaining real-time simulation speed.

Keywords: Computer animation · Crowd simulation · Motion capture

1 Introduction

As far back as 1987 crowds were becoming an interesting research topic for computer-aided animation [1]. Up to that point, using large crowds in live action films required hiring a large number of extras to create the desired crowd. An early example is Cecil B. Demille's The Ten Commandments. Demille hired thousands of extras for the exodus scene. Large crowds of people create the difficulty of directing the crowd to get the desired appearance.

Many approaches have been created to remedy the problem of creating a large crowd that are cost effective and directable. One technique is through animation. Animated crowds used for live action films and animated films are expensive to animate by hand because of the amount of time that the artist would need to spend on each individual in the crowd. Each agent needs to be animated realistically in a fashion that makes them appear as individuals while still maintaining the look and feel of an autonomous crowd. As the size of the crowd increases the complexity of the movement of the crowd increases for the animator.

As computers have become more powerful, solutions to creating dynamic crowds through procedural means has become more viable. In fact, companies have been created just to produce computer animations of crowds [2, 3]. The need for more realistic crowds has pushed research into various areas, each one focusing on weaknesses in the

© Springer International Publishing Switzerland 2016
F.J. Perales and J. Kittler (Eds.): AMDO 2016, LNCS 9756, pp. 66–80, 2016.
DOI: 10.1007/978-3-319-41778-3_7

standard crowd simulation model. Up until now, these areas have focused on making the overall crowd motion look more realistic, rather than focusing on the possible movements of the individuals within the crowd. The result is that you have an overall crowd movement that looks good from a distance but as you get close to the individuals within the crowd there are many artifacts that are distracting for the viewer and destroy the illusion that the crowd is real.

The goal of this work is to address the unrealistic movement of the individual agents of the crowd while maintaining visually pleasing overall crowd movement. This work takes the approach of traditional crowd simulation where the agents are represented by a position in space and a velocity. During each movement-planning phase the agents determine their current desired velocity and orientation. In the planning step of the crowd simulation process the agents are limited to a specific set of movements that have been collected from motion capture data. The motion capture data represents movement that humans are capable of making. This will ensure that the agents move in a realistic fashion. Our solution produces realistic crowd movement along with realistic individual agent movement. We are able to do so in interactive-time with a reasonable number of agents. The main contributions of this work are:

(1) Our use of real-world data in the planning step of crowd simulation
(2) Our weighting function for determining which real-world data will be of best use
(3) Our hybrid obstacle avoidance algorithm called Cell Marking

2   Related Work

2.1   Crowds from Rule-Based Models

In 1985 Amkraut, Girard, and Karl submitted a piece to The Electronic Theater at SIGGRAPH [4]. This piece featured a flock of birds that flew through a virtual environment. This example is one of the first crowds explored in graphics research. Two years later Reynolds published his work on flocking behavior [1] where he presents what has become known as boids or "bird-oid" objects. This system generated significant interest in the area of computer animation. Although animal flocking behavior and human crowd behavior are not identical, Reynolds did adapt pieces of his flocking simulation to human characters [5].

Fiorini and Shiller [6] developed an obstacle avoidance algorithm called velocity obstacles. This algorithm uses the radii and velocities of the objects in a scene to determine the best possible velocity for the current agent. The work of [7] extended the velocity obstacle model by eliminating oscillations in the behavior of the agents as they choose their paths.

Xiong et al. [8] presents a rule-based method for crowd control. This solution considers all of the valid velocities present, then uses a cost function to determine which velocity is the best choice in that scenario.

2.2 Crowds from Social Forces

One of the key papers on human motion in crowds is the paper by Helbing and Molnar [9]. Even though crowds for humans had been addressed before, this was the first paper to describe how social forces can be applied to human crowds. Braun et al. expanded that work to give agents their own personality [10]. Later work by Pelechano et al. [11] improved the social forces method by allowing for a higher number of agents as well as including social actions such as pushing and emotional forces.

Ricks and Egbert [12] explore research in psychology to model the behavior of crowds. Through the use of transactional analysis they create crowds that stop to talk to each other or even walk side by side while continuing toward their destinations. Kim et al. [13] use a similar approach in what they term General Adaptation Syndrome to model how individuals in a crowd will react in certain circumstances and to certain levels of stress.

These papers present a simple underlying model for how crowds should be constructed. However, they fall short in the area of individual motion.

2.3 Crowds from Cellular Automata

Cellular Automata models for crowd simulation provide a very basic representation of crowd simulation. For example, [14–17] demonstrate how cellular automata can be used for crowd simulation. The cellular automata approach focuses on moving entire crowds through an environment such that a reasonable global motion of the crowd is maintained.

Chenney [18] improved on cellular automata techniques by creating velocity fields in individual tiles. The tiles are then stitched together and the edges and boundaries are corrected to accommodate the flow between tiles.

Tecchia et al. [19] also improved upon existing cellular automata algorithms to build crowds. In their system a crowd is divided into 4 cellular automata layers. Each layer performs one portion of the collision detection algorithm. This provides for agent directability in creating realistic dynamic crowds.

The simplicity of the cellular automata algorithm makes these methods desirable. Since the world is discretized, it is easy to know where the agents are and how to keep them from interpenetrating each other. However, these algorithms alone are inadequate for representing real crowds. Realistic motion requires a high resolution grid, and they do not take into account planning the motion and trajectory of an individual in the crowd from the possible real world actions and movements that are available to a specific agent.

2.4 Crowds from Learning

Several researchers have used various learning techniques to assist in crowd motion. Musse et al. [20] use computer vision techniques to help in the simulation of computer agents. Zhong et al. [21] use videos of crowds to learn behavior patterns, then apply those patterns to their crowds. Ahn et al. [22] reuse trajectories based on how well those trajectories allow for regional goals to be met. The goal of each of these systems is to learn about crowd movement then apply that knowledge to their given crowd.

2.5 Crowds from Motion Capture Data

More recently, work has been done to bring motion capture and real world data into crowd simulations [23–26]. These papers present various techniques for crowd animation using motion capture data. Although the techniques have differences, the underlying principles are similar. They film crowds and capture the motion of individual agents within a crowd. They are then able to place agents within the virtual environment and get realistic crowd motion. This motion capture focuses on the overall movement of the crowd but does not address the individual agent's movement as a product of motion capture data and traditional crowd simulation techniques.

Lee et al. [27] uses motion patches to annotate motion data in crowd simulation. Lemercier et al. [28] uses motion capture data as part of the crowd simulation process, but uses it as a study tool for the simulation.

Lerner et al. [29] also use motion capture to create realistic crowd motion. Their technique extracts individual behavior in certain situations that might be experienced in a virtual world. While they do use real world data in their system, their work focuses on creating crowds through example by searching a database for reactions to certain scenarios.

Our system differs from these in that we are trying to take traditional crowd simulation algorithms that have proven to create visually appealing crowds and improve the individual's movements within those crowds.

In summary the current crowd simulation models fail to address the problem of the movement of individuals within a crowd. The main focus in current systems is the overall motion of the crowd. Individual motion is largely ignored. By ignoring the individuals' motion, a wide range of possible crowd motions and uses are lost.

Even though some systems have begun using motion capture data, the data is typically used to enhance overall crowd movement, or is used tangentially in the individual motion. On the other hand, our system uses the motion capture data as the basis for all individual movements.

3   Realistic Motion in Crowds

The main problems with current crowd simulation models are that they primarily focus on the behavior of the crowd but largely ignore the actual real-world motions of the individuals. When crowds are formed without real-world data playing a part in the planning step, the agents are able to make movements that are unrealistic. Our work is able to overcome these obstacles by introducing real-world data into the planning step of the agents in the simulation. As mentioned earlier, the main contributions of this work are our use of real-world data in the planning step of crowd simulation, our weighting function for determining which real-world data will be of best use and our hybrid obstacle avoidance algorithm called Cell Marking. We will now discuss these techniques.

3.1   Base Simulation

Making a simulation that runs quickly over hundreds or thousands of agents is important for crowd simulations. In order to do this, much of the research in crowd simulation turned to a very simple model for representing agents. Each individual within the crowd is typically represented as a point in space and a velocity vector. The simplicity of this model allows the simulation to scale well.

After the paths of the agents have been planned, an animation cycle is applied to the agents, moving them toward their goal locations. However, this process allows for a lot of undesirable artifacts. Individuals in the crowd are able to run faster or slower than their animation is moving, turn without making similar body motion and miss valuable human movements such as sidestepping and pivot turning. Our work overcomes the movement artifacts seen in current crowd systems with our algorithm for agent planning using real-world data to determine realistic agent movement.

3.2   Augmented Simulation

Our simulation uses the common approach of representing each agent as a point in space and a velocity vector. The first thing we want to do in each planning step is to have each agent determine what its desired velocity is going to be. The desired velocity represents the velocity that the agent needs in order to move itself closer to its goal while still avoiding other agents and obstacles within a scene.

To find the desired velocity we first find the velocity that will point the agent closest to its goal. To determine that we find the vector from the agent to the goal. This will give the desired velocity and direction needed to move closer to the goal. Next we change the desired velocity to avoid other obstacles and agents within the simulation. Our obstacle avoidance algorithm is a hybrid algorithm that combines rule based methods like Reciprocal Velocity Obstacles, RVO, [7] with our grid based obstacle avoidance algorithm. We discuss the details of this algorithm in Sect. 4. With the new desired velocity produced from the velocity to the agent's goal and the obstacle avoidance algorithm, we choose a motion capture clip that will move the agent toward its goal while still avoiding other agents.

3.3   Motion Capture Data

The motion capture data we use for this system comes from the Carnegie Melon Motion Capture Library [30]. The motion capture data from this library represents the real-world data that we use for planning. The motion segments represent long movements like a walking turn, a side step, and a turn and walk. Most of the motion segments are about two seconds in length. In order to get the most realistic motion for the agent we would ideally use the entire segment recorded. However, to get the most realistic motion for the overall crowd the agent must be able to choose its motion more frequently than that. We found that a full second of motion capture data applied to the agent is a reasonable compromise, in that agents move realistically while maintaining plausible motion for the overall crowd.

This means that we can choose a small one-second segment from all of the motion capture data and apply it to our agent. The agent will execute the selected motion capture clip, then choose the next one-second segment of motion capture data to run. Left as is, the resulting compilation would be a series of unrelated motions. The agents' movements would spontaneously pop and seem disjointed. The next section describes how we overcome this problem.

3.4   Transitions

To overcome the unrealistic movement caused by shifting from one motion to another, we apply transitions between the two motion capture segments being played. Our approach is similar to the work presented in [31, 32]. To successfully use the transitions in our project we change a few of the assumptions we originally made when selecting motion. Instead of choosing just one second of motion we choose 10 more frames beyond the number of frames in one second of motion. We then interpolate between the last 10 frames of the first motion and the first 10 frames of the second motion. This gives a smooth and reasonable transition between motions at a small cost.

3.5   Choice Function

Knowing which motion capture segment to choose next can be a hard decision to make. The segment needs to move in the direction of the desired velocity and be as fast as the desired velocity. The final orientation of the movement needs to be close to the desired orientation for the agent. It also needs to be collision free and able to minimize foot skate and error in the motion when the transitions happen. Our system uses a choice function that takes all of these requirements into account to select the best motion segment to use in the next timeframe. We score the motions with the following function:

$$motionScore = diff(m1, m2) * w_m + (vel_{opt} - vel_m) * w_{vel} + ||(loc_{opt} - loc_m)|| \\ * w_{loc} + (\theta_{opt} - \theta_m) * w_\theta$$

$$(1)$$

$m1$ and $m2$ are the previous and next motions respectively. w_m is the weight that the difference in transition clips has on the overall score of that specific motion. vel_{opt} is the optimal, or desired velocity, vel_m is the new motion's overall velocity and w_{vel} is the velocity weighting factor. loc_{opt} is the desired end location, loc_m is the location that the new motion will end at and w_{loc} is the location weighting factor. θ_{opt} is the desired orientation of the agent, θ_m is the new orientation of the agent, and w_θ is the orientation weighting factor. $diff(m1, m2)$ is defined as follows:

$$diff(m1, m2) = \sum_{i=0}^{10} \sum_{j=0}^{n} (m1_i^j - m2_i^j)$$

$$(2)$$

For n joints in a motion capture skeleton $m1_i^j$ represents the position of joint j at frame i of the transition for the previous motion and $m2_i^j$ represents the same joint and frame for the new motion.

The choice function scores every possible motion segment using Eq. 1 and then orders the motions from lowest score to highest score. The lowest scoring motion is the best possible motion that can be used by that particular agent for that particular one-second interval.

Including Eq. 2 in the motion scoring function allows the agent to put a preference on segments that will create better looking transitions because it will reward motions that are closer to the previous motion for the transition frames.

The choice function developed is capable of moving agents towards their goals while still avoiding most collisions. However, the choice function alone cannot guarantee complete collision free movement for the agents. This problem is also compounded by the fact that each agent only chooses a new movement every second. One second is a large amount of time for an agent to move without adjusting its velocity so as to not collide with obstacles in the scene. Our system overcomes these collisions through our hybrid obstacle avoidance algorithm called Cell Marking.

4   Cell Marking

Cell Marking is a hybrid obstacle avoidance algorithm that uses a rule-based algorithm, such as RVO and a Cellular Automata algorithm to guarantee that no collisions can occur in a crowd simulation.

4.1   The Grid

The underlying cellular automata structure is important for being able to move the agents around the world collision free. The grid stores information on which cells are occupied by each agent over a sequence of frames. We store multiple frames in a grid cell that each hold individual information as to which agents will be occupying that cell and in which frame.

Adding the time element to the grid cell allows an agent to occupy a cell in the first few frames of its movement and then open up that cell for other agents to occupy later in that movement. This will allow the agents to plan the best route possible in a large crowd or when multiple agents are next to each other.

The grid is updated each time step and the current frame in the grid is updated accordingly. This is shown in Fig. 1.

4.2   The Algorithm

Our simulation uses RVO to score all of the possible velocities for the next time step with velocities resulting in a collision scoring low and velocities resulting in collision free movement scoring high. After computing all of the RVO scored velocities, we

Fig. 1. An agent advancing through its chosen movement. The small spheres in the grid cells represent the occupancy grid cells the agent will occupy during the clip.

select the velocity with the highest score. We then use Eq. 1 to select the best motion for this agent at this time.

Once the motion capture segments have been scored appropriately, the system runs the agent through the selected motion segment and checks the grid at each frame to see if there is a potential collision between two agents during this motion segment. If the agent is able to plan a route on the grid for the time frame without hitting a square that is occupied it flags that motion as its chosen motion and marks the cells in the grid for the given frames that it will be occupying. The next agent then plans its move.

When an agent finds that the chosen motion segment will collide with an obstacle or agent in the simulation it will discard that motion segment and test the next highest scored motion segment in the scored motion segments list. The agent proceeds through motions in the scored list until a motion is found that will generate a collision free path.

There are times when an agent will check every motion in its scored motion list and not find a suitable motion to keep it from colliding with other agents. In this situation, the agent can simply transition to a stop and wait until it finds a collision-free movement in the future.

5 Results

The goal of this work is to create a crowd simulation that maintains the overall realism of current crowd simulation systems while giving the individual agents within the crowd realistic movements and actions. We now discuss the results of our simulations.

5.1 Realistic Crowd Motion

We use four different scenarios to test our crowd's ability to adapt to different situa tions. The four scenarios we use are similar to the examples used in [33]. The scenarios we use are shown in Fig. 2 and described below.

Circle: In the circle scenario we line the agents up in a circle all facing the center of the circle. The agents are then given goals on the opposite side of the circle. This scenario tests how well agents will be able to interact with each other when they are all converging onto the same point. The circle does well with a small number of agents but as the number of agents is increased there is potential for congestion. The manner in which an algorithm deals with the congestion is what makes this particular scenario interesting.

Group Swap: The group swap scenario has two groups of agents facing each other. The agents in each group are given locations that match the agents in the group opposite them. This particular scenario challenges how the agents will handle confrontation from another group when there are others around them heading in the same direction.

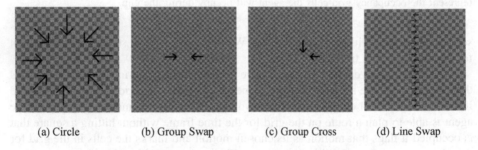

    (a) Circle   (b) Group Swap   (c) Group Cross   (d) Line Swap

Fig. 2. Different scenarios for testing the crowd simulation

Group Crossing: In the group crossing scenario, two groups of agents are placed perpendicular to each other. They are then given goals directly in front of them that will require them to move through the center of the scene. Both groups will meet in the middle and must figure out how to get around each other while progressing toward their desired goal.

Line Swap: The line swap scenario has two parallel lines of agents facing each other. Each agent is given a goal that is occupied by the corresponding agent in the line across from it. The agents attempt to pass each other with as little deviation as possible while still maintaining realistic interactions.

These four examples display the ability of our system to maintain realistic crowd motion with respect to current crowd simulation systems. We show the times required for the agents to reach their goals and compare our results with RVO in Table 1.

The RVO model performs better on the Group Swap, Crossing, and Line Swap. The two algorithms perform comparably on the Circle scenario. One reason that RVO is able to perform better than the Cell Marking algorithm is due to collision avoidance. In the RVO algorithm there are cases where it is impossible to choose a velocity that will guarantee collision free movement. In this case the agent chooses the velocity that will penalize it the least or make its collisions minimal.

On the other hand, Cell Marking does not allow collisions to occur. If the agent realizes there will be a collision present it will either stop or choose another route.

Table 1. Comparison between RVO and Cell Marking

	Circle	Group Swap	Crossing	Line Swap
RVO	50.5 s	96.62 s	88.12 s	16.97 s
CM	50.8 s	121.94 s	94.12 s	22.29 s

The end result is that agents in congested areas spread out more and create longer paths to follow. In the case of the circle this is not as evident because the velocity obstacles push the agents around the outside of the circle like a vortex. In the other cases, the agents converge on each other at a central mixing point. They tend to clump and push to the outside. The result is that it takes longer for the agents to resolve their paths. However, they are eventually able to reach their goals collision free.

5.2   Realistic Individual Motion

The focus of this research is on achieving realistic movement from the individual agents. We have shown that our system produces realistic crowd formations. We also desire to show that the individuals within our crowds make more realistic movements than current crowd simulation systems.

Two specific areas of comparison between our system and current systems are in the reduction of footskate and on larger scale turns. Footskate occurs when an agent's foot movement does not map well to the overall movement of the agent's body. In current systems footskate will happen at any point in the agent's movement but is most pronounced when the agent is turning. In many systems the agent will continue to walk forward while turning on a point on the ground. Some systems try to hide the footskate by having the agents move in an arc. The use of motion capture data for our system significantly reduces footskate.

Since the motion capture date we are using is from actual human movement, the actor's feet will move in a realistic fashion. Transitioning between two segments of real world data can potentially introduce some footskate, but we have found that this can be minimized through the correct application of our choice function.

Figure 3 demonstrates some differences between our system and other current systems. The agents are planning a path along a straight line. Our system is shown in Fig. 3a. The agent moves toward its goal based on the motion capture data it selected. As a result the agent uses natural motion to move toward its goal. Figure 3b shows the movement of current systems. The actor moves toward its goal, then the animation is applied to that actor as a post-processing step. In this case the animation causes the actor to lean to the right, creating an unnatural movement. In addition, sliding occurs at the feet because the agent does not move in the direction of the motion capture data.

Another obvious visual difference between our system and other systems is the individual agent's turns. In our system, agents choose their velocity and orientation based on the motion capture data. This means that making a turn is not as simple as rotating around a point and heading to a destination. When an agent needs to turn it must find a movement in the motion capture data that supports the turn it wishes to make. The result is that the agent makes a realistic looking turn. In addition the agent

(a)   (b)

Fig. 3. Image (a) shows an agent in our system using motion capture data to move in a natural manner. In image (b) an agent plans its path and then uses motion capture data in a post-processing step, as is done in current systems. This often produces an unnatural motion, shown here as a lean to the left.

has several different turn motions it can choose from, thus allowing variation in movement.

A side effect from current systems that our system overcomes is the fact that oftentimes all of the agents in the system make the same or similar movements each frame. The result might be compared to synchronized walking. Our system has the benefit of having a variety of different movements available and because of the cost function involved, each agent will have different needs and will therefore choose different types of movements based on those needs. The result is that the agents will use different movements as they turn. The agents are also able to make quick pivot turns, side steps and any other type of turning motion that is represented in the motion capture dataset. In the case of a side step our agents are able to move in a direction they are not facing.

Figure 4 shows a close up of both types of crowds. Figure 4a shows our system, in which the agents are all facing different directions and in the middle of different types of movement. Figure 4b shows the results of using a post-processing approach, typical in current systems. Note how each agent is in the middle of the same movement, facing the same direction, and moving in the same way.

An informal user study was done to give us a sense of how users would perceive the advantages of our system. The user study was done with 31 participants. Each participant was shown three videos. The first two videos were close-ups of current crowd simulation systems and our own system. The order in which the videos were played was alternated between participants. The participants were then asked to rate which of the two videos had a more realistic appearance, based on the overall feel of the agents' movements as well as how the agents' movements looked with regards to their feet and interactions. The third video was a zoomed out view of the crowd. This video was a video of our current system and the participants were asked if they thought the visible crowd movement was plausible or not.

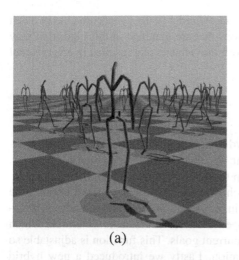 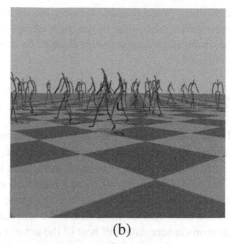

(a)   (b)

Fig. 4. Image (a) shows agents in our system with varying motions and directions. Image (b) shows the current system approach.

23 out of 31 participants said that our system produced more realistic individual movements than the crowds produced using RVO with motion capture applied post process, while seven said that the crowds produced using RVO were more realistic, and one person said that neither one was better than the other.

On the third video 27 out of the 31 participants said that the overall crowd movement produced by our system was plausible, while four of the participants said the results were not plausible.

6 Discussion and Future Work

We have presented a system for crowd animation in which viable actor movements are produced while maintaining the integrity of the overall crowd. We have been able to do this by providing a database of motion capture data, then having the actors select the most appropriate motion sequence based on their current situation and environment. Coupled with our Cell Marking algorithm, this has allowed us to produce realistic individual actor motion while maintaining plausible crowd motion.

There are a few areas of future work that could enhance this system. One is in extending the number of actors that can be simulated in real-time. Optimizing the manner in which the grid is used could potentially help with this situation.

Another area of future work is the way in which transitions are performed. The solution used for this work was fairly simplistic and there are other algorithms available that could potentially produce better results. A solution for transitions that can be done in real time and reduce footskate would increase the overall realism of this simulation.

For our research we took a strictly collision free approach to crowd simulation. Some of the current systems allow for collisions within their models. It would be interesting work to find a balance between collision free movement and allowing collisions. Some possible benefits would be in how quickly the agents are able to reach their goals. Also some of the more abrupt stops that are manifest in this algorithm may be diminished if agents were allowed to choose movements that resulted in a very small collision.

7 Conclusion

In summary our system takes current crowd simulation systems and uses their techniques for forming realistic crowd movement. We then improve upon their weaknesses. Current systems do not use real world data in the agent planning step of their algorithm. This limits the ability of those systems to achieve a totally realistic crowd because the agents within the crowd are able to move in ways that are unrealistic and not representative of human movement. We developed a choice function to determine which motion capture data will best fit the actor's current goals. This function is adjustable so that it can be tuned for the desired application. Lastly we introduced a new hybrid obstacle avoidance algorithm called Cell Marking. This allows the agents to move along collision free paths while choosing the best motion capture data for their current situation. We were able to show that the crowds produced by our simulation were plausible and that the individuals' movements and interactions are realistic and natural.

References

1. Reynolds, C.: Flocks, herds and schools: a distributed behavioral model. In: ACM SIGGRAPH Computer Graphics, vol. 21, pp. 25–34. ACM (1987)
2. Massive Software (2015). http://massivesoftware.com
3. Golaem Software (2015). http://golaem.com
4. Amkraut, S., Girard, M., Karl, G.: Eurythmy. SIGGRAPH Video Rev. **21**, 329–336 (1985)
5. Reynolds, C.: Steering behaviors for autonomous characters. In: Game Developers Conference (1999). http://wwwred3d.com/cwr/steer/gdc99
6. Fiorini, P., Shiller, Z.: Motion planning in dynamic environments using the relative velocity paradigm. In: Proceedings of 1993 IEEE International Conference on Robotics and Automation, pp. 560–565. IEEE (1993)
7. Van den Berg, J., Lin, M., Minocha, D.: Reciprocal velocity obstacles for real-time multi-agent navigation. In: ICRA 2008, IEEE International Conference on Robotics and Automation, pp. 1928–1935. IEEE (2008)
8. Xiong, M., Lees, M., Cai, W., Zhou, S., Low, M.Y.H.: A rule-based motion planning for crowd simulation. In: CW 2009, International Conference on CyberWorlds 2009, pp. 88–95. IEEE (2009)
9. Helbing, D., Molnar, P.: Social force model for pedestrian dynamics. Phys. Rev. E **51**(5), 4282 (1995)
10. Braun, A., Musse, S.R., De Oliveira, L.P., Bodman, B.E.: Modeling individual behaviors in crowd simulation. In: 16th International Conference on Computer Animation and Social Agents, 2003, pp. 143–148. IEEE (2003)

11. Pelechano, N., Allbeck, J., Badler, N.: Controlling individual agents in high-density crowd simulation. In: Proceedings of the 2007 ACM SIGGRAPH/Eurographics Symposium on Computer Animation, pp. 99–108. Eurographics Association (2007)
12. Ricks, B.C., Egbert, P.K.: More realistic, flexible, and expressive social crowds using transactional analysis. Vis. Comput. **28**(6–8), 889–898 (2012)
13. Kim, S., Guy, S.J., Manocha, D., Lin, M.C.: Interactive simulation of dynamic crowd behaviors using general adaptation syndrome theory. In: Proceedings of the ACM SIGGRAPH Symposium on Interactive 3D Graphics and Games, pp. 55–62. ACM (2012)
14. Blue, V.J., Adler, J.L.: Cellular automata microsimulation for modeling bi-directional pedestrian walkways. Transp. Res. Part B: Methodological **35**(3), 293–312 (2001)
15. Schadschneider, A.: Cellular automaton approach to pedestrian dynamics-theory. arXiv preprint cond-mat/0112117 (2001)
16. Burstedde, C., Klauck, K., Schadschneider, A., Zittartz, J.: Simulation of pedestrian dynamics using a two-dimensional cellular automaton. Phys. A **295**(3), 507–525 (2001)
17. Hamagami, T., Hirata, H.: Method of crowd simulation by using multiagent on cellular automata. In: IAT 2003, IEEE/WIC International Conference on Intelligent Agent Technology, pp. 46–52. IEEE (2003)
18. Chenney, S.: Flow tiles. In: Proceedings of the 2004 ACM SIGGRAPH/Eurographics symposium on Computer animation, Eurographics Association, pp. 233–242 (2004)
19. Tecchia, F., Loscos, C., Conroy-Dalton, R., Chrysanthou, Y.L.: Agent behaviour simulator (abs): A platform for urban behaviour development (2001)
20. Musse, S.R., Jung, C.R., Jacques, J., Braun, A.: Using computer vision to simulate the motion of virtual agents. Comput. Animation Virtual Worlds **18**(2), 83–93 (2007)
21. Zhong, J., Cai, W., Luo, L., Yin, H.: Learning behavior patterns from video: a data-driven framework for agent-based crowd modeling. In: Proceedings of the AAMAS (2015)
22. Ahn, J., et al.: Long term real trajectory reuse through region goal satisfaction. In: Allbeck, J. M., Faloutsos, P. (eds.) MIG 2011. LNCS, vol. 7060, pp. 412–423. Springer, Heidelberg (2011)
23. Lee, K., Choi, M., Hong, Q., Lee, J.: Group behavior from video: a data-driven approach to crowd simulation. In: Proceedings of the 2007 ACM SIGGRAPH/Eurographics Symposium on Computer Animation, pp. 109–118. Eurographics Association (2007)
24. Courty, N., Corpetti, T.: Crowd motion capture. Comput. Animation Virtual Worlds **18**(4–5), 361–370 (2007)
25. Pelechano, N., Spanlang, B., Beacco, A.: Avatar locomotion in crowd simulation. In: International Conference on Computer Animation and Social Agents (CASA) (2011)
26. Kim, J., Seol, Y., Kwon, T., Lee, J.: Interactive manipulation of large-scale crowd animation, ACM Trans. Graph. **33**(4), Article 83 (2014)
27. Lee, K.H., Choi, M.G., Lee, J.: Motion patches: building blocks for virtual environments annotated with motion data, In: ACM SIGGRAPH 2006 Papers (SIGGRAPH 2006), pp. 898–906. ACM, New York (2006)
28. Lemercier, S., Moreau, M., Moussaïd, M., Theraulaz, G., Donikian, S., Pettré, J.: Reconstructing motion capture data for human crowd study. In: Allbeck, J.M., Faloutsos, P. (eds.) MIG 2011. LNCS, vol. 7060, pp. 365–376. Springer, Heidelberg (2011)
29. Lerner, A., Chrysanthou, Y., Lischinski, D.: Crowds by example. In: Computer Graphics Forum, vol. 26, pp. 655–664, Wiley Online Library (2007)
30. Carnegie Mellon University. CMU graphics lab motion capture database. http://www.mocap.cs.cmu.edu

31. Egbert, C., Egbert, P.K., Morse, B.S.: Real-time motion transition by example. In: Perales, F.J., Fisher, R.B. (eds.) AMDO 2010. LNCS, vol. 6169, pp. 138–147. Springer, Heidelberg (2010)

32. Kovar, L., Gleicher, M., Pighin, F.: Motion graphs. In: ACM SIGGRAPH 2008 Classes, p. 51. ACM (2008)

33. Ondrej, J., Pettre, J., Olivier, A.H., Donikian, S.: A synthetic-vision based steering approach for crowd simulation. ACM Trans. Graph. (TOG) 29(4), 123 (2010)

Leveraging Orientation Knowledge to Enhance Human Pose Estimation Methods

S. Azrour[✉], S. Piérard, and M. Van Droogenbroeck

INTELSIG Laboratory, Department of Electrical Engineering and Computer Science,
University of Liège, Liège, Belgium
samir.azrour@ulg.ac.be

Abstract. Predicting accurately and in real-time 3D body joint positions from a depth image is the cornerstone for many safety, biomedical, and entertainment applications. Despite the high quality of the depth images, the accuracy of existing human pose estimation methods from single depth images remains insufficient for some applications. In order to enhance the accuracy, we suggest to leverage a rough orientation estimation to dynamically select a 3D joint position prediction model specialized for this orientation. This orientation estimation can be obtained in real-time either from the image itself, or from any other clue like tracking. We demonstrate the merits of this general principle on a pose estimation method similar to the one used with *Kinect* cameras. Our results show that the accuracy is improved by up to 45.1 %, with respect to a method using the same model for all orientations.

1 Introduction

Markerless pose estimation has attracted much interest since the release of low-cost depth cameras like the *Microsoft Kinect*. Shotton *et al.* and Girshick *et al.* made an important step by presenting methods that infer a full-body pose reconstruction in real-time. Their details were explained, chronologically, in [3,8,9]. Despite this technological breakthrough, the accuracy of human pose estimation from single depth images remains insufficient for some applications.

The straightforward strategy to improve the pose estimation is to substantially increase the size and the diversity of the learning set, but this is costly, impractical, and often impossible. Other ideas to improve the method of Shotton *et al.* have also been developed. Yeung *et al.* [11] presented a way to combine the predictions of two *Kinect* cameras in order to reduce the problems related to unwanted joints positions vibration and bone-length variation observed with the method described in [9]. Wei *et al.* [10] used a method equivalent to [8] in combination with a tracking algorithm and showed that it improved the robustness and the accuracy on the estimation of the joint positions. In this paper, we present a principle for improvement that can be used with any markerless pose estimation method based on machine learning techniques. Instead of taking advantage of additional cameras or filtering the predictions in a post-processing step, we start by estimating the orientation of the observed person.

© Springer International Publishing Switzerland 2016
F.J. Perales and J. Kittler (Eds.): AMDO 2016, LNCS 9756, pp. 81–87, 2016.
DOI: 10.1007/978-3-319-41778-3_8

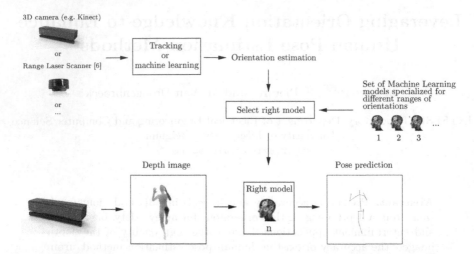

Fig. 1. Outline of our method. The orientation estimation can be obtained from the image itself or thanks to any kind of sensors through a machine learning or a tracking algorithm for instance. The last image shows the skeleton linking the estimated joints.

Our contribution is to show how an estimation of the orientation of the observed person improves the accuracy of a pose estimation algorithm. Our idea consists in slicing the full orientation range into smaller ranges and learning a different model for each of these smaller ranges. When the models are used to recover the pose, given the estimation of the orientation of the observed person, we use the appropriate model to make the predictions for the joints positions. To take into account the uncertainty on the orientation estimation, we consider slightly overlapping orientation ranges when the models are learned. An illustration of our method is shown in Fig. 1.

2   Principle of Leveraging an Orientation Estimation

The intuition for having several models depending on smaller orientation ranges is the following. From our experience, when it comes to analyze silhouettes annotated with depth in each pixel (see Fig. 3), machine learning methods tend to grant a high importance to the information related to the external contour and not enough importance to the information related to the depth signal. The problem is that there are two different poses corresponding to the same silhouette shape [7] (when the small details of the silhouette corresponding to the perspective effects are neglected), and this ambiguity leads to large errors when an average solution is predicted. Note that with the arbitrary convention taken in this paper (see Fig. 2), one of the two possible poses is associated with an orientation of θ, while the other one is associated with an orientation of $360° - \theta$.

Therefore, except for the rare cases where the observed person has an orientation very close to $0°$ (seen from his right side) or $180°$ (seen from his left side),

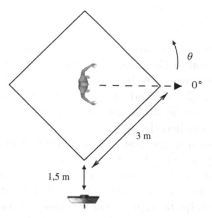

Fig. 2. The configuration considered in this paper. The person can be anywhere in the area (a square of 3 m side) with any pose and any orientation. The camera is placed 1 m above the floor; its optical axis is horizontal.

the knowledge of the orientation is sufficient to overcome the pose ambiguity, even if it is only roughly estimated. Our method is based on the idea that it is preferable to rely on an additional method that is specifically designed for orientation estimation instead of trying to recover the joint positions and disambiguate the silhouette orientation all at once. We observed that when a machine learning method does not have to simultaneously estimate the orientation and the pose, and can focus on the pose estimation given that a rough orientation estimation is provided to it, its task is eased and the accuracy of the predictions is improved.

Several clues can be used to estimate the orientation. When the observed person is walking, his orientation is given by his velocity vector, and can therefore be estimated by tracking. This tracking can be done directly from the depth camera, or from range laser scanners [6]. The orientation can also be estimated directly from a single depth image [5].

One way of forcing the pose estimation method to take the orientation into account is to consider several ranges of orientation and to learn a different model for each range. During the pose estimation step, given the orientation estimation, we use the appropriate model to predict the pose. Note that the overlap between consecutive ranges should be adapted to the maximum uncertainty of the selected orientation estimation method. In the case of the estimation from the depth image, Piérard et al. [5] showed that it is possible to achieve an average uncertainty of 4.3° (measured on synthetic, noise-free data), but no bound was given. In practice, the errors are larger, but the temporal variance can be filtered out, leading to reliable estimates as shown on the video on the author's website. We take an overlap of 20° for this orientation estimation method.

3   Experiments

To assess the effectiveness of our principle, we implement a simplified (for practical reasons) version of the pose estimation method described in Girshick *et al.* [3]. The main differences are that we use a general regression random forest model (the *ExtRaTrees* [2]) instead of a custom one, that we use 500 features rather than 2,000 to describe the pixels environments, and that the models are learned from another, smaller, dataset.

To generate the learning and test datasets, we followed a method similar to the one described in [9] except that we used the open source softwares *Blender* and *MakeHuman*. Moreover, we used only one human model and did not add clothes to it. Without loss of generality, our small dataset is sufficient to establish that our principle helps to improve the accuracy of the pose estimation. The poses used to generate the data were taken randomly from the *CMU motion capture database* [1]. A few unrealistic poses, that do not correspond to a standing person, have been manually excluded (less than 1 %). A total of 24,000 silhouettes annotated with depth have been generated from the same amount of poses for the learning set, and 10,000 for the test set. In the generated depth images, the distance from the human model to the camera varies from 1.5 to 5.74 meters. Note that we used the specifications of the *Kinect v2* of *Microsoft* to generate the depth images and we added a Gaussian noise with the characteristics given in [4]. Some examples of our input depth images are shown in Fig. 3 with the projection of the ground truth body joints positions in green.

Fig. 3. Examples of generated depth images used in our experiments. The ground truth body joints are displayed in green. (Color figure online)

We report the results obtained with 1, 4, and 12 models specialized according to the orientation. We analyze 8 body joints: neck, head, shoulder, elbow, wrist, hip, knee, ankle. We only consider the right joints given that the prediction accuracy will be symmetrical for the left ones.

3.1   Improvement with a Constant Global Learning Dataset Size

Our first experiment shows what happens when we increase the number of models, with smaller orientation ranges, while keeping a constant learning dataset size.

Table 1. Mean errors on the positions of the considered body joints for different number of models used with a constant learning dataset size. There is an optimal number of models (4 in this experiment) for a constant learning dataset size (8000 samples).

	amount of models:	1		4		12
	learning samples per model:	8000		$8000/4 = 2000$		$8000/12 \simeq 666$
	range of each model:	360°		$360°/4 + 2 \times 10° = 110°$		$360°/12 + 2 \times 10° = 50°$
	neck	2.9 cm	>	2.4 cm (- 15.3 %)	<	2.4 cm (- 14.4 %)
	head	3.1 cm	>	2.8 cm (- 7.6 %)	<	2.9 cm (- 3.9 %)
mean error	right shoulder	5.4 cm	>	3.0 cm (- 45.1 %)	<	3.0 cm (- 44.1 %)
	right elbow	9.1 cm	>	5.9 cm (- 35.3 %)	<	6.0 cm (- 34.0 %)
	right wrist	13.7 cm	>	9.9 cm (- 27.3 %)	<	10.3 cm (- 24.4 %)
	right hip	4.2 cm	>	2.8 cm (- 34.0 %)	<	2.8 cm (- 33.6 %)
	right knee	5.8 cm	>	4.5 cm (- 23.4 %)	<	4.6 cm (- 21.8 %)
	right ankle	8.3 cm	>	6.2 cm (- 25.5 %)	<	6.3 cm (- 23.9 %)

Table 1 gives the mean Euclidean errors for 1, 4 and 12 models. We see a significant reduction of the error for all joints when going from 1 to 4 models. These results underline that using multiple models designed for narrow ranges of orientations is preferable than using a unique model. However, going from 4 to 12 models slightly worsens the performance.

With a learning dataset, whose size cannot be increased, there is a trade-off between, on the one side, the improvement that is obtained from the knowledge of an approximative orientation estimation by the use of specialized pose estimation models, and on the other side, the deterioration due to the reduction of the learning set size. Nevertheless, the optimal solution takes advantage of a few models, and benefits from the knowledge of the orientation.

Note that the predictions for the head and the neck are less influenced by the number of models used. Indeed, the joints on the spine (that is the person's rotation axis) are less affected than those in the limbs by a change of the orientation. Moreover, we observe the largest errors on the wrist, as it is the joint that has the higher freedom to move in space. The magnitude of the mean error is thus related to the variety of poses in the test set. The general trend is higher errors at limb extremities, and lower errors at joints close to the torso.

The curves of Fig. 4 depict the mean Euclidean errors (estimated with a Gaussian filter of $\sigma = 8°$) affecting the pose estimation at every joint with respect to the orientation of the observed person. The results obtained with a single 360°-model is shown in red, while the one with four 110°-models is shown in blue. As can be seen, the errors are anisotropic, and the best improvement obtained thanks to our principle is for people facing the camera, or seen from their back. Moreover, for all the joints of the right limbs, we observe larger errors when the person is seen from his left side, which is probably due to the fact that these joints have a higher chance of being occluded.

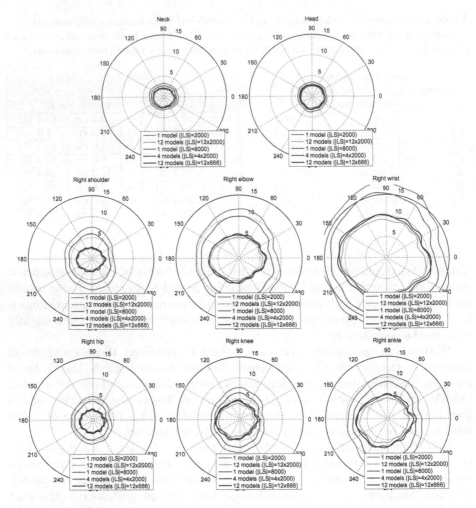

Fig. 4. Mean errors (in cm) on the positions of the considered body joints for different number of models specialized for reduced ranges of orientation. By convention, a person with an orientation of 0° is seen from the right side. (Color figure online)

3.2 Improvement with a Constant Learning Dataset Size per Model

Figure 4 also shows the behavior when the same experiment is performed with all models derived from the same amount of learning samples. The dark gray curves correspond to a single 360°-model, the purple ones to four 110°-models, and the light gray ones to twelve 50°-models. Each of these models has been learned from 2,000 samples. To the contrary of our first experiment, we observe a systematic decrease of the error when the number of models is increased. However, the small difference between 4 and 12 models suggests a plateau is reached after 4 models.

Therefore, relying on too many models is useless. This suggests that a rough orientation estimation suffices to improve the performance of pose estimation.

4   Conclusion

This work presents the principle of using an estimation of the orientation of the observed person to improve the accuracy of a pose estimation algorithm. Instead of learning a unique model over the 360°-range of orientation, we learn several models designed for smaller ranges of orientations. We tested this principle for different amounts of models and showed that the accuracy is significantly improved when the number of models increases while keeping a constant learning dataset size.

References

1. Carnegie Mellon University: Motion capture database. http://mocap.cs.cmu.edu
2. Geurts, P., Ernst, D., Wehenkel, L.: Extremely randomized trees. Mach. Learn. **63**(1), 3–42 (2006)
3. Girshick, R., Shotton, J., Kohli, P., Criminisi, A., Fitzgibbon, A.: Efficient regression of general-activity human poses from depth images. In: International Conference on Computer Vision (ICCV), Barcelona, Spain, pp. 415–422, November 2011
4. Kerl, C., Souiai, M., Sturm, J., Cremers, D.: Towards illumination-invariant 3D reconstruction using ToF RGB-D cameras. In: International Conference on 3D Vision (3DV), Tokyo, Japan, vol. 1, pp. 39–46, December 2014
5. Piérard, S., Leroy, D., Hansen, J.-F., Van Droogenbroeck, M.: Estimation of human orientation in images captured with a range camera. In: Blanc-Talon, J., Kleihorst, R., Philips, W., Popescu, D., Scheunders, P. (eds.) ACIVS 2011. LNCS, vol. 6915, pp. 519–530. Springer, Heidelberg (2011)
6. Piérard, S., Pierlot, V., Barnich, O., Van Droogenbroeck, M., Verly, J.: A platform for the fast interpretation of movements and localization of users in 3D applications driven by a range camera. In: 3DTV Conference, Tampere, Finland, June 2010
7. Piérard, S., Van Droogenbroeck, M.: On the human pose recovery based on a single view. In: International Conference on Pattern Recognition Applications and Methods (ICPRAM), Vilamoura, Portugal, vol. 2, pp. 310–315, February 2012
8. Shotton, J., Fitzgibbon, A., Cook, M., Sharp, T., Finocchio, M., Moore, R., Kipman, A., Blake, A.: Real-time human pose recognition in parts from single depth images. In: IEEE International Conference on Computer Vision and Pattern Recognition (CVPR), Providence, Rhode Island, USA, pp. 1297–1304, June 2011
9. Shotton, J., Girshick, R., Fitzgibbon, A., Sharp, T., Cook, M., Finocchio, M., Moore, R., Kohli, P., Criminisi, A., Kipman, A., Blake, A.: Efficient human pose estimation from single depth images. IEEE Trans. Pattern Anal. Mach. Intell. **35**(12), 2821–2840 (2013)
10. Wei, X., Zhang, P., Chai, J.: Accurate realtime full-body motion capture using a single depth camera. ACM Trans. Graph **31**(6), 188.1–188.12 (2012)
11. Yeung, K.-Y., Kwok, T.-H., Wang, C.: Improved skeleton tracking by duplex Kinects: a practical approach for real-time applications. J. Comput. Inf. Sci. Eng. **13**(4), 041007-1–041007-10 (2013)

Erythrocytes Morphological Classification Through HMM for Sickle Cell Detection

W. Delgado-Font[1], M. González-Hidalgo[2], S. Herold-Garcia[1],
A. Jaume-i-Capó[2(✉)], and A. Mir[2]

[1] Universidad de Oriente, Santiago de Cuba, Cuba
silena@uo.edu.cu
[2] Universitat de les Illes Ballears (UIB), Palma, Spain
{manuel.gonzalez,antoni.jaume,arnau.mir}@uib.es

Abstract. In sickle cell disease the cell morphology analysis is used to diagnose due the deformation of the red blood cell caused by the disease. Previous works used, in images of peripheral blood samples, ellipse adjustment and concave point detection due to the elongated shape of the erythrocyte and obtained good results the detection of cells that were partially occluded in cells' clusters. In this work, we propose a new algorithm for detecting noteworthy points in the ellipse adjustment and the use of Hidden Markov Model (HMM) for automatic erythrocyte supervised shape classification in peripheral blood samples. Furthermore, in this study we applied a set of constraints to eliminate the image preprocessing step proposed in previous studies. The method was validated using peripheral blood smear samples images with normal and elongated erythrocytes. In all the experiments, in the classification of normal and elongated cells the sensibility was superior to 96 %.

Keywords: Erythrocytes morphological classification · Hidden Markov Models · Contour representation

1 Introduction

Objects recognition by their shape is a classic problem in image processing and computer vision. The representation of objects can be obtained by considering the contour of the object or region. Several features of the contour can be taken as descriptors: the curvature, the Fourier coefficients, chain code, among others; while for the region can be considered some others like median axes or Zernike moments. The advantage of the descriptors using features contour is preserving local information, which is important in complex studies.

One of the methods that have been used to study 2D shapes are hidden Markov models, HMM [1]. Several authors have conducted studies on the capabilities of the HMM for classifying 2D shapes. In [2] the authors use a HMM together with the local curvature and occlusions are treated as the absence of a part of the contour. The problem of occlusions is also studied in [4]. In [3,5]

© Springer International Publishing Switzerland 2016
F.J. Perales and J. Kittler (Eds.): AMDO 2016, LNCS 9756, pp. 88–97, 2016.
DOI: 10.1007/978-3-319-41778-3_9

different features to define the contours and construct the HMM for shape classification are addressed. The HMMs have also been used for shape analysis in medical images, see by example, [6–9]. In [10] a HMM is used to detect and localize cells in microscope images of embryonic cells taken in a time sequence.

According to our investigations, we have not found references of HMM employment to study erythrocytes shape in blood images. Automated erythrocyte morphologic study has already been developed previously using other different methods [11,12]. There have been studies of other cells present in the blood, such as leukocytes [13] or malaria parasites [14]. Recently, the use of integral geometry based functions for the study of existing cells in the blood images [15,16] provided much more efficient classification results with respect the methods used until the moment. So, the automated morphologic study of cells in blood images is a hot topic, but we have not found references to the use of HMM for automatic representation and study of erythrocyte shape.

This paper aims at testing the effectiveness of the use of HMM capacities in automated erythrocyte supervised shape classification in peripheral blood samples. For the experiments, we considered only images of patients with sickle cell anemia, a disease that causes erythrocyte deformation, which changes its normal shape to an elongated or elliptical shape, like a sickle. Several papers relating to this behaviour conduct their experiments in the images of this disease.

2   Materials and Methods

2.1   Hidden Markov Models to Model Erythrocytes Shapes

A Hidden Markov Model or HMM is a Markov process [20] of unkown parameters. The purpose is to determine the unknown or hidden parameters of the model from the observed parameters.

In a hidden Markov model the state is not visible directly, only the observable values for each state are visible. Each state has a probability distribution on the observable values. Consequently, the sequence of observable values generated by a HMM provides certain information about the sequence of states.

The hidden Markov models are applied to temporary shapes recognition, as speech recognition, handwriting, gestures, grammatical labeled or bioinformatics. A HMM has the following components: (S, V, π, A, B) where:

- S is the set of individual states: $S = \{S_1, S_2, \ldots, S_N\}$. The state in time t is denoted by q_t.
- V is the set of observable values for each state: $V = \{v_1, v_2, \ldots, v_M\}$.
- π: the initial probabilities $\pi = \{\pi_i\}$ where $\pi_i = P[q_1 = S_i]$ where $1 \leq i \leq N$.
- A: the matrix of interstates transition probabilities $A = a_{ij}$, where $a_{ij} = P[q_{t+1} = S_j | q_t = S_i]$.
- B: the matrix of probabilities distribution of the observations $B = b_j(k)$, where $b_j(k) = P[v_k | q_t = S_j)$, that is, the probability of observing v_k, if we are in S_j state at time t, $1 \leq i \leq N$ and $1 \leq k \leq M$.

The observable sequence is denoted by the set $O = \{o_1, o_2, \ldots, o_T\}$, where o_t is an element of set V and T is the number of observations in the sequence. Given suitable values of N, M, A, B and π the HMM can be used to generate the sequence as follows:

1. An initial state $q_1 = S_i$ is chosen from the initial distribution of probabilities π.
2. Set $t = 1$.
3. $O_t = v_k$ is chosen according to the distribution of probabilities of the observable values in S_i, that is, $b_i(k)$.
4. The new state $q_{t+1} = S_j$ is chosen according to the distribution of probabilities of interstate transition for the state S_i, that is, a_{ij}.
5. Upgrade $t = t + 1$;
6. Repeat from the step 3 if $t < T$; otherwise, finish the process.

There are three canonical problems associated with the HMM:

Problem 1: given the parameters of the model, how to obtain the probability of a sequence of a particular observable values.

Problem 2: given the parameters of the model, how to obtain the most probable sequence of hidden states that generates a given sequence of observable values.

Problem 3: given a sequence of observable values or a set of such sequences, how to obtain the set of the most probable transition states and the a_{ij} and $b_j(k)$ probabilities. In other words, how to train the parameters of the HMM given a sequence or sequences of the data.

In [22], a more accurate description of these problems and how to solve them is explained.

The HMM is useful to model processes that change in time. Our proposal is to model the erythrocytes taking into account the variation in their contour curvature in the following way: for each pairs of consecutive points of the contour, the difference between the angle tangents of these two points is considered.

If these differences are between certain ranges, we classify the points of the contour into three types: circular, which will be the case of normal erythrocytes where the differences or the curvature is nearly constant (Fig. 1a, α angle), points that belong to elongated or elliptic erythrocytes, which will be the case of drepanocytes where the differences or the curvature is much larger (Fig. 1b, β angle) and points of elliptic erythrocytes where the differences or the curvature is smaller (Fig. 1b, γ angle). More specifically, let d be the considered difference and let u_1, u_2 and u_3 be three thresholds,

1. if $d < u_1$, the point is type 1. (Fig. 1b, γ angle).
2. if $u_1 \leq d \leq u_2$, the point is type 2. (Fig. 1a, α angle).
3. if $d \geq u_3$, the point is type 3. (Fig. 1b, β angle)

We describe the contour from the previous differences of all the considered pairs of points. This description is invariant to translations and rotations, but not to scales.

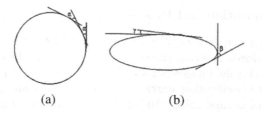

Fig. 1. Variations among tangent angles in the contour for a circle and an ellipse

For each class of erythrocytes (normal, elongated and other deformations) a HMM (S, V, π, A, B) is considered with three states $S = \{$StableVar, SmallVar, BigVar$\}$. Each state represents the contour curvature of the considered erythrocyte. The observable values of each state are $V = \{$Type1, Type2, Type3$\}$, which represents the three types of curvature of points. The other parameters of the HMM for each class of erythrocytes are estimated from the corresponding training set of the corresponding class using the algorithm to solve **Problem 3**.

So, our problem is: given an erythrocyte, it has to be classified into one of the three classes. From the erythrocyte, we can compute a sequence of observable values or a sequence of types of points of the contour. Using the algorithm to solve **Problem 1**, a probability $\hat{p}_i$ of this sequence is found for each of the three HMM of the three classes of erythrocites. ($i = 1$ for normal class, $i = 2$ for ellongated class and $i = 3$ for other deformations class)

Let p_1 and p_2 two probabilities thresholds. The classification algorithm is the following:

- If the probability of normal class $\hat{p}_1$ is greater than p_1, the erythorcyte belongs to the normal class.
- If the probability $\hat{p}_2$ of elongated class is greater than p_2, the erythorcyte belongs to the elongated class.
- Otherwise, the erythorcyte belongs to the class of other deformations.

To refine the previous method and because the probabilities $\hat{p}_i$ increase if the length of sequence of points decreases, we have splitted the contour of the erythrocyte in two parts and two thresholds values s_1 and s_2 were also considered. The refined algorithm is the following:

- If the probability of normal class $\hat{p}_1$ is greater than s_1, the part of the contour is classified into the normal class.
- If the probability $\hat{p}_2$ of elongated class is greater than s_2, the part of the contour is classified into the elongated class.
- If both parts of the contour are classified into the same class, the erythorcyte is classified into that class. Otherwise, the erythorcyte is classified into the class of other deformations.

2.2   Image Acquisition and Processing

We used the images acquired in [21]: 45 images of different fields of 17 prepared samples were obtained. To avoid the cases of overlapped cells and other types of present cells in the image, images of individual cells of 80 × 80 pixels were defined starting from the classification carried out by the specialist, in the following way: 202 images of normal cells, 210 images of elongated cells and 211 images of cells with other deformations. The descriptions of the defined contours were obtained following the process described in the previous section. Examples of each defined class of the used images are shown in Fig. 2. To be able to carry out a morphological analysis of objects in the image, the image should be segmented previously [17].

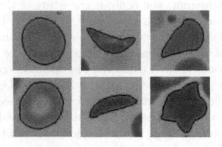

Fig. 2. Cell images of normal, elongated and other deformation class

2.3   Experiments to Realize

To check the effectiveness of the employment of the HMM in erythrocytes supervised classification, the following experiments were conducted:

1. Erythrocytes supervised classification in two classes: normal and elongated.
2. Erythrocytes supervised classification in three classes: normal, elongated and other deformations.
3. Supervised classification with rejection of normal and elongated erythrocytes, with a threshold of belonging to the class object studied. If the probability to belong to the class object does not exceed that threshold, the object is considered as other deformations class.
4. The three previous experiments but with the HMM training with descriptions contours and rotations experiments. This experiment is conducted because, although the contour description can be considered rotation invariant, the HMM training does not have to provide the same probabilities in cases of contour rotations.
5. The previous experiments but rotating the starting point of the contour and training the HMM with this initial description. The aim is to check if it is enough to consider this initial description instead of all contour rotations.

6. Finally, since the HMM has the feature of obtaining smaller probability values if the chain length increases, we have conducted experiments splitting the contour into two segments and classifying each one of them, then apply heuristics to assign the final probability.

A 5×1 process of crossed validation for error estimation [18] was carried out in our experiments and the confusion or contingency matrix with the measures of sensibility, specificity and precision for each class was used [19]. The values of all thresholds were determined by experimentation. In the following section the obtained results are shown and subsequently discussed.

3   Results and Discussion

In all experiments we have used the following notation: $C1$ for normal erythorcyte class; $C2$ for sickle or elongated erythorcyte class; $C3$ for other deformations erythorcyte class; TPR is the True Positive Rate or sensibility; TNR for the True Negative Rate or especificity and P for precision.

Experiment 1: The results obtained in the supervised classification of normal and elongated erythrocytes are very favorable, reaching a sensibility of 96 % and 99 % respectively (Table 1). This is an expected behavior since good differentiation exists among contours of normal and elongated erythrocytes.

Table 1. Erythrocyte classification in 2 classes.

	C1	C2	TPR	P	TNR
C1	194	8	0.96	0.99	0.99
C2	1	209	0.99	0.96	0.96

Table 2. Erythrocyte classification in 3 classes.

	C1	C2	C3	TPR	P	TNR
C1	190	5	7	0.94	0.97	0.79
C2	0	175	35	0.83	0.76	0.84
C3	5	49	157	0.74	0.79	0.89
Total				0.84	0.84	0.84

Experiment 2: In Table 2 the results of the classification considering three types of erythrocytes are shown: the normal ones, those elongated and those that present other deformations. In this case the classification of normal erythrocytes remains high, with 94 % of sensibility, but in the case of the elongated erythrocytes it drops to 83 %, because several objects are classified as belonging to other deformations. In the case of the class of other deformations it stays at 74 %. This is the expected behavior because some elements of this class of other deformations present a relatively elongated form although it is not the feature of the sickle cell.

Experiment 3: In Table 3 the results of the classification are shown when it is considered the class of other deformations like a class of rejection. The sensibility of the sickle cell classification rises to 85 % in this case but in the class of other deformations, it drops to 60 %, this is due to that several objects of this class have relatively elongated form and they are classified as sickle and they are only two classes.

Experiment 4: Experiments 1, 2 and 3 were carried out training each HMM with the initial description of the objects contours and the rotation of those contours. For each contour, all the versions of their description are obtained rotating all 4 points the same angle. In the case of experiment 1 the results were the same and they are shown in Table 1, the values of sensibility remain high in both classes. In Table 4 the results of the classification considering the three classes of erythrocytes and the training of the HMM with the rotations of the contours are shown. In this case, the values of sensibility in normal and elongated classes remains and it goes up the value of sensibility in the class of other deformations. This is the expected behavior because the way we train the models makes stabilize the parameters. In Table 5 the results of the erythrocytes classification with rejection are shown. In this case the results were relatively similar to the case of normal and elongated, but in other deformations the sensibility drops to 57 %, because when there are objects with relatively elongated form they are classified as sickle or elongated.

Table 3. Erythrocyte classification in 2 classes with rejection.

	C1	C2	C3	TPR	P	TNR
C1	188	8	6	0.93	0.99	0.72
C2	0	179	31	0.85	0.66	0.76
C3	1	84	126	0.60	0.77	0.89
Total				0.79	0.81	0.79

Table 4. Erythrocyte classification in 3 classes with contour rotation.

	C1	C2	C3	TPR	P	TNR
C1	189	5	8	0.94	0.98	0.79
C2	0	173	37	0.82	0.77	0.85
C3	3	47	161	0.76	0.78	0.88
Total				0.84	0.84	0.84

Experiment 5: In Table 6 the results of the classification of normal and elongated, training the models with the description of the contours and the rotation of the starting contour point, are shown. In this case the sensibilities remain high in both classes. In Table 7 the results of the classification in 3 classes, training the models with the description of the contour and adding the rotation of its starting point, are shown. In this case the sensibility in the classes of normal and elongated remains high but in the class of other deformations it descends to 67 %. This is because the training of the models is not able to set the parameters with the same efficiency to the case using rotations contours. In Table 8 the results of classifying in normal and elongated with rejection are shown. The sensibility in the case of normal and elongated ascends but in the case of other deformations drops to 37 %. So, most of part of the objects are classified as elongated.

Experiment 6: In Table 9 the results of the classification in three classes but dividing the contour in 2 segments are shown, since the model returns high probabilities if the length of the chain that it receives is small [1]. In this case, the sensibility for the normal class stays high. The sensibility for the class of

Table 5. Erythrocyte classification in 2 classes with rejection and contour rotation.

	C1	C2	C3	TPR	P	TNR
C1	188	9	5	0.93	0.99	0.70
C2	0	178	32	0.84	0.64	0.75
C3	1	90	120	0.57	0.76	0.89
Total				0.78	0.80	0.78

Table 6. Erythrocyte classification in 2 classes with starting contour point rotation.

	C1	C2	TPR	P	TNR
C1	196	6	0.97	0.99	0.99
C2	1	209	0.99	0.97	0.97

Table 7. Erythrocyte classification in 3 classes with starting contour point rotation.

	C1	C2	C3	TPR	P	TNR
C1	192	5	5	0.95	0.96	0.76
C2	0	178	32	0.85	0.73	0.81
C3	8	61	142	0.67	0.79	0.90
Total				0.82	0.83	0.82

Table 8. Erythrocyte classification in 2 classes with rejection and starting contour point rotation.

	C1	C2	C3	TPR	P	TNR
C1	191	6	5	0.95	0.97	0.66
C2	0	198	12	0.943	0.60	0.65
C3	5	128	78	0.37	0.82	0.94
Total				0.75	0.80	0.75

Table 9. Erythrocyte classification in 3 classes with contour division (Experiment 2).

	C1	C2	C3	TPR	P	TNR
C1	184	3	15	0.91	1.00	0.76
C2	0	128	82	0.61	0.87	0.92
C3	0	16	195	0.92	0.67	0.76
Total				0.81	0.85	0.82

Table 10. Erythrocyte classification in 2 classes with rejection and contour division (Experiment 3).

	C1	C2	C3	TPR	P	TNR
C1	186	3	13	0.92	0.99	0.76
C2	0	154	56	0.73	0.78	0.86
C3	1	41	169	0.80	0.71	0.83
Total				0.82	0.83	0.82

other deformations is 92 %. That is the expected behavior since each segment has a high probability of ownership to the class. But in the case of the elongated class, sensibility descends to 61 %, because when the contour is splitted in two parts, in many cases one of the segments is classified as belonging to the normal class, and this makes it to be assigned to the class of other deformations. In Table 10 the results of the classification in two classes with rejection and contour division are shown. In this case the sensibility for the normal class stays high. The sensibility for the elongated class is 73 %, superior to the previous case. In the case of the class of other deformations descends to 80 %, because several objects are classified as normal or elongated.

To evaluate the HMM performance in comparison with other methods in the bibliography, the experiments were carried out under the same conditions as in [15, 16] and using the provided database in [21]. The obtained results with this proposal do not overcome, for now, those shown in these works.

4 Conclusions

We have shown that it is possible to use HMM for classification of erythrocytes in normal and elongated classes. In all the experiments, the sensibility in this case was superior to 96 %. If we take into account the class of other deformations, the sensibility for elongated and other deformations classes did not overcome 83 % and 74 % respectively, because it had several objects with relatively elliptic form in the class other deformations.

The training of the HMM model with the descriptions corresponding to the rotations of the contours makes that the sensibility of the classification in the class of other deformations rises to 76 %. This form of training guarantees a better stability in the parameters of the models. The results of classification considering the rotation of the starting point of the contour to process was not better than the experiments considering the rotations of all the contours of the training set. Classification considering the class of other deformations like a class of rejection was not better than results with respect to the other experiments. The best results were obtained in classification of normal and elongated erythrocytes, due to the differentiation among both classes. The best results for classification in three classes were obtained when carrying out the training of the models with the rotation of all the contours.

Acknowledgements. This work was partially supported by the Projects TIN2012-35427, TIN2013-42795-P, with FEDER support, of the Spanish Government, and "XI Convocatoria de Ayudas Para Proyectos de Cooperación Universitaria al Desarrollo 2014 de la UIB". The authors also thank the Mathematics and Computer Science Department at the University of the Balearic Islands for its support.

References

1. Rabiner, L.: Quantitative red cell morphology. Monogr. Clin. Cytol. **9**, 1–27 (1989)
2. Bicego, M., Murino, V.: Investigating Hidden Markov Models capabilities in 2D shape classification. IEEE Trans. Pattern Anal. Mach. Intell. **26**(2), 281–286 (2004)
3. Cai, J., Liu, Z.Q.: Hidden Markov Models with spectral features for 2D shape recognition. IEEE Trans. Pattern Anal. Mach. Intell. **23**(12), 1454–1458 (2001)
4. Thakoor, N., Gao, J.: Detecting occlusion for Hidden Markov Modeled shapes. IEEE ICIP **2006**, 945–948 (2006)
5. Palazón, V., Marzal, A., Vilar, J.M.: On Hidden Markov Models and cyclic strings for shape recognition. Pattern Recogn. **47**, 2490–2504 (2014)
6. Zhu, Y., et al.: Coupling oriented Hidden Markov random field model with local clustering for segmenting blood vessels and measuring spatial structures in images of tumor microenvironment. In: IEEE International Conference on Bioinformatics and Biomedicine, pp. 353–357 (2011)
7. Qian, X., Byung-Jun, Y.: Contour-based Hidden Markov Model to segment 2D ultra-sound images. In: ICASSP 2011, pp. 705–708 (2011)
8. Min-Chi, S., Kenneth, R.: Hidden Markov Models for tracking neuronal structure contours in electron micrograph stacks. In: ISBI 2012, pp. 1377–1380 (2012)

9. Renuka, S., Min-Chi, S., Kenneth, R.: Hidden Markov Model-based multi-modal image fusion with efficient training. In: ICIP 2014, pp. 3582–3586 (2014)
10. Khan, A., Gould, S., Salzmann, M.: A linear Chain Markov Model for detection and localization of cells in early stage embryo development. In: 2015 IEEE Winter Conference on Applications of Computer Vision, pp. 527–533 (2015)
11. Ritter, N., Cooper, J.: Segmentation and border identification of cells in images of peripheral blood smear slides. In: ACSC 2007, vol. 62, pp. 161–169. Australian Computer Society Inc. (2007)
12. Habibzadeh, M., Krzyzak, A., Fevens, T.: Application of pattern recognition techniques for the analysis of thin blood smear images. J. Med. Inform. Technol. **18**, 29–40 (2011)
13. Eom, S., Kim, S., Shin, V., Ahn, B.-H.: Leukocyte segmentation in blood smear images using region-based active contours. In: Blanc-Talon, J., Philips, W., Popescu, D., Scheunders, P. (eds.) ACIVS 2006. LNCS, vol. 4179, pp. 867–876. Springer, Heidelberg (2006)
14. Daz, G., González, F.A., Romero, E.A.: Semi-automatic method for quantification and classification of erythrocytes infected with malaria parasites in microscopic images. J. Biomed. Inform. **42**(2), 296–307 (2009)
15. Gual-Arnau, X., Herold-García, S., Simó, A.: Erythrocyte shape classification using integral-geometry-based methods. Med. Biol. Eng. Comput. **53**(7), 623–633 (2015)
16. Gual-Arnau, X., Herold-García, S., Simó, A.: Geometric analysis of planar shapes with applications to cell deformations. Image Anal. Stereology **34**(3), 171–182 (2015)
17. Osher, S., Sethian, J.: Fronts propagating with curvature dependent speed: algorithms based on Hamilton-Jacobi formulations. J. Comput. Phys. **79**, 12–49 (1988)
18. Ferri, F.J., Vidal, E.: Comparison of several editing and condensing techniques for colour image segmentation and object location. Pattern Recognition and Image Analysis, Series in Machine Perception and Artificial Intelligence. World Scientific Editorial (1992)
19. Stehman, S.V.: Selecting and interpreting measures of thematic classification accuracy. Remote Sens. Environ. **62**(1), 77–89 (1997)
20. Ross, S.M.: Introduction to Probability Models, 11th edn. Elsevier, Amsterdam (2014)
21. González-Hidalgo, M., Guerrero-Peña, F.A., Herold-García, D., Jaume-i-Capó, A., Marrero-Fernández, P.D.: Red blood cell cluster separation from digital images for use in sickle cell disease. IEEE J. Biomed. Health Inform. **19**(4), 1514–1525 (2015)
22. Rabiner, L.R.: A tutorial on hidden Markov models and selected applications in speech recognition. In: Proceedings of the IEEE, pp. 257–186 (1989)

Providing Physical Appearance and Behaviour to Virtual Characters

María del Puy Carretero[✉], Helen V. Diez, Sara García, and David Oyarzun

Vicomteh-IK4, Paseo Mikeletegi 57, 20009 Donostia-San Sebastián, Spain
{mcarretero,hdiez,sgarcia,doyarzun}@vicomtech.org
http://www.vicomtech.org

Abstract. The goal of the work presented in this paper is to develop a web based authoring tool to create the physical appearance of a virtual character and to provide its behaviour. One of the main characteristics of this tool is its simplicity to create a virtual character, provide its behaviour and the way to integrate it anywhere. The appearance of each virtual character and its behaviour are stored in a database. In order to specify the behaviour, the standard BML (Behaviour Markup Language) is used. It is interpreted by a BML Parser module that indicates to the animation engine how the virtual character has to act. The authoring tool is tested creating different virtual characters and integrating them in two unrelated applications with different roles.

Keywords: 3D virtual character · Authoring tool · Animation

1 Introduction

Nowadays virtual characters are frequently used in several kind of applications. The role of the virtual characters depends on the application; it can act for example as a guide, assistant or as an information presenter. Although they are commonly used, their design, development, animation and integration are not easy tasks. These functionalities are commonly done by 3D designers and animation experts. The goal of the work presented in this paper is to develop an authoring tool to create the physical appearance of a virtual character and to provide its behaviour in order to make it lively. In addition, other objective is to provide different options to integrate and use the created virtual characters in different applications.

One of the most typical method of giving the virtual character's behaviour is by using a mark-up language, which contains different labels to indicate the text to be spoken, emotions, facial and body gestures, and the exact moments when these have to be reproduced. The authoring tool presented in this paper is based on Behavior Markup Language (BML) standard because of the reasons given in Related Work section [1].

The paper is organized as follows; Sect. 2 analyses the related work regarding different methods and possibilities of creating virtual characters and giving them

© Springer International Publishing Switzerland 2016
F.J. Perales and J. Kittler (Eds.): AMDO 2016, LNCS 9756, pp. 98–107, 2016.
DOI: 10.1007/978-3-319-41778-3_10

behaviour. Section 3 explains the method followed to accomplish the goals of this work, describing in detail each authoring tool. Section 4 explains the global architecture to create and integrate virtual characters. Section 5 shows different use cases and applications of the presented work. And the final section is about conclusions and future work.

2 Related Work

The idea of virtual characters editor is not new. Virtual worlds like Second Life[1], or games such as The Sims[2] or World of Warcraft[3] allow the user to configure the appearance of the virtual character who will represent them. However the use of these editors is exclusively of the application (the virtual world or the game) and the virtual character only can be used on them. In addition, the actions of the virtual character are defined by the actions of the user. That is, the behaviour is defined by what wants to do the end user at each moment.

In other kind of applications, behaviour definition usually is done by means of authoring tools and by using scripting and markup languages [2]. During the last years, several markup languages have appeared in order to specify the behaviour of virtual characters such as VHML [3], AML [4] or CML [5]. A comparison between them and other markup languages oriented to virtual characters can be found in [6].

BML [1] is a markup language, developed several years ago, oriented to describe verbal and non-verbal behaviour of virtual characters. BML defines elements like gestures and facial expressions and also allows specifying their temporal alignment. BML has become a standard and other markup languages allow compatibility with it. For example, the aim of PML [7] is to specify knowledge about the environment an non-verbal behaviour to virtual characters and it includes compatibility with BML. Moreover as the authors explain in [8] BML has some advantages such as it is intuitive and simple to implement.

In addition there are several projects based on BML whose main objective is to generate non-verbal behaviour for virtual characters. There are several interpreters like SmartBody [9], BMLRealizer [10] or Elckerlyc [11] that animate virtual character receiving a BML archive as input. However, to generate that input, there is only one behaviour planning developed [12]. This non-verbal generator analyzes the syntactic and semantic of a text and the affective state of a character to decide the behaviour, so it is not oriented to be decided by end users.

An interesting tool for the creation of interactive applications with multiple virtual characters is Visual SceneMaker [13]. It is planed to add BML and other markup languages to integrate non-verbal behaviour generation, so it does not include our main objective.

---

[1] http://secondlife.com/.

[2] https://www.thesims.com/.

[3] http://eu.battle.net/wow/.

Taking all this into consideration, a tool based on BML with the following features has not been found:

- it has to be Web based in order to be accessible from any device and at any time,
- it has to be easy to use,
- it has to be modular in order to add new functionalities,
- it has to allow appearance and behaviour edition,
- the appearance and behaviour have to be easily integrable in other applications.

3   Authoring Tool: Intelligent Animated Agent Editor

The authoring tool is divided in two different functionalities. The first one is to create the physical appearance of the virtual character. The second one is to provide behaviour to an already defined virtual character. The proposed tool is a web based application in order to make it accessible from any device.

Previous to using the Editor the user must have the 3D models to work on. These models have to be created and maintained by 3D graphic designer experts in order to design and create the different options to create the virtual characters.

To change the appearance of the 3D models the texture of their attributes must be changed. To change the behaviour different animations designed for that model have to be loaded. So for each model it is needed to have stored various files; COLLADA files for the 3D models and animations and .jpeg or .png files for the textures.

To handle the application an SQL database is used. This database stores the user profiles, projects, 3D models, textures, animations and Timeline sequence. To store the textures and animations, the route in which each file is found is stored.

3.1   Appearance Editor

The appearance editor has been designed to configure the physical appearance of virtual characters in a simple way. End users do not have to have prior knowledge in design of 3D computer graphics. The appearance of the virtual character is configured by selecting different options in hair, face, eyes, body, clothing and other complements.

Figure 1 shows the interface of the Appearance Editor. As it can be seen, there are three main work areas:

- **3D Visor:** this area shows in real time the appearance of the virtual character. When the end user selects an option from the menu, this change is automatically shown here.
- **Options menu:** it is composed by a series of libraries that facilitate the virtual character editing task. There are three different libraries:

Fig. 1. Appearance editor interface

- *Virtual Characters:* this library stores the 3D models of each virtual character. The end user only has to choose one to customize it.
- *Textures:* each virtual character has several textures associated. The end user can select one of them to customize it and change the appearance according to his/her preferences.
- *Complements:* for each virtual character it is necessary to have a series of accessories or complements. These complements can be hair styles, hats, moustaches, different kind of jewels, etc. The texture can also be selected to change its appearance.
- **Timeline:** although this area can be seen from the Appearance Editor, this functionality is to define the virtual character's behaviour as explained in the next section.

Thus the end user can select the basic appearance with the virtual characters menu, customize it through selecting different textures and have the possibility to add several complements to personalise the physical appearance to his/her liking. Once the end user has finished the appearance configuration of the virtual character, the project containing this character can be saved in the database with a given name.

3.2 Behaviour Editor

The objective of the Behaviour Editor is to animate the virtual character and to provide it with the ability to speak in an easy way without the need of having technical knowledge in animation of virtual characters.

Figure 2 shows the interface of the Behavior Editor. As it can be seen, there are three different areas:

– **Viewer Area:** in this area, end users can watch the defined behaviour by pressing play button.
– **Options Menu:** as in the Appearance Editor, it is composed by a series of libraries that facilitate the task of editing the behaviour. As it was mentioned before, these libraries have to be developed by experts. There are three different libraries:
  - *Expressions:* it contains predefined facial animations to express emotions such as: happiness, sadness, surprise, etc. The user can select the intensity of the expression.
  - *Animations:* it contains different animations to personalise the behaviour such as: greeting with hand, walking, etc.
  - *Loops:* These animations include all those movements that people do unconsciously and they are applied to virtual characters to make their behaviour more natural. For example: blinking, swaying body, etc.

Fig. 2. Behavior editor interface

– **Timeline:** it displays the list of selected options in chronological order. In order to specify the behaviour, the end user has to drag&drop expressions, animations and loops from the Options Menu.

As the aim of virtual character is to emulate the behaviour of a real person, it will be able to communicate in a verbal way. For this purpose there is also an option to introduce the text that the virtual character has to speak. This text is transformed into speech by a Text-to-Speech synthesizer. iSpeech [14] has been used for this purpose. To enter the text there is a button with the 'T' letter above Options Menu that opens a pop-up menu to write the text.

Thus, once the appearance of the virtual character has been defined with the Appearance Editor, this character can be doted with behaviour with this tool. The end user only has to write the text for the virtual character to reproduce. This text is converted into speech and an audio file is stored in the project folder. Then the user has to drag&drop this feature onto the Timeline, and add the animations that the virtual character has to do while acting. The user selects the start time of each action as well as the duration of each one.

The result can be visualized at any moment in the Viewer Area pressing the play button of the interface and the end user can modify it as many time as needed.

The composition created in the Timeline is translated and stored into a BML file. In the following BML example designed with the Behavior Editor, an introduction message has been created.

```
<bml xmlns="http://www.bml-initiative.org/bml/bml-1.0"
     character="Iaan" id="bml1">
  <gesture id="behaviour1" lexeme="hello-waving"
  start="2" end="5"/>
  <faceLexeme id="behaviour2" lexeme="happy" amount="0.8"
  start="2" end="5"/>
  <speech id="speech1" start="4">
      <text>Hello! My name is Iaan
      and I am a virtual character</text>
  </speech>
</bml>
```

This BML file will be the input of the Animation Engine. The following section explains all the process to obtain a virtual character acting.

4   Global Architecture

Figure 3 shows the global architecture in order to define the appearance and behaviour of virtual characters. As it can be seen, both editors are accessible from the same URL, explained in the previous section.

Once the behaviour of the virtual character is defined, it is stored as BML format, which is interpreted by the BML Parser module. This module extracts

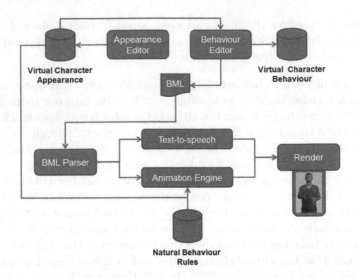

Fig. 3. Global architecture

the text that has to be reproduced by the virtual character and converts it into audio by means of a text-to-speech module. Besides, the BML Parser extracts the behaviour of the virtual character of the BML labels. This behaviour is represented by the Animation Engine Module.

The Animation Engine is composed by several modules developed using JavaScript programming language and following all the HTML5 and Web3D standards. WebGL [15] technology has been used to render the virtual character via web. WebGL is based on OpenGL, which is a widely used open source 3D graphics standard. Besides nowadays, most common browsers support this technology without the need of plug-ins; Google Chrome, Mozilla Firefox, Apple Safari or Opera [16].

The Animation Engine runs as follows: the appearance of the virtual character is loaded from the Virtual Character database. It has natural behaviour, involving blinking, looking sideways, changing the weight of the body between both feet, crossing arms, etc. With this natural behaviour the virtual character emulates the actions of a real person in a waiting state. The natural behaviour rules are the same ones for each character and they are applied when there is no other behaviour running. In order to change the behaviour, the user has to edit one with the web based Behavior Editor.

When the Animation Engine receives the BML input with the designed behaviour, the animation engine stops any default (natural) animation except blinking. Then it starts the sequence of animations, emotions and other defined behaviour.

Thanks to both tools, the creation of virtual characters is very intuitive and fast. Its integration with other contents and applications can be done by two different means:

- By generating a video from the Behavior Editor itself. In order to generate the video FFmpeg [17] is used.
- By integrating the Animation Engine in the application where the virtual character has to appear.

How to integrate the virtual character depends on the characteristics and specifications of the final application. Through a video, the virtual character will only give information. Whereas if the animation engine is integrated, more interactive characters can be created. The following section explains different use cases.

5 Application and Use Cases

As it has been explained before, there are two different ways of integrating the result of the authoring tool. It depends on the final application as well as the role of the virtual character.

The authoring tool has been tested integrating the virtual character with the following roles: a presenter and a virtual teacher.

5.1 Virtual Character as a Presenter

One of the use cases of the Appearance and Behavior Editors has been to create a virtual presenter. The role of the virtual character is to give or present different kind of information. In this case, the main objective was to mix the virtual presenter with other kind of information as pictures, text, videos, etc. The idea was to obtain a video of the virtual character acting in order to use it in other editor to mix it with the rest of the content.

Thanks to the authoring tools, it was possible to create the introduction made by the virtual character in an easy way. The designer only had to select the appearance, write the speech and select the behaviour of the character.

As the virtual character had to be mixed with other contents, a chroma video was obtained in order to integrate it properly. Thus this video of the virtual character acting can be integrated with further multimedia content to create the final video of the presentation.

5.2 Virtual Character as Virtual Teacher

E-learning applications are very commonly used in the academic area. Increasingly frequent use of virtual characters who exercise the role of teachers. The objective is to guide students in their learning process as a real teacher does.

One of the tasks of the virtual character is to introduce the lessons. For this task the authoring tool can be used to create the lessons. Moreover, teachers evaluate students so also the behaviour editor can be used to create these responses.

The difference with the previous application is that one of the advantages of the e-learning is that the student can decide his/her scheduling, so the application is interactive. In addition learning management systems (LMS) are normally used for this purpose. In this case the selected LMS was Moodle, so the animation engine was integrated into Moodle in order to show the virtual teacher. Lessons and possible responses of the teacher were created with the authoring tool and integrated into the Moodle course. Students could see the virtual tutor teaching the lesson and also received feedback from virtual tutor in the exercise phase.

6   Conclusions and Future Work

This paper presents an innovative tool to define the appearance and behaviour of virtual characters. Its design has been thought for users who are not familiar with the design of computer graphics, animation and programming. Thus, the user interface is specifically designed to be intuitive and very easy to use.

The integration of the result can be easily done by two different means: by generating a video and playing it; and by integrating the animation engine into the final application. We plan to evaluate the usability of the system with real users of the application.

As future work, we are working on reusing the defined behaviour in other virtual characters. As the authoring tool presented in this paper works now, the behaviour is defined for a particular virtual character. This is because each virtual character has its own defined animations. These animations cannot be used in other characters because each one has its particular characteristics. Although human virtual characters are normally used, and all of them have similar physiognomy, the length of the skeleton bones is not equal, so during the animations can be non detected collisions. Reusing the defined behaviour is an interesting functionality in order to reuse scripts, or to have the opportunity to change the selected virtual character, etc.

Another useful functionality is to define behaviour to several virtual characters at the same time. Thus, it would be possible to have several characters in the same scene with different or similar roles. For example to emulate news presenters or other kind of simulations.

References

1. Vilhjálmsson, H.H., et al.: The behavior markup language: recent developments and challenges. In: Pelachaud, C., Martin, J.-C., André, E., Chollet, G., Karpouzis, K., Pelé, D. (eds.) IVA 2007. LNCS (LNAI), vol. 4722, pp. 99–111. Springer, Heidelberg (2007)
2. Jung, Y., Wagner, S., Jung, C., Behr, J., Fellner, D.: Storyboarding and pre-visualization with X3D. In: Proceedings of the 15th International Conference on Web 3D Technology, pp. 73–82. ACM (2010)
3. Marriot, A.: VHML (2001). http://www.vhml.org/

4. Kshirsagar, S., Magnenat-Thalmann, N., Guye-Vuillme, A., Thalmann, D., Kamyab, K., Mamdani, E.: Avatar markup language. In: ACM International Conference Proceeding Series, vol. 23, pp. 169–177, May 2002
5. Arafa, Y., Mamdani, A.: Scripting embodied agents behaviour with CML: character markup language. In: Proceedings of the 8th International Conference on Intelligent User Interfaces, pp. 313–316. ACM, January 2003
6. Oyarzun, D., Ortiz, A., Carretero, M.P., Gelissen, J., Garcia-Alonso, A., Sivan, Y.: A framework for representing inhabitants in 3D virtual worlds. In: Proceedings of the 14th International Conference on 3D Web Technology, pp. 83–90. ACM (2009)
7. Scherer, S., et al.: Perception markup language: towards a standardized representation of perceived nonverbal behaviors. In: Nakano, Y., Neff, M., Paiva, A., Walker, M. (eds.) IVA 2012. LNCS, vol. 7502, pp. 455–463. Springer, Heidelberg (2012)
8. Čereković, A., Pejša, T., Pandžić, I.S.: A controller-based animation system for synchronizing and realizing human-like conversational behaviors. In: Esposito, A., Campbell, N., Vogel, C., Hussain, A., Nijholt, A. (eds.) Second COST 2102. LNCS, vol. 5967, pp. 80–91. Springer, Heidelberg (2010)
9. Thiebaux, M., Marsella, S., Marshall, A.N., Kallmann, M.: Smartbody: behavior realization for embodied conversational agents. In: Proceedings of the 7th International Joint Conference on Autonomous Agents and Multiagent Systems, vol. 1, pp. 151–158. International Foundation for Autonomous Agents and Multiagent Systems, May 2008
10. Árnason, B.P., Porsteinsson, A.: The CADIA BML realizer. http://cadia.ru.is/projects/bmlr/
11. van Welbergen, H., Reidsma, D., Ruttkay, Z.M., Zwiers, J.: Elckerlyc: a BML realizer for continuous, multimodal interaction with a virtual human. J. Multimodal User Interfaces 3(4), 271–284 (2010). ISSN: 1783-7677
12. Lee, J., Marsella, S.C.: Nonverbal behavior generator for embodied conversational agents. In: Gratch, J., Young, M., Aylett, R.S., Ballin, D., Olivier, P. (eds.) IVA 2006. LNCS (LNAI), vol. 4133, pp. 243–255. Springer, Heidelberg (2006)
13. Gebhard, P., Mehlmann, G., Kipp, M.: Visual SceneMaker: a tool for authoring interactive virtual characters. J. Multimodal User Interfaces 6(1–2), 3–11 (2011)
14. iSpeech. http://www.ispeech.org/. Accessed May 2016
15. Leung, C., Salga, A.: Enabling WebGL. In: Proceedings of the 19th International Conference on World Wide Web, pp. 1369–1370. ACM (2010)
16. WebGL - 3D Canvas graphics. http://caniuse.com/. Accessed April 2016
17. FFmpeg. https://ffmpeg.org/. Accessed May 2016

On Combining Edge Detection Methods for Improving BSIF Based Facial Recognition Performances

Pierluigi Tuveri, Luca Ghiani[✉], Mohanad Abukmeil,
and Gian Luca Marcialis

Department of Electrical and Electronic Engineering,
University of Cagliari, Cagliari, Italy
{pierluigi.tuveri,luca.ghiani,mohanad.abukmeil,
marcialis}@diee.unica.it

Abstract. Lighting variation is a major challenge for an automatic face recognition system. In order to overcome this problem, many methods have been proposed. Most of them try to extract features invariant to illumination changes or to reduce illumination changes in a pre-processing step and to extract features for recognition.

In this paper, we present a procedure similar to the latter where the two steps are complementary. In the pre-processing step we deal with the illumination changes and in the features extraction step we use the BSIF (Binarized Statistical Image Features), a recently proposed textural algorithm.

In our opinion, a method capable of reducing the lighting variations is ideal for an algorithm like the BSIF.

The performance of our system has been tested on the FRGC dataset and the presented results show the validity of our approach.

Keywords: Face recognition · Edge detection · Binarized Statistical Image Features · Textural algorithm

1 Introduction

Face analysis is a difficult task for an automatic system. Additional issues as different head poses, illumination changes or partial occlusions make it even more challenging. That is true today more than ever, with the widespread presence of hand devices and security cameras with embedded face detection and recognition modules.

Over the years several face recognition algorithms have been developed [1] starting from linear subspace methods like PCA [2] first and, then, LDA [3]. Subspace Learning goal is to find a subspace into which all faces are projected since a lower dimension leads to better performance and, more important, the feature vectors projected in the subspace are supposed to be more separable, thus easier to recognize.

© Springer International Publishing Switzerland 2016
F.J. Perales and J. Kittler (Eds.): AMDO 2016, LNCS 9756, pp. 108–116, 2016.
DOI: 10.1007/978-3-319-41778-3_11

There are also local feature-based methods like Elastic Bunch Graph Matching [4] or Active shape models [5]. They process the input image in order to identify and extract (and also measure) distinctive facial features such as the eyes, mouth, nose, etc., as well as other fiducial marks and compute the geometric relationships among those facial points reducing the input facial image to a vector of geometric features. Standard statistical pattern recognition techniques are then employed to match faces using these measurements.

Another kind of facial image representation is based on texture features like those extracted by Local Binary Pattern (LBP) [6], Local Phase Quantization (LPQ) [7], BSIF [8]. These local descriptors have gained attention lately due to their robustness to challenges such as pose and illumination changes. The idea of using a textural algorithm for face description is motivated by the fact that faces can be seen as a composition of micro-patterns which are well described by such operators.

Among these algorithms, BSIFs have shown to perform better than others in face recognition [8], even when only one colour channel is available, namely, the Y one. BSIFs are based on textural filters learnt from natural images. These can be generated on the basis of an appropriate set of training images. Generally, obtained filters are similar to Gabor's ones, and appear to be effective for describing the textural information around the edges of the face image. For this reason, we believe that a preliminary step of edge enhancement and/or detection, instead of standard pre-processing methods as histogram equalization, could contribute to further improve the performance. Moreover, it has been observed that these filters can reduce the lighting variations of an image. Therefore, in this paper we present an experimental analysis of such filters coupled with BSIFs. Experiments are carried out on the FRGC dataset, Experiment 4, where lighting variations in the test set (Probe set) are significant with respect to those in the Gallery set. Results showed that the improvement of the performance is remarkable when edge enhancement methods are applied instead of edge detectors or filters explicitly conceived for reducing lighting conditions only, and they are competitive with other state-of-the-art methods using the Y colour channel.

2   BSIF and Edge Enhancement-Based Pre-processing

Since [9], textural algorithms have been widely used in face recognition. These local image descriptors have fully proved the capability of efficiently describe faces. In this work we adopted the BSIF (Binarized Statistical Image Features) algorithm, another textural algorithm recently proposed by Kannla and Rathu and we selected it since it outperformed similar algorithms like LBP or LPQ [8]. A fixed set of filters is automatically learnt from a small set of natural images. The algorithm is based on a convolution between the input image $X(u,v)$ and a set of n of these pre-learnt filters.

Such convolution can be written as:

$$s_i = \sum_{u,v} W_i(u,v)X(u,v) = w_i^T x$$

The feature vector extracted by the BSIF algorithm is the histogram of pixels code values of the image. Each bit is associated with a different filter and the length of the bit string is determined by the number of filters used. The filters W_i are learnt using independent component analysis (ICA) by maximizing the statistical independence of s_i. In our experiments, we used the set of filters provided by the authors of [8] and learnt from a set of 13 natural images. We then define a function:

$$Z(s_i) = \begin{cases} 1 & if\, s_i > 0 \\ 0 & otherwise \end{cases}$$

on which we can build the value:

$$X = \sum_{i=0}^{n-1} Z(s_i) 2^i$$

In order to implement our version of the face recognition module, we selected a stack of 12 filters, each one of 5×5 pixels. Figure 1 represents the 12 filters used.

The observation of the BSIF filters, similar to many others edge detection filters, suggests that the analysis of an image from which the noise and the variations due to the lighting have been removed and in which details of the edges have been enhanced will produce better results.

As a matter of fact the more the edges are distinct the more the response to a BSIF filter will be effective. Pre-processing an image will reduce the less detailed areas and this helps in particular to better describe the areas that are under or overexposed to lighting.

Many pre-processing algorithms have been proposed in order to reduce illumination changes in face images. In this paper, we adopted the following ones [10]:

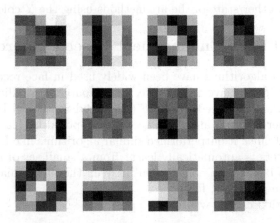

Fig. 1. Filters used in the BSIF algorithm.

Sobel: it an approximation of the derivative in the horizontal and vertical directions. The difference with respect to similar filters is that Sobel, while deriving in one direction, it also apply a gaussian average in the other. It is very basic but has a good capability to detect edges and reduce noise [11].

Canny: first a gaussian filter is applied in order to reduce the noise smoothing the image. The gradient of the image is calculated horizontally and vertically and, from that, it is easy to determine the edge direction. Then each edge point is compared with its neighbours and the so called nonmaximum values are suppressed, so the edge line is thinned by the elimination of those values. Finally a double threshold is applied to maintain high valued and reject low valued edge pixels while intermediate values are maintained only if close to high valued ones. With the right parameters tuning it has a good edge detection ability [11].

Single Scale Retinex (SSR): This algorithm is based on the logarithmic difference between the original image, and the image convoluted by a gaussian filter. The main parameter is the bandwidth of the gaussian, as a matter of fact the right tuning avoids the halo effects. This problem is present when the image is affected by not gradual luminosity [12].

Multi Scale Retinex (MSR): The algorithm is an improvement of the SSR. It tries to alleviate the halo effect problem, using three Gaussian filters, hence using three different bandwidth. In other words the MSR is a weighted sum of three SSR [13].

Self Quotient Image (SQI): it is based on two steps, illumination estimation and illumination effect subtraction. An image with the same illumination and shape as the original one is generated. The difference between the logarithms of the original and the modified images allows to normalize the illumination and to enhance the edges [14].

Weber Low Descriptor (WLD): it is based on the Weber's Law. The principle states that the ratio between the increment threshold and the background is a constant. Thus the algorithm calculates the difference between the center and its neighbors divided by the value of the center in order to estimate that constant. It has a great edge enhancement capability [15].

Difference of Gaussians (DoG): it is a filter computed as the difference of two Gaussian functions that have different standard deviations. Basically it is a band-pass filter capable of removing the lighting variations in the low band and, at the same time, the noise in the high band. It is very effective displaying the contours [16].

In Fig. 2(a) we show an example where the face has been underexposed during the acquisition. We show the pre-processing results as well (Fig. 2(b-i)). It can be seen that, apart from the Sobel and Canny filters as well as the histogram equalization, the analyzed filters return a clearer image. From the images it is evident that we can divide the filters in different groups: edge detection based (Sobel and Canny), lighting enhancement (Retinex) based (SSR and MSR) and edge enhancement based (SQI, WLD and DoG).

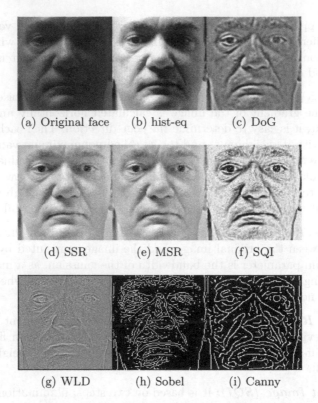

(a) Original face   (b) hist-eq   (c) DoG

(d) SSR   (e) MSR   (f) SQI

(g) WLD   (h) Sobel   (i) Canny

Fig. 2. Original face (a), face pre-processed with a simple histogram equalization (b), face pre-processed with DoG (c), SSR (d), MSR (e), SQI (f), WLD (g), Sobel (h), Canny (i).

3   Experimental Results

All the colored images have been converted to grayscale. As the size of the faces might change from one picture to another, the eyes position is used to rotate the image in order to have a roll angle equal to zero and to normalize the distance between the eyes [1]. A normalization distance of 64 pixels has been selected and a square of 128×128 pixels containing the face is cropped from the image. The image is converted to grayscale, then one of the presented pre-processing methods is applied. Finally, the cropped face image is divided in NxN (6×6 in our case) squares and a BSIF histogram is calculated and inserted in a feature vector (1024 integer values) for each of these squares. The concatenation of the individual feature vectors produces a vector that is compared with those of all the other available templates using a cosine distance.

We tested all the presented pre-processing methods coupled with the BSIF algorithm on the FRGC dataset, Experiment 4, ROCIII. The experiment 4 of the FRGC version2 is one of the hardest challenge in face recognition. The images of the query set are captured in uncontrolled illumination, instead the images of the target set are captured in controlled environment.

Moreover images from the target set are captured during Fall while those from the query during Spring [17].

ROC curves are presented in Fig. 3 and compared with those obtained by the BSIF algorithm without any pre-processing (no-prep) or with just a simple histogram equalization (hist-eq). Performance obtained with the latter two is

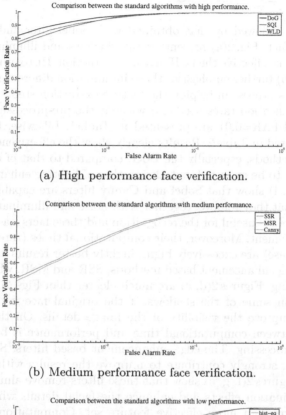

(a) High performance face verification.

(b) Medium performance face verification.

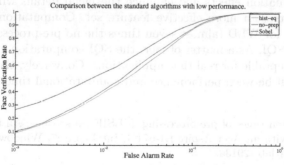

(c) Low performance face verification

Fig. 3. Results obtained by the BSIF algorithm without any pre-processing (no-prep) and with eight different pre-processing methods. (Color figure online)

Table 1. Face verification rates at FAR=0.001 and FAR=0.01 for the different pre-processing methods + BSIF.

	no-prep	hist-eq	Edge Detection		Lighting Enhancement		Edge Enhancement		
			Sobel	Canny	SSR	MSR	SQI	WLD	DoG
FVR@FAR=0.001	0.105	0.089	0.239	0.421	0.457	0.489	0.752	0.763	0.819
FVR@FAR=0.01	0.421	0.389	0.549	0.762	0.785	0.805	0.935	0.945	0.960

the worst result followed by that obtained with Sobel filter and Canny filter. As a matter of fact, Fig. 2(a) presents many shadows and illumination changes that does not make effective the BSIF feature extraction. Histogram equalization shown in Fig. 2(b) further emphasizes those illumination differences and explains the failure of this process in helping the feature extraction step.

The face verification rates with and without the pre-processing methods at FAR=0.001 and FAR=0.01 are presented in Table 1. Likewise, the processing times are presented in Table 2. Results clearly show the effectiveness of the edge enhancement methods, especially the DoG, compared to that of edge detection methods, as was to be expected, but also to that of lighting enhancement methods. Figures 2(h, i) show that Sobel and Canny filters are capable of detecting the edges but that they remove, together with noise and illumination effects, all the other face details useful for the recognition and these facts leads to an unsatisfactory improvement. Moreover, their computational times (three times the no pre-processing case) are excessively high. Slightly better results are obtained by using the lighting enhancement based methods, SSR and MSR, which explicitly model the lighting. Figures 2(d, e) are much clearer than Figs. 2(a, b). Surprisingly they retain some of the shadows of the original face image since their purpose is to improve the visibility of the image details. On the other hand, the trade-off between computational time and performance is better than the case of no-preprocessing. The edge enhancement based filters, SQI, WLD and especially DOG, strongly contribute to improve the results with a remarkable performance. Figures 2(f, g, c) show that these filters remove almost completely noise and illumination effects and enhance the facial details which help BSIF algorithm to extract a more effective feature set. Computational time is the biggest problem for WLD (almost seven times the no pre-processing case) and, much more, for SQI. As a matter of fact, the SQI computational time (about 1 second) is unacceptable for real-time applications. Conversely, the DoG exhibits the best trade-off between performance and computational time.

Table 2. Execution times of pre-processing + BSIF (in second). All the experiments were performed with an Acer Aspire E1-571G, Intel core i7, Windows 8.1 64 bit, 12 GB ram using Matlab r2013a.

no-prep	hist-eq	Edge Detection		Lighting Enhancement		Edge Enhancement		
		Sobel	Canny	SSR	MSR	SQI	WLD	DoG
0.010	0.012	0.034	0.037	0.023	0.033	0.912	0.067	0.018

Finally, we would like to mention another paper in which a textural feature extractor on one channel has been coupled with edge enhancement method. Tan and Triggs [16] used the DoG LBP (FVR=0.80 @FAR=0.001) and Gabor filters (FVR=0.80 @FAR=0.001). Reported results is an indirect confirmation of our claim on the complementarity between edge enhancement and textural algorithms.

4 Conclusions

In this paper, we analyzed the performance of several edge detection and enhancement algorithms coupled with BSIF approach by using only one channel and under lighting variations. We showed that filters conceived for edge enhancement performed even better than filters explicitly conceived for modeling the illumination variations and for edge detection. Therefore, the ability of a pre-processing method to enhance information specifically useful to BSIF is strictly correlated with the performance improvement.

Future work will include experiments with other pre-processing methods and feature extraction algorithms in order to further confirm our claims.

Acknowledgement. The research leading to these results has received funding from the European Union's Seventh Framework Programme managed by REA - Research Executive Agency http://ec.europa.eu/research/rea (FP7/2007-2013) under Grant Agreement n 606058.

References

1. Jain, A.K., Li, S.Z.: Handbook of Face Recognition. Springer-Verlag, New York, USA (2005)
2. Turk, M., Pentland, A.: Eigenfaces for recognition. J. Cogn. Neur. **3**(1), 71–86 (1991)
3. Belhumeur, P.N., Hespanha, J.P., Kriegman, D.: Eigenfaces vs. fisherfaces: recognition using class specific linear projection. PAMI, IEEE Trans. **19**(7), 711–720 (1997)
4. Wiskott, L., Fellous, J.M., Krüger, N., von der Malsburg, C.: Face recognition by elastic bunch graph matching. IEEE Trans. PAMI **19**(7), 775–779 (1997)
5. Cootes, T.F., Taylor, C.J., Cooper, D.H., Graham, J.: Active shape models-their training and application. Comp. Vis. Im. Underst. **61**(1), 38–59 (1995)
6. Ojala, T., Pietikäinen, M., Mäenpää, T.: Multiresolution gray-scale and rotation invariant texture classification with local binary patterns. IEEE Trans. PAMI **24**(7), 971–987 (2002)
7. Heikkilä, J., Ojansivu, V.: Methods for local phase quantization in blur-insensitive image analysis. In: Proceedings of the International Work on Local and Non-Local Approx. in Im. Proceedings (LNLA 2009), pp. 104–111 (2009)
8. Kannala, J., Rahtu, E.: Bsif: binarized statistical image features. In: Proceedings of the 21stInternational Conference on Pattern Record (ICPR 2012), Tsukuba, Japan, pp. 1363–1366 (2012)

 9. Ahonen, T., Hadid, A., Pietikäinen, M.: Face recognition with local binary patterns. In: Pajdla, T., Matas, J.G. (eds.) ECCV 2004. LNCS, vol. 3021, pp. 469–481. Springer, Heidelberg (2004)
10. Jain, A.K.: Fundamentals of Digital Image Processing. Prentice-Hall Inc, NJ, USA (1989)
11. Solomon, C.J., Breckon, T.P.: Fundamentals of Digital Image Processing: A Practical Approach with Examples in Matlab. Wiley-Blackwell, Hoboken (2010). ISBN-13: 978-0470844731
12. Land, E.H., Mccann, J.J.: Lightness and retinex theory. J. Opt. Soc. Am. **61**, 1–11 (1971)
13. Rahman, Z., Woodell, G.A.: A multiscale retinex for bridging the gap between color images and the human observation of scenes. IEEE Trans. Image Proc. **6**, 965–976 (1997)
14. Wang, H., Li, S.Z., Wang, Y., Zhang, J.: Self quotient image for face recognition. In: 2004 International Conference on Image Processing, 2004. ICIP 2004, vol. 2, pp. 1397–1400, October 2004
15. Chen, J., Shan, S., He, C., Zhao, G., Pietikainen, M., Chen, X., Gao, W.: Wld: A robust local image descriptor. PAMI, IEEE Trans. **32**(9), 1705–1720 (2010)
16. Tan, X., Triggs, B.: Enhanced local texture feature sets for face recognition under difficult lighting conditions. IEEE Trans. Image Process. **19**(6), 1635–1650 (2010)
17. Phillips, P.J., Flynn, P.J., Scruggs, T., Bowyer, K.W., Chang, J., Hoffman, K., Marques, J., Min, J., Worek, W.: Overview of the face recognition grand challenge. In: Proceedings of the of the 2005 IEEE Computer Society Conference on Computer Vision and Pattern Recognition, Washington, DC, USA, CVPR 2005, pp. 947–954. IEEE Computer Society (2005)

Implementing Elements of Fear Invoking Anxiety Using a Game Platform

Joshua Lawson and Sudhanshu Kumar Semwal$^{(\boxtimes)}$

University of Colorado, Colorado Springs, CO 80918, USA
{jlawson,ssemwal}@uccs.edu
http://www.uccs.edu/semwal

Abstract. This paper explains implementation details of a game in Unity3D® with a focus on immersion and fear. Through immersion, our goal is to draw and encompass the player as much as possible into the simulated environment. During game play, the user is presented with disturbing situations with a hostile and unfamiliar environment. Quick problem solving and finding the means to escape is necessitated with limited resources, as the player tries to survive and as the game becomes less forgiving over time. The final product is a game that is able to keep the player both engaged and terrified through immersion and the sense of approaching doom.

Keywords: Anxiety · Fear · Game design · Interaction · Problem solving · Virtual environment

1 Introduction

Immersion is related to illusion, and simulation can be used to create an environment where our senses interact with the simulation, creating a sense of immersion. Understanding senses and theoretical basis of perception [Car72, Riv84, Von62] is not the focus of this paper. Our work is motivated by the glow-flow, metaplay and psychic space [Kru91] setups. Entertainment and technology concepts are combined to create emotional engagement with participants, encouraging interaction between the participant and their surrounding environment.

One of the emotions is fear. Fear is felt when a threat is percieved. Responses and actions to these threats vary depending on the indiviudal as well as the neccesary amount of stimulation. This makes it critical to explore ways to disseminate stimulation across multiple senses and avenues of approach. Game play can provide a safe yet engaging and interesting environment to experience fear and can be appealing and sought by many. Consider long lines at haunted house exhibits, or movies and plays invoking a sense of fear. Multi-tiled LCD displays [Aga10], or single user head mounted displays, e.g. [Ocu14], both provide an opportunity to create 3D virtual environments which are immersive, and therefore provide an opportunity to generate a variety of emotions. Sound was the focus to generate fear and anxiety [Top11]. Four perspectives under which emotions can be studied are discussed in [Top11].

F.J. Perales and J. Kittler (Eds.): AMDO 2016, LNCS 9756, pp. 117–124, 2016.
DOI: 10.1007/978-3-319-41778-3_12

Exposition: Our setting is a deep sea environment. The player is required to interact and explore the level in an effort to find a four digit code which is necessary for completing the game. There is also an entity in the game which will attempt to locate, impede, and ultimately, terminate the player. This entity, which shall be referred to as *the Monster* is provided with an AI script which tells it to search and destroy. When the AI comes into contact with the player, the player must cope with the Monster through evasion and escape.

Location: Many people have an innate and understandable fear of the mystery and being in a situation that they cannot control. Being in the water removes this control since the player knows that they are not in their natural environment but instead one belonging to some possible fierce and unknown predators.

2   Dynamic Environment

The deep sea is mostly a vast expanse of flat sea bed but there are occasional characteristic differences that dwarf any features on dry land. Such characteristics include deep canyons and mountain chains. The vast expansion of the open and flat seabed provides an excellent means of confusing the player and purposely trying to make them lose their bearing in the absence of landmarks. A drop-off can appear unexpectedly, potentially causing the player to wander off the edge and to their demise. Figure 1(a) provides an example of a drop off/gorge in the level. Another characteristic of the environment is that there are man-made structures throughout the level to indicate that this is some type of deep sea mining facility.

Game set up and goal: The player has a total of six starting locations. These locations are in different portions of the map and help confuse and disorientate the player. This encourages the player to try a different approach to each play through. The monster has a total of three starting locations which can potentially place it very close to the player's starting location or very far away. This helps provide a dynamic element to how soon the player will bump into the monster and be forced to escape. A four digit code required to open the door

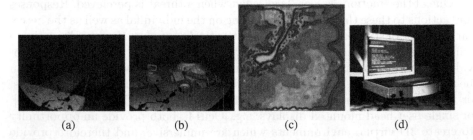

(a)   (b)   (c)   (d)

Fig. 1. (a) Example of a drop-off gorge. (b) Scene indicating that someone was here. (c) Dynamic starting locations in the level. (d) Computer Terminal, providing code.

to complete the game, and is randomized at the start of each play through. The code is displayed to the user one piece at a time from twelve computer terminals scattered throughout the level. Not all of these terminals in the level will contain a piece of the code. In fact, only four will actually provide a single digit of the code which are randomly selected at startup. The player is therefore forced to find and activate each terminal until the complete code has been determined. Another immersive element added to this feature is for the game to force the player to keep track of which digits have been recovered, the specific terminals that revealed these digits, as well as the order of the digits provided. The player must provide the four digit code at the end of the level to escape. Forgetting one of the digits or their order forces the player to find the terminal that provided that digit to verify what they forgot. This provides an excellent level of paranoia and desperation to the player during the entire process. Figure 1(c) provides an image of the level layout and the dynamic starting locations. Yellow Xs are the six starting locations for the player. Purple Xs are the three starting locations for the monster. Red Os are the twelve locations for each computer terminal.

The terminals are not hidden and do not blend in with the background but they are still small enough to be hard to visually spot. Figure 1(d) shows one of the computer terminals up close.

Player Visibility: The game takes place in the deep sea which is a cold and pitch dark environment where no sunlight can penetrate. Without a source of light, the player will not be able to see anything. The player is provided with two light sources attached to the camera; one is looking down and lighting the area around the player's feet while the other is looking directly ahead under linear fog conditions.

Light Interaction: The player places a great deal of dependency on their only real light sources in the game. Thus, anything happening to these lights would be quite catastrophic. The game plays with this fact and will randomly decide to either restrict the player's light source through dimming or by simply turning them off for an extended period of time. This makes one the player's greatest asset in the game to appear to posses a mind of its own that is passively hostile.

Ambient Effects: Ambient effects come in two forms which are both utilizing the Unity® particle simulator; small particles and randomized clouds. The small particles are used for falling particles as well as air bubbles. The falling particles are simulating small pieces of organic matter that are slowly sinking to the sea bed. These particles are typically easy to spot due to the light reflecting off the particle in contrast to the pitch black background. There are also bubble particles to simulate the player's breathing apparatus on the suit. The bubbles will appear in bursts on a continuous interval to make the affect more obvious and less annoying. Figure 2(a) shows the bubbles rise over the player's view screen and assumedly to the surface. Cloud particles are added to simulate the effects of small clouds of dust being disturbed by the current as well as any other visual disruption in the deep sea such as random temperature variations in the water or different clouds of material floating around.

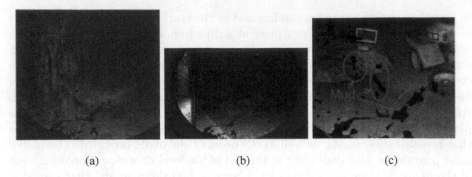

(a)   (b)   (c)

Fig. 2. (a) Sample bubble particles. (b) Player's view port. (c) Mud on the view port glass.

Movement Effects: The player has a small arrangement of movement options which include walking, running, and jumping. Walking and running activates an animation sequence which simulates taking a heavy and cumbersome step. This encourages immersion by making the player see the weight of the suit shifting with each step. Walking activates the animation sequence at a normal rate while running doubles the animation rate. Jumping in the game is very limited and only intended to help the player get past small hurdles in their path.

Visual Effects: Since the player is in a deep sea environment, they must be in a suit of some kind. The bulky nature of the suit is simulated as well as the view hole the diver must see through. This circular view hole must be kept rather small and does not allow the diver to see things in their peripheral, they can only look forward. Figure 2(b) shows the circular view port implemented in our game. This forces the player to move the entire suit to change their line of sight. An additional feature of the helmet is the glass. This allows for additional immersion into the game by including imperfections in the glass as well as image distortions. Each effect on the glass is applied to a transparent plane and then stacked in layers next to each other. The first imperfection simulates large clumps of mud on the outer surface of the glass and directly obscures the player's view. The mud on the glass can be seen as black splotches in Fig. 2(c). The second imperfection is to simulate general wear and tear on the glass such as small smudges, surface scratches, and water residue. Against a dark surface the imperfections are difficult to see but they are easy to see against a lit surface. Figure 3(a) shows this type of imperfection.

Helmet effects are simulated by applying two types of distortions to the glass. The first type of distortion simulates moisture on the glass surface on the interior of the port view. This is also applied to a transparent plane, like the other glass effects, but it is the closet layer to the player. The amount of distortion caused by this layer is directly related to the endurance level of the player. Figure 3(b) shows a comparison between the view port without any distortion and the view port with full distortion. The second glass distortion effect simulates broken

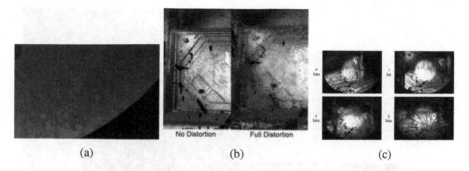

Fig. 3. (a) Water Residue on the Glass. (b) Distortion Effects on the View Port. (c) Progression of the Glass Cracking on the View Port.

glass from impacts. The state of the glass also serves as a health indicator for the player. This was a more immersive method of keeping track of the player's health since it did not involve creating a health gauge or some type of GUI that would display this information directly to you. The player interprets the broken glass as the current state of the suit and its remaining endurance to the outside pressure of the deep sea. The broken glass utilizes the same distortion shader as the moisture glass layer except that it utilizes a series of shattered glass texture for each stage of the glass' remaining endurance. Figure 3(c) shows the propagation of the glass cracks.

A single visual effect disrupts the player's overall line of sight. This effect introduces additional immersion though simulating hypoxia. Hypoxia develops from oxygen deprivation. The level of hypoxia effect is directly related to the endurance level of the player. Figure 4(a) compares the levels of hypoxia on the player.

Endurance Levels: If the player is moving (walking, running, jumping) then their endurance level will drop. If the player has the lights off or is able to see the monster then their endurance level will also drop from terror. Additional elements control the base level of the maximum endurance the player can have. These reflect the player's current state of mind and the durability of the suit. The assumption here is that the more damage inflicted on the suit the more terror the player has for being closer to death. There is only one way for the endurance level to be restored and that is when the player stands still with light and allow for their heart rate and breathing to return to normal.

Algorithms for the Monster's behaviour: The monster is the antagonist in the game and its main purpose is to stop the player from escaping. The monster's appearance is very similar to that of a human but with some small changes in its proportions. The disproportions are that it is over 7 feet tall, has long arms that reach past its knees, and also has a large neck that makes the connection between the body and the head confusing. Figure 4(b) shows the monster in a lit environment. This is an attempt to place the monster into the uncanny valley where the closer something non-human is to looking human, the

122   J. Lawson and S.K. Semwal

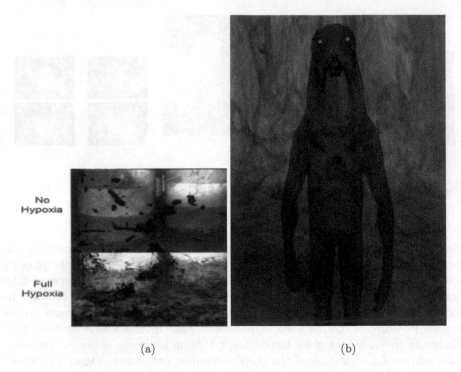

(a)   (b)

Fig. 4. (a) Hypoxia effects. (b) Monster - game antagonist.

greater the unfamiliarity. Additional features of the monster are the transparent body as well as the reflective eyes and teeth. The transparent body makes the creature slightly difficult to characterize and become familiar with due to the inability to determine its true color and detailed features. The reflective eyes and teeth can only be seen if there is a light source shining directly on them. This adds some realism to the fact that this creature lives in the deep sea and needs adaptations for taking in more light. Additional measures have been put in place to prevent the player from being able to get a clear visual of the monster. When the monster gets too close to the player and the player has their light directly on it then the light will fail and begin to sporadically turn on and off, while a loud high pitched screech sound will play. The player usually also receives a large amount of intended terror, from looking at the monster which then quickly raises the player's simulated heart rate during game play. The flickering lights become more unresponsive and the sound becomes more horrid the closer the player is to it. This is to distract the player from being able to clearly see the monster as well as encourage the player to look away. The monster works on a search and destroy mentality. The monster will initially scan its current position until the player has performed an action to give away their position. The monster will then rush to this position and search for the player there. When the player is encountered the monster will pursue and attempt to approach and attack the player.

The monster keeps track of a threat indicator that is used to indicate how much effort the monster uses in the chase i.e. the player is getting close to winning the game. There are a few things in the game that increase the threat level. One is when the player finds a piece of the four digit code and the other is set off on a predetermined time interval. Both give away the player's position which encourages them to keep moving. When a higher threat level is reached it becomes significantly more difficult for the player to escape.

3   Sound Effects

Ambient Sound Implementation: The desired outcome from using the ambient is to give the player the feeling of isolation as well as paranoia. The isolation and paranoia effect is generated by playing recordings belonging to the National Oceanic and Atmospheric Administration (NOAA). The benefit of this sound is that it is genuine sound from the deep ocean which makes it much more believable than one generated in a sound studio. The sound itself has a very creepy element with a constant low hum in the background. There is also an occasional louder higher pitch hum which may give the player the impression that whatever they are hearing is moving. This seems to imply some form of intelligence to whatever is generating the sound. A second sound is played which was recorded from a satellite orbiting Mercury from electromagnetic noise coming off of the planet. This was used because of its very unique nature and the incredible alien feeling from the sound. This sound is constantly playing in the background but is usually being played with a volume level of zero. A script is running that will occasionally play the sound for a few seconds before returning the volume back down.

Player Generated Sounds Algorithms: One sound is generated from their movement and simply adds immersion to the feeling of walking around in a heavy and cumbersome suit. The sound is a simple paft noise one would typically make when taking a step through loose dirt. The sound is timed with the animation effect of the body moving down and towards the step to link the cause of the sound being from making a heavy and slow step forward. Additional critical sound effects are the ones used to provide the player information about their current state of endurance. These sounds are the heartbeat and breathing. When the player performs an action or becomes terrified, then the pitch of the heartbeat increases as does their breathing rate. When the player stands still then their heart and breathing rate will begin to slowly drop. Additional sound effects occur when the player activates a holographic map as well as when the player's helmet is taking damage. The map is there to help prevent them from getting lost, but the information being provided to them initially seems to break from immersion. The problem is that the player should not have any knowledge of their current location outside of the game. One way to make it seem that the map is in fact in game and is part of the suit functionality is to provide a simple clicking sound when the map is activated. When the player is hit by the monster or when the suit is taking damage a sound effect is activated with the animation that has a cracking sound. This provides the player additional information about what is currently happening to the suit. A cracking sound when in a deep sea suit is never a good indicaton.

Monster Sounds: The monster has a grunting that can only be heard when it is very close. This provides the player a small chance of hearing the monster as it passes close by. This is implemented to raise their paranoia because every strange sound in the distance could possibly be interpreted as the monster which causes them to perform evasion tactics which wastes time and energy.

4   Conclusions and Future Research

The game was demonstrated to eighteen advanced gamers in a classroom setting. The game debued in the evening time. Gamers felt anxious and stressed with the sounds and effect generated by the game. The effects of the breaking glass on the helmet created a sense of urgency and quiet, making it somewhat dramatic experience. We plan to create an exhibit in a large room to get more feedback. We imagine a large projection system surrounding the player with a group watching an interaction and being engages with the sound generated by the game environment. One item that would be a great advantage to the game would be the utilization of the Oculus Rift virtual reality kit. This would allow for the player to be greatly immersed into the game by restricting the player's peripherals and allowing them to control motions by moving their head.

References

[Aga10] Agana, A., Devalath, M., McNamara, A., Parke, F.: The effect of tiled display of performance in multi-screen immersive virtual environment. IEEE Virtual Reality, Waldham, MA (2010)

[Car72] Carr, D.E.: The forgotten Senses. Doubleday and Company, pp. 1–331 (1972)

[DeL91] Deloura, M.: Game Programming Gems, 3rd edn. Charles River Media, Hingham (2000)

[Kru91] Krueger, M.W.: Artificial Reality II. Addison Wesley, Reading (1991)

[Ocu14] Oculus Rift Virtual Reality Kit (2014). https://www.oculusvr.com

[Riv84] Rivlin, R., Gravelle, K.: Deciphering the Senses, Simon and Schuster, pp. 1–28, and 157–189 (1984)

[Top11] Toprac, P., Abdel-Meguid, A.: Causing Fear, Suspense, and Anxiety using Sound Design in Computer Games, in book: Game Sound Technology and Player Interaction: Concepts and Developments, Chapter 9, Publisher IGI Global, Editors, Mark Grimshaw, pp. 176–191 (2011)

[Ass14] Unity 3D Asset Store (2014). https://www.assetstore.unity3d.com

[Uni14] Unity 3D Game Engine, May 2016. http://unity3d.com/

[Von62] Von Buddenbrock, W.: The Forgotten Senses, The University of Michigan Press, Ann Arbor, Transltaed by Frank Gaynor, Third Printing, pp. 1–53 (1962)

Balance Clinical Measurement Using RGBD Devices

Ines Ayed[1,2], Biel Moyà-Alcover[2], Pau Martínez-Bueso[3], Javier Varona[2],
Adel Ghazel[1], and Antoni Jaume-i-Capó[2(✉)]

[1] GresCom Lab. Ecole Supérieure des Communications de Tunis,
Université de Carthage, Tunis, Tunisia
[2] Unitat de Gràfics, Visió i Intel.ligència Artificial. Departament de Ciències
Matemàtiques i Informàtica, Universitat de les Illes Balears, Palma, Spain
antoni.jaume@uib.es
[3] Grupo de Investigación en Evidencia, Estilos de Vida y Salud.
Departamento de Enfermería y Fisioterapia,
Universitat de les Illes Balears, Palma, Spain

Abstract. RGBD capture devices have been proven as an ICT realistic approach for clinical prevention of falls. RGBD devices facilitate the capture of human movement and are known because of its low cost. According to that, its use is widespread and has been validated in different interactive applications for balance rehabilitation. In this type of rehabilitation, it is very important to have information on clinical patient outcomes. Moreover, it would be helpful to use RGBD devices in case the patient performs the rehabilitation treatment at home because the physiotherapist could use the RGBD devices to assess the balance. This paper demonstrates that the Microsoft Kinect device is reliable and adequate to calculate the standard functional reach test (FRT); one of the most widely used balance clinical measurements. To do so, an experiment was performed on 14 healthy users to compare the FRT calculation manually and using a RGBD device. The results show an average absolute difference of 2.84 cm (± 2.62), and there are no statistically significant differences applying a paired t-student test for the data.

Keywords: Computer vision · Microsoft Kinect · RGBD · Clinical evaluation · Balance · Motor rehabilitation

1 Introduction

One of the priorities of Horizon 2020, the European program which finances research and innovation projects, is tackling the challenges of the society. Its main challenges cover healthcare throughout life and the welfare of all, including those who are in active and healthy ageing, through ICT (Information and communications technology) for risk detection and early intervention [1, 2].

The European ageing population is in fast grow. According to the World Bank, 18% of the population in Spain is over 65 years and it is at increased

© Springer International Publishing Switzerland 2016
F.J. Perales and J. Kittler (Eds.): AMDO 2016, LNCS 9756, pp. 125–134, 2016.
DOI: 10.1007/978-3-319-41778-3_13

risk of cognitive impairment, frailty, and social exclusion together with significant negative effects on their quality of life and on of those who are in charge of them. This also can affect the sustainability of healthcare systems and the assistance quality. Early detection of risks associated with aging, using ICT approaches, may allow earlier intervention to alleviate its negative consequences [3,4]. Concretely, among the elderly people, falls can lead to a major social problem. It influence significantly in life expectancy and lead to subsequent clinical problems with high social and health costs. The loss of autonomy is the most prominent consequence. Different studies have demonstrated the importance of falls prevention, and its effectiveness when specific programs of physiotherapy are used to improve balance [5–7].

RGBD capture devices have been proven as an ICT realistic approach for clinical prevention of falls. They facilitate the capture of human movement and are popular because of their low cost. Therefore they have been used widely and have been validated in several studies about motor rehabilitation: postural control [8], clinical functional analysis and rehabilitation [9], gait retraining [10], activities of daily living [11], guidance and movement correction [12], training static balance [13], and games to improve balance and postural control [14]. These systems can be used at the patients' homes so that they do not have to displace to a hospital or a rehabilitation center, and can therefore devote more time to their rehabilitation. In fact, it is common for a patient to do rehabilitation exercises independently at home, and from time to time a physiotherapist visits him to check his performance and the effectiveness of the treatment [15–17]. For a therapy to be effective it is necessary to measure its clinical outcomes using reliable and valid tests. There is a wide range of tools and tests that allow physiotherapists to measure the progress of patients, but there are few mechanisms to assess the effectiveness of rehabilitative therapy at home without the equipments and facilities usually found in hospitals and rehabilitation centers [18–20]. For this reason, in telerehabilitation for fall prevention, the patient has to visit from time to time a physiotherapist or vice versa, to measure the therapeutic evolution and to be able to adjust his/her therapy.

The functional reach test (FRT) [21], is one of the most used tests for measuring balance clinically because it measures the limits of stability while standing. Also it detects limitations in activities of daily living (ADL) and indicates falls risk. In this paper we want to validate the calculation of the FRT using a RGBD device. Since the user uses interactive applications for balance rehabilitation using RGBD device, the physiotherapist could use the same device to measure the FRT of the patient at home without having to carry any additional material. Therefore, the calculation of the FRT manually and with an experimental system that uses a RGBD device, namely the Microsoft Kinect was compared.

The remaining work is organized as follows. In Sect. 2, we present the experimental system which allows assessing the FRT automatically using a RGBD device. In Sect. 3, we explain the experiment used to preliminarily validate the experimental system. In Sect. 4, results are presented and analyzed. Finally, the last section is devoted to conclusions and proposed further work.

2   Experimental System

The experimental system is designed to preliminarily validate if RGBD devices can evaluate correctly the FRT. To do this, we implemented an experimental system that allows a physiotherapist to calculate the FRT of the user in 3 steps.

2.1   The Functional Reach Test (FRT)

In this test, as shown in Fig. 1, the patient is first instructed to stand close to a wall. While standing in a comfortable position and looking straight ahead, the patient is asked to raise the arm that is closer to the wall at 90 degrees of shoulder flexion with a closed fist: here the position of the head of the 3rd metacarpal is marked on the wall (this is the initial position, B). From this position, the patient is asked to flex the trunk and reach forward as far as he can without taking a step or touching the wall: here the physiotherapist marks on the wall the end position of the 3rd metacarpal (this is the final position C).

The final score of FRT is the distance between the start and end positions. Three trials are done and the average of the last two is noted. Results of less than 25 cm indicate a limitation in activities of daily living (ADL) and a risk of falls [22, 23].

2.2   Proposed System

The FRT was transferred to our experimental system as interaction mechanisms so that it can automatically measure the maximum distance that a user can reach forward. Our experimental system allows the physiotherapist to calculate the FR in three steps. As input method for our system we use a RGBD device, namely the Microsoft Kinect. This device consists of a RGB camera, an infrared depth sensor, a microphone and custom processor. It allows motion capture of the whole human body in 3D, and has facial recognition and voice recognition capabilities. This capture device was chosen because it facilitates the capture of human movement besides to his low cost.

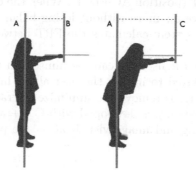

Fig. 1. Method for measuring the functional reach test (FRT)

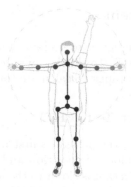

Fig. 2. Skeleton model returned by SDK 1.8 of Microsoft Kinect

The RGBD device has a Software Development Kit (SDK) that allows access to the RAW images of its sensors (depth and color images), and retrieve skeletal tracking information of the user situated in front of the sensor in order to implement gesture interactive applications, like in our case. The skeleton model consists of 20 joints with 3 degrees of freedom each. In Fig. 2 the skeleton model returned by Microsoft Kinect SDK 1.8 is shown.

In order that the physiotherapist can calculate the FRT through our system, the user must stand in front of the RGBD device and a screen, as shown in Fig. 3. This is the typical architecture of a video game in which the user's movements are captured. The patient must be familiar with the use of interactive applications for motor rehabilitation of balance with RGBD devices thus he will know this architecture. Before the user performs the FRT, he watches a video about how the experimental system works, so he can know afterwards what to do. Figure 4 shows the functioning sequence of the experimental system.

First, the therapist asks the user to peform the initial position of the FRT (position AB Fig. 1). When the physiotherapist thinks that the user does it correctly, the starting position is indicated to the system and the system stores the position of the user's hand. Then the user is asked to reach forward to the final position of the FRT (position AC Fig. 1). When the clinician considers that the user can not advance anymore without losing balance, the final position is stored. At the end, the system calculates the FRT between the initial position and the end position.

In order to motivate the user, he can see himself on the screen (see Fig. 5). Text messages are displayed to inform the user about his movement execution and the background image is removed to minimize distractions.

The experimental system was developed with C ++ and Unity. The capture process, image processing and image visualization are performed by means of Microsoft Kinect SDK.

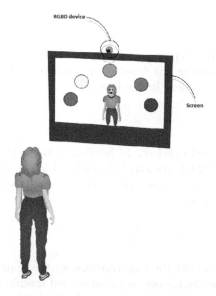

Fig. 3. Architecture of the system environment

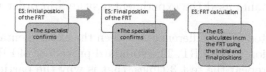

Fig. 4. Functioning sequence of the experimental system(ES)

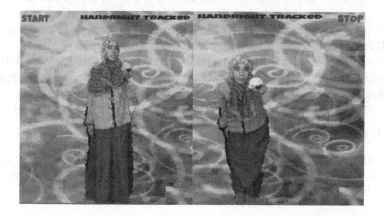

Fig. 5. Screenshot of the experimental system

3   Experiment

The experiment in this work was realized with the aim to validate the use of RGBD devices in measuring the functional reach test, so these devices can be used for clinical teleassessment in the future.

3.1   Participants

The experiment was performed on 14 healthy adults (11 men); aged between 22 and 48 years (mean 29.4, standard deviation 7.2). None of the subjects had cognitive and/or motor problems. All participants signed an informed consent form before the experiment.

3.2   Process

In order to validate whether the experimental system can assess automatically the FRT with the same confidence as the standard mechanism, by a physiotherapist in a manual way, a test study was conducted with real users. On the one hand, all participants performed the FRT in the standard way. On the other hand, the participants used the experimental system in order to automatically calculate the FRT.

We are interested in the differences between the experimental system and the standard application of the FRT. The standard procedure of FRT indicates that each user should repeat the test 3 times, that is why the participants also used the experimental system 3 times. To avoid the factor of pre-learning, the order in which the FRT is performed by the standard way and experimental system is decided randomly, as well as each repetition. An example of an experimental sequence for a user might be: FRT1, Experimental System 1 (ES1), ES2, FRT2, ES3, FRT3.

As it can be seen, a within-subjects design was used with the standard FRT as a control group. So that users know how to use the experimental system a demonstration was conducted before starting the experiment.

3.3   Measurements

The experimental system was assisted at all times by a physiotherapist and was monitored by the research team. All experiments were performed using a PC with the following settings:

1. Intel Core i3 Dual-core (2 Core) CPU P8400 @2.40 GHz
2. 4 GB RAM
3. Graphic card Mesa DRI Mobile Intel GM45 Express
4. Windows 7
5. Microsoft Kinect

The system performance was 30 fps. This result ensured a real-time response from the experimental system [24]. The interaction features of Kinect work better when the user is facing the sensor, for this reason the experimental system was designed to work in a frontal way and not laterally with respect to the user.

The measures used were the distance in cm between the initial position and the final one, for both the experimental system (MES) and the standard FRT (MFRT). An independent statistical Student t-test for paired samples (paired t-test) was applied to these measures in order to determine whether there were significant statistical differences between them. The statistical analysis tool R was also used where a confidence interval of 95 % was applied.

4   Results

Table 1 shows the measurements made in our experiment.

Table 1. Results of the 6 measurements in cm, made by each user

User	M_{FRT}^1	M_{FRT}^2	M_{FRT}^3	M_{ES}^1	M_{ES}^2	M_{ES}^3	$|M_{FRT} - M_{ES}|$
1	35.50	36.50	42.00	37.06	38.13	31.57	2.41
2	42.00	44.50	48.00	36.00	40.50	37.00	7.00
3	48.00	47.50	45.70	49.16	51.28	41.97	0.40
4	47.00	42.20	46.60	39.79	53.94	46.11	1.34
5	55.20	56.20	52.90	60.94	50.75	56.38	1.12
6	33.50	35.50	38.90	30.00	28.44	37.08	4.12
7	49.50	45.50	51.50	50.75	57.00	50.51	3.86
8	45.00	43.50	40.00	46.23	37.34	40.60	1.44
9	45.50	42.00	42.00	50.03	45.30	36.41	0.74
10	34.50	44.00	43.00	44.83	38.93	38.91	0.39
11	38.50	44.00	45.00	34.45	36.66	43.28	4.37
12	36.00	33.00	34.50	37.40	32.59	43.60	3.36
13	33.00	36.00	41.00	46.10	43.05	47.54	8.89
14	42.50	41.50	41.50	40.10	41.90	42.70	0.26
Mean	41.84	42.31	43.76	43.05	42.56	42.40	0.03

At first glance, the results of each measurement for each user are very similar. To get a more graphical view, Fig. 6 shows for each user the mean of the 3 measurements MFRT and the mean of the three measurements MES. We calculate the difference between the means for each user (MFRT - MES), and the results showed an average absolute difference of 2.84 cm (±2.62).

To check if there was significant statistical difference on these means, the paired t-test of the difference was applied, and as shown in Table 2, there is no

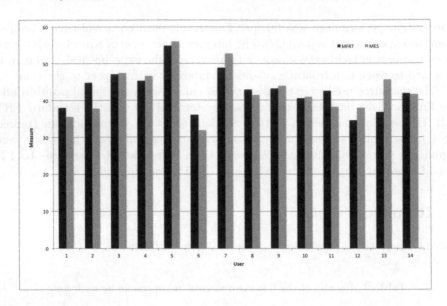

Fig. 6. Comparison Chart of the mean FRT and the mean of the experimental system for each user (in cm)

Table 2. Results of statistical test (paired t-test) applied to the results obtained

$t(13) = -0.034$
$p - value = 0.973$
$Difference = -0.036$

statistical significant difference since p = 0.973, much higher than 0.05; the p value which is usually used to consider statistical significance. The alternative hypothesis was that the mean difference was not equal to zero.

Also an Ad-hoc analysis of the statistical power of the test performed was applied, and the result indicated that the lowest statistical difference that could be detected between the FRT and the experimental system with 14 subjects is 3.9 cm.

5   Conclusions

This paper presents an experimental system to assess the functional reach test with RGBD device, namely the Microsoft Kinect. The system, with the help of a physiotherapist, indicates to the user what to do step by step, and internally measures its functional reach test (FRT). The system presented is preliminary validated, the results showed an average absolute difference of 2.84 cm (±2.62) and applying a paired t-student test for the data, where the hypothesis was there is no difference in the average, indicates that there are no statistically significant differences.

Moreover, the analysis of statistical power test indicated that the lower statistical difference that could be detected with 14 subjects was 3.9 cm, therefore it would be appropriate to perform the experiment on a larger sample to detect minor differences between the FRT and the experimental system and thus to validate more efficiently the RGBD devices for functional reach test.

These preliminary results suggest that the RGBD devices, namely Microsoft Kinect, are suitable for measuring the FRT.

Acknowledgments. This work was partially funded by European commission under Alyssa Program (ERASMUS-MUNDUS action 2 lot 6), by the Projects TIN2012-35427 and TIN2015-67149-C3-2-R of the Spanish Government, with FEDER support. The authors also thank the Mathematics and Computer Science Department at the University of the Balearic Islands for its support.

References

1. Edirippulige, S., Wootton, R.: Telehealth and communication: Using the Internet in Healthcare. Heal Informatics Transform Healthc with Technol Sydney Thomson (2006)
2. Pineau, G., Moqadem, K., St-Hilaire, C., Perreault, R., Levac, E., Hamel, B., et al.: Telehealth: clinical guidelines and technological standards for telerehabilitation. Montreal: Agence d'Evaluation des Technologies et des Modes d'Intervention en Sante (AETMIS) (2006)
3. Botsis, T., Demiris, G., Pedersen, S., Hartvigsen, G.: Home telecare technologies for the elderly. J. Telemed Telecare **14**(7), 3337 (2008). SAGE Publications
4. McCue, M., Fairman, A., Pramuka, M.: Enhancing quality of life through telerehabilitation. Phys. Med. Rehabil. Clin. N. Am. **21**(1), 195205 (2010)
5. Elavsky, S., McAuley, E., Motl, R.W., Konopack, J.F., Marquez, D.X., Hu, L., et al.: Physical activity enhances long-term quality of life in older adults: Efficacy, esteem, and affective influences. Ann. Behav. Med. **30**(2), 13845 (2005)
6. Metz, D.: Mobility of older people and their quality of life. Transp Policy. **7**(2), 14952 (2000)
7. Rubenstein, L.Z., Josephson, K.R.: Falls and their prevention in elderly people: what does the evidence show? Med. Clin. North. Am. **90**(5), 80724 (2006). Elsevier
8. Clark, R.A., Pua, Y.H., Fortin, K., Ritchie, C., Webster, K.E., Denehy, L., Bryant, A.L.: Validity of the Microsoft Kinect for assessment of postural control. Gait Posture **36**(3), 372–377 (2012)
9. Bonnechere, B., Jansen, B., Salvia, P., Bouzahouene, H., Omelina, L., Moiseev, F., Jan, S.V.S.: Validity and reliability of the Kinect within functional assessment activities: comparison with standard stereophotogrammetry. Gait Posture **39**(1), 593–598 (2014)
10. Clark, R.A., Pua, Y.H., Bryant, A.L., Hunt, M.A.: Validity of the Microsoft Kinect for providing lateral trunk lean feedback during gait retraining Gait Posture **38**(4), 1064–1066 (2013)
11. Cogollor, J.M., Hughes, C., Ferre, M., Rojo, J., Hermsdrfer, J., Wing, A., Campo, S.: Handmade task tracking applied to cognitive rehabilitation. Sensors **12**(10), 14214–14231 (2012)

12. Gama, A.D., Chaves, T., Figueiredo, L., Teichrieb, V.: Guidance and movement correction based on therapeutics movements for motor rehabilitation support systems. In: 2012 14th Symposium on Virtual and Augmented Reality (SVR), pp. 191–200. IEEE, May 2012
13. Lange, B., Koenig, S., McConnell, E., Chang, C.Y., Juang, R., Suma, E., Rizzo, A.: Interactive game-based rehabilitation using the Microsoft Kinect. In: 2012 IEEE Virtual Reality Short Papers and Posters (VRW), pp. 171–172. IEEE, March 2012
14. Jaume-i-Capó, A., Martinez-Bueso, P., Moya-Alcover, B., Varona, J.: Interactive rehabilitation system for improvement of balance therapies in people with cerebral palsy. Neural Syste. Rehabil. Eng. IEEE Trans. 22(2), 419–427 (2014)
15. Lourido, B.P., Gelabert, S.V.: La perspectiva comunitaria en la fisioterapia domiciliaria: una revisin. Fisioterapia 30(5), 231–237 (2008)
16. Mehta, S.P., Roy, J.S.: Systematic review of home physiotherapy after hip fracture surgery. J. Rehabil. Med. 43(6), 477–480 (2011)
17. Keays, S.L., Bullock-Saxton, J.E., Newcombe, P., Bullock, M.I.: The effectiveness of a pre-operative home-based physiotherapy programme for chronic anterior cruciate ligament deficiency. Physiotherapy Res. Int. 11(4), 204–218 (2006)
18. Durfee, W.K., Savard, L., Weinstein, S.: Technical feasibility of teleassessments for rehabilitation. Neural Syst. Rehabil. Eng. IEEE Trans. 15(1), 23–29 (2007)
19. Hailey, D., Roine, R., Ohinmaa, A., Dennett, L.: Evidence on the effectiveness of telerehabilitation applications. Institute of Health Economics (2010)
20. Hailey, D., Roine, R., Ohinmaa, A., Dennett, L.: Evidence of benefit from telerehabilitation in routine care: a systematic review. J Telemed Telecare 17(6), 281–287 (2011)
21. Duncan, P.W., Weiner, D.K., Chandler, J., Studenski, S.: Functional reach: a new clinical measure of balance. J. Gerontol. 45(6), M192–M197 (1990)
22. Riolo, L.: Attention contributes to functional reach test scores in older adults with history of falling. Phys. Occup. Ther. Geriatr. 22(2), 15–28 (2004)
23. Lovallo, C., Rolandi, S., Rossetti, A.M., Lusignani, M.: Accidental falls in hospital inpatients: evaluation of sensitivity and specificity of two risk assessment tools. J. Adv. Nurs. 66(3), 6906 (2010). Wiley Online Library
24. Varona, J., Jaume-i-Cap, A., Gonzlez, J., Perales, F.J.: Toward natural interaction through visual recognition of body gestures in real-time. Interact. Comput. 21 (1–2), 3–10 (2009)

Evaluation of K-SVD Method in Facial Expression Recognition Based on Sparse Representation Problems

Eloy Rafael Oliveros[1], Grethel Coello[1], Pedro Marrero-Fernández[1], Jose Maria Buades[2], and Antoni Jaume-i-Capó[2(✉)]

[1] Universidad de Oriente, Santiago de Cuba, Cuba
[2] Universitat de les Illes Balears, Palma, Spain
antoni.jaume@uib.es

Abstract. The following machine learning scheme is commonly used for the recognition of facial expressions: First, the face is detected in the image. Second, tracking techniques are applied, based on active shape models; then, from the tracking of the characteristic points, a description of the facial expression is carried out, using characterization methods based on shape and/or texture; in the case of high dimension vectors, methods of features selection are applied; and finally they are classified in one of the basic expressions. In the latest years, techniques based on sparse representation methods to classify facial expression have been successfully developed. This paper aims at evaluating these methods' performance from the training of the representation model using K-SVD. A characterization scheme of facial expression is assessed using JAFFE y CK+ databases, with or without the use of the K-SVD method, achieving a value of 0.9755 of accuracy in the classification. The obtained results prove the feasibility in the use of this method in the facial expressions classifiers based on sparse representation.

1 Introduction

Automatic understanding of human behavior has attracted great interest in the last two decades, especially its many applications in a wide range of fields; like psychology, computer technologies, medicine and security. It was not until recent years, when a group of MIT (Massachusetts Institute of Technology) researchers named this computer field as affective computing. It can be defined as the branch of artificial intelligence aimed to design systems and technologies able to recognize, interpret and process emotions.

Facial expression is the strongest natural way humans use to communicate emotions, confirm or emphasize, express intention, and in a more general way, to manage interactions with people and environment [1]. Charles Darwin wrote a treaty in 1872, in which he established the general principles of human and animal expressions [2] and proved that facial expressions are universal. In 1970, Paul Ekman y Wallace V. Friesen published a paper in [3] in which facial expression and emotional patterns were associated for the first time. They set six facial expressions with distinctive features

© Springer International Publishing Switzerland 2016
F.J. Perales and J. Kittler (Eds.): AMDO 2016, LNCS 9756, pp. 135–146, 2016.
DOI: 10.1007/978-3-319-41778-3_14

each, known as basic emotions. In 1978, Suwa et al. [4] presented a preliminary research on automatic analysis of facial expressions (AAFE) in image sequences.

Figure 1 shows the general scheme for (AAFE) that has been used in the last years. First, from the image obtained, face detection is carried out, as well as its characteristic points. They can be detected using active shape models or active appearance model [5]. These methods show good results in a general way. That is why, the last works on the topic focus on the other components. For the characterization, there are many papers that propose the use of Gabor Wavelets [6–8], Local Binary Patterns (LBP) [9], among others. Due to the high dimensionality of feature vectors, features selection has been carried out with more common methods, like Principal Component Analysis (PCA) and the Linear Discriminant Analysis (LDA). Manifold learning is a popular recent approach to nonlinear dimensionality reduction [10], as it is the case of Locality Preserving Projections (LPP) [11].

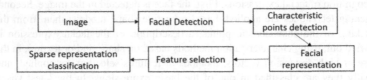

Fig. 1. General Scheme for the facial expression classification based on sparse representation.

For the classification step, there have been used the most traditional methods, like the nearest neighbors classifiers, support vectors machine, and others. Recently, classifiers based on sparse representation (SRC) has started to be used [12–14], This has called the interest of the scientific community, due to the good results in different areas of image processing.

In [9] the use of a variant of LBP is proposed as a characterization method, taking into consideration the features obtained as invariants of intensity changes and the distinctive information that reduce the correlation between elements of different facial expressions. This proposal has, among its advantages, the results obtained from its application to noisy images and the computational complexity of the expression representation method. The main disadvantage lies on the fact of not using any method for dimension reduction, which allows improving the system efficiency.

This proposal, as well as others that have been studied, like [13, 15–17], shows a deficiency that may affect the results of automatic classification of facial expressions. None of the analyzed papers uses methods of knowledge base adjustment, which is equivalent, in general terms, to train the classifier.

In [18] the K-SVD algorithm was presented to adjust dictionaries of sparse representations of signals, with which, excellent results have been obtained, but in the studied literature there is no evidence of its application to the problems of AAFE. However, its use allow a preprocessing of the expression dictionary, making it more representative and generic inside the space of each expression independently, to establish a framework capable of dynamically update the knowledge base for the AAFE. This procedure would be analogous to what is known as training a classifier. Therefore, these work aims at evaluate the application of K-SVD method into the facial expression recognition based on sparse representation problems.

2 Scheme Description

In this section there are briefly presented the elements that are part of the general scheme for the AAFE used in this work.

2.1 Features Extraction

The phase of features extraction is fundamental in the whole process of expressions classification. There have been many ideas to propose the most distinctive features to represent an expression. According to [15] the methods for characteristic extraction can be classified into: based on geometric analysis and based on appearance. Several techniques have been used in the appearance based method. Some of them can be PCA, Independent Components Analysis, LBP, Gabor Wavelets filters. It has been demonstrated that the latter obtain better results in facial analysis [19].

Representation techniques using Gabor Wavelets filters have developed since the paper [20], due to its relevance from the biological point of view and the computational properties it offers. It is stated the image coding of facial expressions by using a multiorientation and a multiresolution set of Gabor Wavelets filters. Works as [6] and [7] use this technique for facial recognition. [8] presents a method for AAFE using Gabor Wavelets filters, obtaining the features in the regions that show significant changes according to the natural face. Filters are defined as:

$$\Psi_{\mu,v}(z) = \frac{\|k_{\mu,v}\|^2}{\sigma^2} e^{-\frac{\|k_{\mu,v}\|^2\|z\|^2}{2\sigma^2}} \left[e^{ik_{\mu,v}z} - e^{-\frac{\sigma^2}{2}} \right] \tag{1}$$

Where μ y v represent the orientation and the scale of Gabor kernels, $z = (x, y)$, $\|\cdot\|$ denotes the norm operator, and the wave vector $k_{\mu,v}$ is defined as $k_{\mu,v} = k_v e^{i\phi_\mu}$, where $k_v = k_{max}/f^v$ and $\phi_\mu = \pi\mu/8$. k_{max} is the maximum frequency, and f is the space factor among the kernels in the frequency domain. Each kernel is the product of a Gaussian envelope and a complex plane wave. In most cases, there used five different scales $v \in \{0, \ldots, 4\}$ and eight orientations, $\mu \in \{0, \ldots, 7\}$. In Fig. 2 it is shown the real part of Gabor filters with five scales and eight orientations, using the following parameters: $\sigma = 2\pi$, $k_{max} = \frac{\pi}{2}$ and $f = \sqrt{2}$. An image representation, using Gabor Wavelets is obtained by means of the convolution of the image with a Gabor filters bank. If $I(z)$ is an image in grey scale, the, convolution of I with a Gabor filter $\Psi_{\mu v}$ is defined as:

$$G_{\mu,v} = I(z) \times \Psi_{\mu,v}(z) \tag{2}$$

Where $z = (x, y)$, $\times$ denotes the convolution operator and $G_{\mu,v}(z)$ is the convolution result. The magnitude of the resulting complex image is defined as:

$$|G| = \sqrt{Re(G)^2 + Im(G)^2} \tag{3}$$

A way of representing the image with this model is by means of the magnitudes of the transformes images, using each Gabor filter. A variant would be by the link of the resulting values in G, considering all the pixels or a part of them. Another way of facial representation is the proposal in [15], where the characteristic vector $F_{k,N}$ is set by the following expression:

$$F_{k,l} = \sum_{i=x_l-k}^{x_l+k} \sum_{j=y_l-k}^{y_l+k} |G_{ij}|, l = 0,1,\ldots,N, k = 1,3,5,7,9 \tag{4}$$

where N represents the number of characteristic points in the face image, x_l and y_l are the coordinates of the characteristic points and k defines the number of neighbors to be analyzed. This variant groups more information in each feature according to the published results. This way of expression representation is used in this work for the scheme proposed.

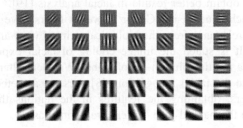

Fig. 2. Gabor filters 8 orientations (columns) and 5 scales (rows).

2.2 Features Selection

Once we have the features vector, it is necessary to make a selection of them. In several situations, in spite of having a high dimension, the information or features vectors give the idea that the important or significant values are in a minor dimension space. Therefore, the techniques for dimension reduction aim at extracting the most relevant information from the obtained original data, representing them in a space of minor dimension which components contain the largest amount of relevant information possible.

Manifold learning is a popular recent approach to nonlinear dimensionality reduction [10]. LPP [11] is an algorithm that uses this technique. This method creates a representation of the entry space as a complete graph W where each of the n samples is linked with the other $n-1$ with a weight $0 \le w_{ij} \le 1, i,j = 1\ldots n$. A 0 weight represents that there is no connection, while 1 represents the strongest connection possible. The way of creating the edges between the two nodes i and j can be: (1) $\in$-neighborhood, the vertices i y j are connected if $\| x_i - x_j \|^2 < \in$, with $\|\cdot\|$ the Euclidian norm in $\Re^n$; (2) k nearest neighbors, the vertices i and j are connected if i is in the k nearest neighbors of j or j is in the k nearest neighbors of i. The point is minimize the following objective function $\sum_{i,j}(y_i - y_j)^2 w_{ij}$, being y_i and y_j the vectors in their new dimension.

There are different alternatives to choose the way of establishing the edges weights of the constructed graph. One of them is known as Gaussian kernel, which states that, if the vertices i and j are connected, then $w_{ij} = e^{-\frac{\|x_i - x_j\|^2}{t}}$. In supervised cases, a variant to use is establishing connections only among vertices of the same class with a weight equal to $1/k_n$ where k_n is the number of samples of the class, $w_{ij} = \frac{1}{k_n}$. The previous equation can be named as kernel LDA. In [17] it is stated an alternative for the construction of W, in which both ways of establishing the edges' weights are combined, recognizing that some problems are not linearly separable. A convex combination is proposed:

$$W = \alpha W_{LDA} + (1 - \alpha)W_{Gaussian} \tag{5}$$

where $0 \leq \alpha \leq 1$. For datasets with high differences between classes, any value for $\alpha > 0$ is justified. In general cases, any value for α (except 0 or 1), obtains better results that taking the independent vertices. This variant is named SLPP for having semisupervised characteristics, and it is the one proposed in this paper.

2.3   Classification

After the dimension reduction of the features vectors, the classification is carried out. In this work, a classifier is used, based on sparse representations because in recent years the interest in the application of the sparse representation of signals in the computer vision and image processing has increased [16]. Using a dictionary $D \in \Re^{n*K}$ that contains signals prototypes K as columns, known as atoms, a signal $y \in \Re^n$ can be represented as a sparse linear combination of those atoms. The representation can be exact, $y = Dx$ or an approach, $y \approx Dx$ satisfying $\|y - Dx\|_p \leq \epsilon$, where $x \in \Re^K$ contains the representation coefficients and $\|\cdot\|_p$ represents the "norm" ℓ^p, defined as:

$$\|x\|_p = \left(\sum_i |x_i|^p\right)^{\frac{1}{p}} p \geq 1 \tag{6}$$

being $p = 1, 2, \infty$, the most used values for this norm.

According to [21] compression, features extraction and the analysis of activities are some of the advantages and applications of sparse representation. In the case of AAFE, the general idea is based on representing an expression as the combination of an expression set to later classify it using a decision rule on the obtained representation, [22].

The first phase is the sparse coding, that, according to [21], it is the process of finding representative coefficients x based on the signal y and the D dictionary. Usually, it is achieved by a *pursuit algorithm*, which computes an approximate solution to the problem, because the exact solution is an NP-complete problem. In recent years, there have been designed efficient methods for obtaining good representations. Some of the most recognized and simple ones are the *matching pursuit*. They are greedy algorithms that go atom by atom, selecting the most appropriate one. The method used in this work is known as OMP (*Orthogonal Matching Pursuits*) [23].

Another important aspect in sparse representation of signals lies on the dictionary selection. There are different ways of selecting it. It is known that the basis of Fourier and Discrete Cosine transformed are a good selection for a complete dictionary. Another well used strategy is to take as initial dictionary, a set of the own signals you want to represent and then adjust them for a generalization. In [18] it was introduced the K-SVD method, for the adjustment of dictionaries which has provided excellent results, in different areas. In this method, the adjustment is carried out atom by atom, based on the signals that use them for their representation and by means of the decomposition in singular values of the matrix resulting from eliminating the not used signals.

To apply sparse representation to classification problems, the D dictionary is created as the union of subdictionaries, this is $D = [A_i, \ldots, A_z]$, where each A_i represents a base of the subspace, in which the i-th class vectors are represented. Therefore, when a vector y is represented by a D dictionary, the atoms that should have the biggest contribution should be the ones belonging to the y class. For the case of expressions, Fig. 3 shows the process of the dictionary shape. Once we find the representation of a signal or expression, it is necessary a decision rule for the classification. In this work, an expression is classified in the class that minimizes the error in its reconstruction. This variant is known as error reconstruction, and according to literature, it is one of the best results providers [17]. Defined as $c^* = \min_{c=1\ldots z}|y - D\alpha^c|$, being z the total of the expressions in the dictionary and α^c the corresponding subvector of c-th subdictionary.

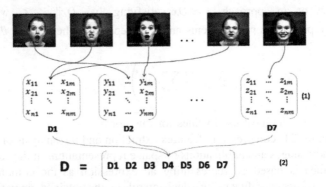

Fig. 3. Dictionary build process: (1) expression representation and placed in corresponding subdictionary phase. (2) Subdictionaries linking phase.

2.4   General Scheme

The expression representation is carried out with the convolution of the image with 40 Gabor filter (5 scales and 8 orientations), using the Eq. 4, then we applied the SLPP method to reduce the features vectors dimension. A dictionary of expressions it is form and adjusted using K-SVD. The sparse representation of a new expression is obtained with OMP algorithm and classified according to the decision rule described before.

3   Results and Discussion

3.1   Experimental Environment

For the experiment in this work we use two of the most widely used databases to facials expressions recognition; JAFFE and Extended Cohn-Kanade (CK+). The JAFFE database, [24] has 213 images of 10 Japanese woman facial expressions, with a resolution of 256X256 each; representing seven basic expressions (neutral, surprise, happiness, disgust, fear, sadness, anger). The selected actresses posed the same expression several times, this is why there are "identical" samples. This characteristic has to be take into consideration, once we applied the techniques for error estimation with cross validation (specifically leaving-one-out). Because when the set is divided, there exist a high probability of having "identical" elements in the training subset and the testing subset. For this work the images of the same actor with the same expression in JAFFE were eliminated.

The CK+ database, [25], is an augmented version of Cohn-Kanade database, 18. It counts with 593 sequences of 123 subjects. The image sequence varies in duration (i.e. 10 to 60 frames) and incorporates the onset (which is also the neutral frame) to peak formation of facial expressions. From the 593 sequences, only 327 of 118 different subjects are tagged with some emotion. The established protocol to work with CK+ , estipulate the use of leaving-one-out technique for cross validation. Only the last frame of the sequence was used for the experiment, because it contains the maximum expression. This database represents seven basics expressions (neutral, surprise, happiness, disgust, fear, sadness, anger).

$$ACC = \frac{True\,Positives + True\,Negatives}{Total\,Predictions} \tag{7}$$

For the experiments we use the accuracy measure, defined in the Eq. 7, representing the proximity between the result and the exactly classification. The leaving-one-out technique is used for classifying; it means that each subject is classify independently using it as test set and the rest of subjects as training. Different ways of expression characterization are used to compare the classification results against the general scheme propose in this work. The experiments are made gradually regarding the phases, to highlight the importance in the application of each one as a way of improve the results. In the case of JAFFE database, the points of interest refers to a 100 points, uniformly distributed over the center of image, as it is show in Fig. 4, this center

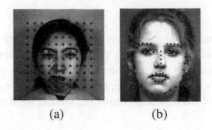

(a)   (b)

Fig. 4. (a) Landmarks in JAFFE database. (b) Landmarks in CK+ database.

match up with the center of the face. This is because JAFFE, unlike CK+ , have not landmarks on the faces.

3.2 Results Analysis Using Different Characterization Methods

The value of the accuracy using both databases with six different representations methods are given in Table 1. The first column represent the values using JAFFE, while the second one represent the results over CK+ . *RAW* is the representation of the expression that take into account just the pixels values, without any processing, in the whole image. *WGP* is the characterization resulting of the convolution of the landmarks in the image with 40 Gabor filters linking in only one vector. The next rows used the following representation method:

$$F_{k,l} = \sum_{i=x_l-k}^{x_l+k} \sum_{j=y_l-k}^{y_l+k} |G_{ij}|, l = 0, 1, \ldots, N, k = 1, 3, 5, 7, 9$$

altering the values of parameter k, $N = 68$ for CK+ , and, $N = 100$ for JAFFE. The features vectors dimension is represented with the subindexes on each value. These considerations are the same for each one of the tables in this paper.

Table 1. Accuracy values over different representation methods.

	JAFFE	CK+
RAW	0.8122 $_{d=65536}$	0.9179 $_{d=3060}$
WGP	**0.8694** $_{d=4000}$	0.9702 $_{d=2720}$
$F_{3,N}$	0.8690 $_{d=4000}$	0.9750 $_{d=2720}$
$F_{5,N}$	0.8653 $_{d=4000}$	**0.9764** $_{d=2720}$
$F_{7,N}$	0.8612 $_{d=4000}$	0.9762 $_{d=2720}$
$F_{9,N}$	0.8653 $_{d=4000}$	0.9753 $_{d=2720}$

It can be noticed that the classification results using the schemes based on Gabor Wavelets are better than the representation based on the pixels values. This is an expected result for the properties of Gabor basis and the features vectors dimensionality.

The difference in the results between both databases lies on the vectors dimension and the landmarks of the images. In the same way, the amount of elements in the databases is quite different, being CK+ the one with most images, which allow a larger dictionary.

3.3 Dimension Reduction

As shown in Table 1, the dimension of features vectors is always superior to 2000 components. The number of components of a vector and the space in which they are represented influence in the classification results. In this experiment, the SLPP method is used to reduce the dimension of the vectors obtained as part of the characterization process. The values of the accuracy in the classification are shown in Table 2. For this experiment, the *RAW* representation is refused for being the one with worst results and for the criteria previously detailed. The dimension reduction is achieved; projecting the vectors in $\Re^{30}$. The best results for each database are superior to the best results with no dimension reduction (previous experiment). The representation based on Eq. 4 is superior in almost every case of *WGP*. The shown values were obtained using $\alpha = 0.95$ in the Eq. 5, for having the best results among all the experiments that have been carried out.

Table 2. Accuracy values using SLPP method.

	JAFFE	CK+
WGP	0.8653	0.9790
$F_{3,N}$	0.8694	0.9786
$F_{5,N}$	**0.8898**	0.9826
$F_{7,N}$	0.8816	0.9821
$F_{9,N}$	0.8694	**0.9850**

3.4 K-SVD Algorithm Application

In this work, it is necessary to obtain a dictionary that optimally represents any new signal that enters the system. The K-SVD algorithm finds precisely that dictionary. In this case, the use is applying it to every subdictionary separately. We create dictionaries with half of the signals of an expression as initialization, and then, do the adjustment with the other half. This methodology creates a drawback due to the final dictionary dimension is reduced. Therefore, the classifier knowledge base takes into account less samples for the classification process. For this experiment, only the CK+ database was selected, because there are too few samples in JAFFE; and the *WGP* representation was refused for being the one with worst results in every previous case.

Table 3 shows the classification results using the complete scheme detailed in the paper. The highest result is reached with the $F_{3,68}$ representation, even when they are very similar among them. In this case, the decision rule coincides precisely with the objective of the K-SVD algorithm, because it tries to minimize the error in the signals

Table 3. Accuracy values using K-SVD algorithm.

	$F_{3,N}$	$F_{5,N}$	$F_{7,N}$	$F_{9,N}$
CK+	**0.9755**	0.9729	0.9703	0.9694

representation of the same class. Eventough, the results reduction is justified in the few elements of the database. The dictionary adjustment constitutes an important strategy in the classification using sparse representation. The posibility of improving the use of a learning technique as the K-SVD allows to count on a dynamic scheme for the recognition of facial expressions.

3.5   Summary Results

Table 4 shows the classification values obtained with the use of the most recently used schemes and some of their variation. This is the case of the scheme presented in [9]. It uses LBP as a characterization method and classifies by sparse representation. Another model upon which this work is based on is the proposed by [17], which uses the intensity values of image pixels as expression representation. They all use classifiers based on sparse representation with the decision rule described in this work.

Table 4. Comparison between several AAFE schemes.

Scheme	Accuracy
RAW+SRC	0.9205
RAW+SLPP+SRC [17]	0.9345
LBP+SRC [9]	0.9626
LBP+SLPP+SRC	0.9563
$F_{5,68}$+SRC	0.9747
$F_{9,68}$+SLPP+SRC	**0.9825**
$F_{3,68}$+SLPP+K-SVD+SRC	**0.9755**

It can be checked that the results using representation based on Gabor Wavelet, with Eq. 4, are higher than LBP method even using SLPP. In the same way is significant the increase reached by the last two variants that are shown. Achieving an accuracy of **0.9755**, only overcome by the $F_{9,68}$+SLPP+SRC scheme, justified in the reduce of the total elements; support the use of the K-SVD method for the knowledge base adjustment. Even when the use of K-SVD considerably increases the computation cost of the final scheme, its use can be proposed, take into account that the adjustment is made only during the training phase, meaning that, the complexity of the expression classification it is not affected. Besides the knowledge base, could be updated dynamically, being this a strength of the scheme.

4   Conclusion

It was carried out a study about the main characterization methods of facial expressions, and according to the results obtained in the experimentation, the Gabor Wavelets filters, are the ones with the best performance according to the classification. There were analyzed the influences of the features selection method SLPP. In the results of automatic classification of facial expression, it reached a value of **0.9825** in the effectiveness of the classification. The evaluation of the of the K-SVD method in the problems AAFE is achieved. The achievement of a **0.9825** value in the accuracy shows the feasibility in applying the adjustment of the knowledge base using this method. Likewise, a new scheme is obtained for the AAFE, which is composed of the following methods: Gabor Wavelets filter, for the characterization of facial expressions; SLPP method for features extraction; application of K-SVD algorithm for the adjustment of knowledge base and classification by sparse representation with the decision rule of error reconstruction.

Acknowledgements. This work was partially supported by the Projects TIN2012-35427 and TIC2015-67149-c3-2-R with FEDER support, of the Spanish Government, and "XI Convocatoria de Ayudas Para Proyectos de Cooperación Universitaria al Desarrollo – 2014 y 2015 de la UIB". The authors also thank the Mathematics and Computer Science Department at the University of the Balearic Islands for its support.

References

1. Sandbach, G., et al.: Static and dynamic 3D facial expression recognition: a comprehensive survey. Image Vis. Comput. **30**(10), 683–697 (2012)
2. Darwin, C.: The expression of the emotions in man and animals, USA (1998)
3. Ekman, P., Friesen, W.V.: Manual for the Facial Action Coding System. Consulting Psychologists Press, Palo Alto (1978)
4. Suwa, M., Sugie, N., Fujimora, K.: A preliminary note on pattern recognition of human emotional expression. In: International Joint Conference on Pattern Recognition, pp. 408–410 (1978)
5. Fasel, B., Luettin, J.: Automatic facial expression analysis: a survey. Pattern Recogn. **36**(1), 259–275 (2003)
6. Nanni, L., Maio, D.: Weighted sub-Gabor for face recognition. Pattern Recogn. Lett. **28**(4), 487–492 (2007)
7. Lyons, M.J., et al.: Classifying facial attributes using a 2-d gabor wavelet representation and discriminant analysis. In: Proceedings of the Fourth IEEE International Conference on Automatic Face and Gesture Recognition, 2000, pp. 202–207
8. Mourao, A., et al.: Sparse reconstruction of facial expressions with localized gabor moments. In: 2013 Proceedings of the 22nd European Signal Processing Conference (EUSIPCO), pp. 1642–1646 (2014)
9. Ouyang, Y., Sang, N., Huang, R.: Robust automatic facial expression detection method based on sparse representation plus *LBP* map. Optik-Int. J. Light Electron. Opt. **124**(24), 6827–6833 (2013)

10. Cayton, L., Algorithms for manifold learning. Univ. of California at San Diego Technical report, pp. 1–17 (2005)
11. Niyogi, X.: Locality preserving projections. In: Thrun, S., Saul, L., Schölkopf, B. (eds.) Neural Information Processing Systems. MIT Press, Cambridge (2004)
12. Cotter, S.F.: Sparse representation for accurate classification of corrupted and occluded facial expressions. In: 2010 IEEE International Conference on Acoustics Speech and Signal Processing (ICASSP). IEEE (2010)
13. Weifeng, L., Caifeng, S., Yanjiang, W.: Facial expression analysis using a sparse representation based space model. In: 2012 IEEE 11th International Conference on Signal Processing (ICSP), pp. 1659–1662 (2012)
14. Buciu, I., Pitas, I.: A new sparse image representation algorithm applied to facial expression recognition. In: Proceedings of the 2004 14th IEEE Signal Processing Society Workshop Machine Learning for Signal Processing, pp. 539–548 (2004)
15. Zavaschi, T.H., et al.: Fusion of feature sets and classifiers for facial expression recognition. Expert Syst. Appl. **40**(2), 646–655 (2013)
16. Xia, H., Xu, R., Song, S.: Robust facial expression recognition via sparse representation over overcomplete dictionaries. J. Comput. Inf. Syst. **1**, 425–433 (2012)
17. Ptucha, R., Savakis, A.: Manifold based sparse representation for facial understanding in natural images. Image Vis. Comput. **31**(5), 365–378 (2013)
18. Aharon, M., Elad, M., Bruckstein, A.: K-SVD: An algorithm for designing overcomplete dictionaries for sparse representation. IEEE Trans. Signal Process. **54**(11), 4311–4322 (2006)
19. Liu, C., Wechsler, H.: Gabor feature based classification using the enhanced fisher linear discriminant model for face recognition. IEEE Trans. Image Process. **11**(4), 467–476 (2002)
20. Lyons, M., et al.: Coding facial expressions with gabor wavelets. In: Proceedings of the Third IEEE International Conference on Automatic Face and Gesture Recognition, pp. 200–205 (1998)
21. Elad, M.: Sparse and Redundant Representations: from Theory to Applications in Signal and Image Processing. Springer, New York (2010)
22. Wright, J., et al.: Robust face recognition via sparse representation. IEEE Trans. Pattern Anal. Mach. Intell. **31**(2), 210–227 (2009)
23. Pati, Y.C., Rezaiifar, R., Krishnaprasad, P.: Orthogonal matching pursuit: Recursive function approximation with applications to wavelet decomposition. In: 1993 Conference Record of the Twenty-Seventh Asilomar Conference on Signals, Systems and Computers, pp. 40–44 (1993)
24. Kamachi, M., Lyons, M., Gyoba, J.: The japanese female facial expression (jaffe) database, vol. **21** (1998). http://www.kasrl.org/jaffe.html
25. Lucey, P., et al.: The extended cohn-kanade dataset (Ck+): A complete dataset for action unit and emotion-specified expression. In: 2010 IEEE Computer Society Conference on Computer Vision and Pattern Recognition Workshops (CVPRW). IEEE (2010)

3D Object Recognition Based on Volumetric Representation Using Convolutional Neural Networks

Xiaofan Xu[1,2]([✉]), David Corrigan[2], Alireza Dehghani[1], Sam Caulfield[1,2], and David Moloney[1]

[1] Movidius Ltd., 1st Floor, O'Connell Br House, D'Olier St, Dublin, Ireland
{xiaofan.xu,alireza.dehghani,sam.caulfield,david.moloney}@movidius.com
[2] Trinity College Dublin, College Green, Dublin, Ireland
corrigad@tcd.ie

Abstract. Following the success of Convolutional Neural Networks on object recognition and image classification using 2D images; in this work the framework has been extended to process 3D data. However, many current systems require huge amount of computation cost for dealing with large amount of data. In this work, we introduce an efficient 3D volumetric representation for training and testing CNNs and we also build several datasets based on the volumetric representation of 3D digits, different rotations along the x, y and z axis are also taken into account. Unlike the normal volumetric representation, our datasets are much less memory usage. Finally, we introduce a model based on the combination of CNN models, the structure of the model is based on the classical LeNet. The accuracy result achieved is beyond the state of art and it can classify a 3D digit in around 9 ms.

Keywords: 3D object recognition · Volumetric representation · 3D digit dataset · CNN

1 Introduction

Object Recognition (OR) is widely used in our daily life for the purposes of inspection, registration, and manipulation [1]. The well-known applications such as Google, Facebook and Baidu are probably the most famous websites which use OR on a large scale. Generally, object classification is performed using colour based segmentation methods or from grayscale images using classification methods such as HoG [2]/SVM [3] or other classifiers. However, nowadays deep learning is becoming ubiquitous. We are now able to solve some of the problems once considered impossible in fields such as computer vision, natural language processing, and robotics with recent advancements in deep learning algorithms.

Machine learning techniques use data (images, signals, text) to train a model (or machine) to perform image classification or object detection. Although classical machine learning techniques are still being used to solve challenging image

© Springer International Publishing Switzerland 2016
F.J. Perales and J. Kittler (Eds.): AMDO 2016, LNCS 9756, pp. 147–156, 2016.
DOI: 10.1007/978-3-319-41778-3_15

classification problems, they don't work well when applied directly to images. This is because they ignore the structure and compositional nature of images. The state-of-art CNN technique which is a specific type of deep learning algorithm, addresses the gaps in traditional machine learning techniques. CNNs not only perform classification, but they can also learn to extract features directly from raw images which eliminates the need for manual feature extraction. The performance of deep learning which uses CNNs has rapidly grown to over 95 % accuracy (GoogLeNet [4], VGG [5], AlexNet [6] etc.) in recent years with the availability of large labelled datasets and powerful GPUs. These methods, while appealing from an accuracy standpoint, are computationally extremely intensive requiring up to hundreds and millions of multiplications per classification. Baidu has achieved the best result to date in the ImageNet classification challenge [7] with custom-built supercomputer called Minwa [8]. Minwa contains 72 powerful processors and 144 GPUs, and it has 6.9 TB of host memory, 1.7 TB of device memory. These high computational requirements for existing CNN models, such as the Baidu winning model, makes it impossible to deploy CNNs onto mobile devices without modification.

Following the success of CNNs on OR using 2D images [4–6]; in this work we extended the framework to process 3D data. Although architectures with volumetric convolutions have been successfully used in video analysis [9, 10] where time acts as the third dimension, the nature of our data is very different conceptually. In our proposed approach, CNN classifiers are trained to recognize 3D objects from complete or partial 3D volumetric representations. Many online catalogues of such information are already available which have been generated using 3D scanning devices such as Microsoft's Kinect, or designed using packages such as Blender, 3DMax, Maya or even Minecraft. Unlike the other existing 3D CNNs using 3D point cloud data as training data [11], our dataset is more effective and efficient for training CNNs. The core-structure of our 3D objects is called Volumetric Accelerator (VOLA) which uses a bit-per-voxel representation where the bit corresponding to voxel would be 1 if the volume is occupied by the object and 0 if it is free space. VOLA itself has been shown to offer substantial memory savings compared to other common methods of representing volumetric data, with savings up to 95 % for realistic scenes. Based on this, VOLA representation offers the potential to drastically reduce the computational complexity of a CNN as CNNs require huge numbers of multiplications and VOLA can make them trivial as it only requires multiplications by 1 or 0. Therefore, our trained CNN models will be much easier to deploy onto any embedded platform and the computational requirement for classification will be incredible small. For low-cost robotics, the computational complexity and speed of operation are essential for safe interoperation with environments, humans and animals.

The rest of the paper is outlined as follows: Sect. 2 explains the several datasets have been created for this project along with the CNN models developed based on the proposed datasets. Performance evaluation of CNN models including their accuracy and classification run-time will be presented in Sect. 3. Finally, conclusions and feature works will be discussed in Sect. 4.

2   Technical Content

In this section we introduce the datasets structure. A new way to represent volumetric data is explained. The procedure required for generating the dataset is also included.

2.1   Dataset Structure

There are several datasets used in this work in order to evaluate the performance of the CNN models based on volumetric representation. The datasets have been generated using several approaches.

3D MNIST Datasets. The 3D MNIST dataset has been built based on the original well-known 2D MNIST dataset using MATLAB. It is built in order to train the 3D CNN, performance of which can be compared to the existing LeNet [12] trained on images. Different rotations of the 3D MNIST along x, y, z axes respectively are also included in the dataset as in 3D space rotation is an important component. The degree of rotations was randomly generated between 0° to 360° along 3 axes. Each of these datasets contains a training dataset and a test dataset. Furthermore, the training dataset contains a total number of 59667 3D digits and the test dataset contains a total of 9957 3D digits.

3D-Fonts Dataset. The 3D Font dataset has been created based on the free fonts available online using Blender. Some examples of the 3D digits are shown in Fig. 1. Specifically, the training dataset contains 256 different fonts and the test dataset contains 79 different fonts. The fonts in the training and test datasets are completely different. The reason for building this dataset is to build a CNN model which can recognize the artificial digits in the real world scenario i.e. 3D digit candles. Similar to the 3D MNIST dataset, separate datasets have been created based on different rotations along the x, y, and z axes and the step of every rotation used in this dataset is 10°. The training set contains a total number of 91440 3D digits and test dataset contains 27000 3D digits. A dataset of compound rotations between x, y and z axes are also created based on 25 different fonts for training and 5 different fonts for testing. The rotation step in the combined rotation dataset is 40° for x, y and z axes because the 3D digits with smaller rotation steps would create a huge dataset with similar performance. This combined rotation dataset has a training set of 144000 3D digits and a test set of 28800 3D digits. What is more, a CNN model based

Fig. 1. 3D digits based on different fonts and rotations.

Fonts/ 2D image → Blender/ Matlab —.stl→ Binvox —.binvox→ VOLA → VOLA representation

Fig. 2. Steps require for generating VOLA representation.

on combinational rotation fonts have been trained to recognize the real world 3D digits. In order to test the CNN model based on these fonts, combinational rotation around x&y, x&z and y&z axes respectively with 10° rotation step was also created. Depth images of different resolutions were captured based on the 3D font dataset. In addition, separate CNN models have been trained using depth images to compare the performance of the 3D Font CNN model and details of the accuracy are included in Sect. 3.

2.2 Volumetric Accelerator (VOLA)

Unlike other existing 3D CNNs using 3D point cloud data as training data [11] or RGB channel along with depth channel for building 3D CNNs [13–17], CNNs in this study can be applied directly to recognize the 3D volumetric representation of the 3D digits. The core-structure of the 3D objects is called Volumetric Accelerator (VOLA). VOLA is a software library for creating, manipulating and visualizing volumetric data. (It is under examination as a patent). More specifically, VOLA deals with regular volumetric grids, also known as voxels and VOLA stores only a single bit of information in each voxel. VOLA uses an octree data structure to store the voxels.

2.3 Data Format for CNNs

In order to generate the VOLA representation a few steps are required, shown in Fig. 2 below. Specifically, 3D digits with .stl format are converted into .binvox format which is a program that reads a 3D models, rasterizes it into a 3D voxel grid and generates the resulting voxel file. The reason for using VOLA as it only requires 1 bit per voxel, and in .binvox format it requires 1 byte per voxel. VOLA can save more memory usage then the .binvox representation.

Regarding to the structure of the datasets in Sect. 2.1, different rotations are considered for training and testing the CNN models. Figures 3 and 4 show the

Fig. 3. Digit 2 in binvox format along z-axis rotation with 0°, 40°, 80° and 100° rotation respectively.

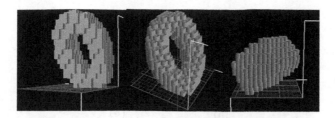

Fig. 4. Digit 0 in binvox format with combinational rotations along x, y and z axes.

different rotations in .binvox format. Binvox represents the occupancy in a grid and each voxel in the .binvox represents 1 byte.

In this work, all 3D digits are based in a small volume of 16×16×16 voxels. The reason for choosing 16×16×16 voxels is because it gives the best performance in terms of computation and visualization. In Fig. 5, it shows the different resolution of binvox and three different resolutions were tested. In 8×8×8 volumetric grid, most of the useful information of Digit 0 is missing. Although in 32×32×32 volumetric grid the binvox gives the best visualizing output, it would increase the computational requirement for training the CNNs. With 16×16×16 voxels representation, the binvox contains enough useful information for it to be recognized as a zero. Therefore, 16×16×16 volumetric grid was chosen in this work.

After converting the 3D digits to binvox, VOLA can be applied directly to the binvox files. VOLA outputs a binvox file into a single string of 1 s and 0 s. VOLA starts at point (0, 0, 0) which corresponding to the circle shown in Fig. 6 it moves from right to left along the x axis, bottom to top along the y axis and font to back along the z axis. The output of a single string from VOLA then reshape into a VOLA image which shown in Fig. 6. The intensity of the image contains only 1s and 0s. Each yellow box on the image represent 1 slice of the binvox in X-y plane along the z axis. The size of these yellow boxes are 16×16 which is the size of the x and y dimension in the volumetric grid. These yellow boxes form into a VOLA image which then be used as the training image.

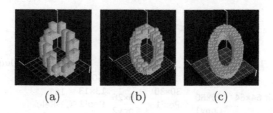

(a)   (b)   (c)

Fig. 5. 3D Same digit 0 with different resolution of binvox:(a) 8×8×8 voxel; (b) 16×16×16 voxel;(c) 32×32×32 voxel.

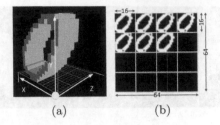

(a)   (b)

Fig. 6. Binvox to VOLA conversion process:(a) Binvox representation visualization; (b) VOLA representation.

2.4 CNN Architecture

In this work, a few CNN models have been designed based on the famous LeNet model [12] shown in Fig. 7 using CNN framework Caffe [18]. However, the CNN model in Fig. 7 only consists 1 rotation of the 3D digits, the combination rotation CNN model is described in Sect. 2.5. Unlike the traditional LeNet model takes in the input of size 28×28, this CNN takes in the input as VOLA image of size 64×64 without any resize, the VOLA image is based on the .binvox of size 16×16×16 3D digit. The first convolutional layer contains 20 kernels of size 5×5, and second convolutional layer contains 50 kernels of size 5×5. In the Pool layers, max pooling of 2×2 is applied on each of the feature maps achieved from the convolutional layers. After passing through multiple convolutional layers, max pooling layers and fully connected layer, the 2D VOLA image has been converted into a vector of size 10 contains the probability of the input belongs to each class which can be used for 3D digit classification. All the trainable parameters in each layer are initialized randomly and trained using online error back-propagation algorithm described in [12].

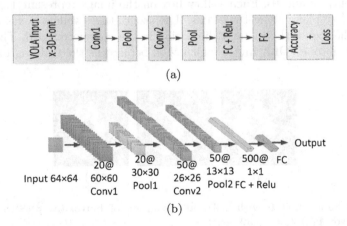

Fig. 7. The CNN model layout for 1 rotation 3D digit recognition. (a) The architecture contains 2 convolution layers, 2 max pooling layers, 2 fully connected layer; (b) The architecture in details.

2.5 Model Combination

Based on the model description in Sect. 2.4, a combination CNN models is designed for recognize the real world 3D digits. Four CNNs with the structure shown in Fig. 7 are trained based on X-rotation, y rotation, z rotation and xyz rotation 3D digits respectively. Maximum output will be voted as the final output. In real world 3D object contains different rotations, the selection of optimal CNN model for a problem is difficult. Therefore, we construct multiple models and combine the outputs from these models in order to make a best prediction. This has been used in combining traditional neural networks [19]. The input to these models is the same VOLA image. Output results demonstrate that the combination CNN models achieve good prediction on real 3D digit.

3 Experimental Results and Discussion

3.1 Accuracy

The test accuracy based on the test dataset of the individual trained CNNs based on the 3D fonts with different rotations is shown in Table 1. The average accuracy achieved for the 3D font CNN is 81.85 %. The reason for having a lower accuracy in z-rotation is due to the fact that Digit 6 and Digit 9 have similar features when these 2 digits rotate in the z direction. Based the 3D MNIST dataset, the average test accuracy reached to 89.14 %. The VOLA input to the CNN models are size 64×64 with only 1-bit representation for each pixel. Depth images of size 16×16 with 4-bit representation (16 grayscale level) for each pixel achieved only 63.05 % accuracy and achieved 70.04 % with 32×32, 6-bit representation per pixel. The details are shown in Table 2. The reason for using this depth image representation is to match the memory footprint with VOLA representation. Low accuracy result for the depth images suggested the features from the 3D shape are important in the recognition process. In order for the depth image to reach the same accuracy level as the VOLA image, it requires image size of

Table 1. Test accuracy and loss for 3D font CNNs & 3D MNIST CNNs with different rotation.

3D font CNN	Test Accuracy	Test Loss
X-rotation	82.95 %	0.757495
Y-rotation	84.70 %	0.774017
Z-rotation	77.33 %	1.0494
XYZ-rotation	82.43 %	0.700333
3D MNIST CNN	Test Accuracy	Test Loss
X-rotation	91.80 %	0.342894
Y-rotation	92.32 %	0.322077
Z-rotation	83.31 %	0.738499

Table 2. Accuracy & Loss for depth image.

Depth images	Accuracy	Loss
16×16 4-bit representation for each pixel	63.05 %	0.757495
32×32 6-bit representation for each pixel	70.04 %	0.774017
64×64 8-bit representation for each pixel	90.56 %	1.0494

64×64 with 8-bit representation for each pixel. This cause much more memory usage compared to the VOLA image. A separate test was performed based on the xy-plane projection of the 3D digits. However, the accuracy achieved for this case is only 57.85 %. This proves that for 3D digit recognition z plane information is important and it also suggests that our proposed CNN models have a good performance.

3.2   Classification Run-Time

We use a Titan-X GPU in the experiments. The performance for classification based on the trained models are listed in Table 3. The results show that for the original LeNet based on 2D MNIST dataset gives slowest classification. It takes 13 ms when classifying 1 image. For the trained 3D digit CNNs, takes around 9 ms to classify 1 3D digit. The results show that our implementation of CNNs based on VOLA representation is fast for classification especially in the convolutional layers. As the VOLA representation made the multiplications more trivial.

Table 3. Classification time for CNN models.

Layers	3D MNIST X-rotation	3D Fonts X-rotation	3D Fonts xyz-rotation	2D MNIST
Data	0.050	0.043	0.071	0.064
Conv1	2.207	2.147	2.245	3.343
Pool1	0.133	0.129	0.133	0.063
Conv2	5.841	5.721	5.824	9.759
Pool2	0.070	0.066	0.085	0.036
Ip1	0.379	0.361	0.392	0.157
Relu	0.011	0.009	0.013	0.012
Ip2	0.059	0.049	0.058	0.053
Loss	0.179	0.154	0.179	0.168
Average	0.992	0.964	1.000	1.517
Total	8.929	8.679	9.000	13.655

4   Conclusion

We developed CNN models for recognize 3D digits in this paper and we also created several datasets based on the 3D digits using VOLA representation. The final output of the CNN is obtained by combining the information from all the CNN models based on different rotation of the 3D digits. We also analysis the performance of the CNN models based on our VOLA volumetric representation. The test accuracy we achieved is around 80 %. In this paper we only tested the performance based on the test dataset. We can also test our model with the real world 3D digits which can be captured using Kinect or any other devices in the future.

Acknowledgment. This work has been partially supported by Project Eyes of Things (EoT) Grant n. 643924 from the European Union's Horizon 2020 Research and Innovation Program.

References

1. Lowe, D.G.: Object recognition from local scale-invariant features. In: The Proceedings of the Seventh IEEE International Conference on Computer Vision 1999, vol. 2, pp. 1150–1157. IEEE (1999)
2. Dalal, N., Triggs, B.: Histograms of oriented gradients for human detection. In: IEEE Computer Society Conference on Computer Vision and Pattern Recognition 2005 CVPR 2005, vol. 1, pp. 886–893. IEEE (2005)
3. Burges, C.J.: A tutorial on support vector machines for pattern recognition. Data Min. Knowl. Disc. **2**(2), 121–167 (1998)
4. Szegedy, C., Liu, W., Jia, Y., Sermanet, P., Reed, S., Anguelov, D., Erhan, D., Vanhoucke, V., Rabinovich, A.: Going deeper with convolutions. In: Proceedings of the IEEE Conference on Computer Vision and Pattern Recognition, pp. 1–9 (2015)
5. Simonyan, K., Zisserman, A.: Very deep convolutional networks for large-scale image recognition (2014). arXiv preprint arXiv:1409.1556
6. Krizhevsky, A., Sutskever, I., Hinton, G.E.: Imagenet classification with deep convolutional neural networks. In: Advances in Neural Information Processing Systems, pp. 1097–1105 (2012)
7. Russakovsky, O., Deng, J., Su, H., Krause, J., Satheesh, S., Ma, S., Huang, Z., Karpathy, A., Khosla, A., Bernstein, M., et al.: Imagenet large scale visual recognition challenge. Int. J. Comput. Vis. **115**(3), 211–252 (2015)
8. Wu, R., Yan, S., Shan, Y., Dang, Q., Sun, G.: Deep image: scaling up image recognition, vol. 22, p. 388 (2015). arXiv preprint arXiv:1501.02876
9. Ji, S., Xu, W., Yang, M., Yu, K.: 3d convolutional neural networks for human action recognition. IEEE Trans. Pattern Anal. Mach. Intell. **35**(1), 221–231 (2013)
10. Karpathy, A., Toderici, G., Shetty, S., Leung, T., Sukthankar, R., Fei-Fei, L.: Large-scale video classification with convolutional neural networks. In: Proceedings of the IEEE Conference on Computer Vision and Pattern Recognition, pp. 1725–1732 (2014)

11. Maturana, D., Scherer, S.: Voxnet: a 3d convolutional neural network for real-time object recognition. In: 2015 IEEE/RSJ International Conference on Intelligent Robots and Systems (IROS), pp. 922–928. IEEE (2015)
12. LeCun, Y., Bottou, L., Bengio, Y., Haffner, P.: Gradient-based learning applied to document recognition. Proc. IEEE **86**(11), 2278–2324 (1998)
13. Song, S., Xiao, J.: Deep sliding shapes for amodal 3d object detection in rgb-d images (2015). arXiv preprint arXiv:1511.02300
14. Lenz, I., Lee, H., Saxena, A.: Deep learning for detecting robotic grasps. Int. J. Robot. Res. **34**(4–5), 705–724 (2015)
15. Socher, R., Huval, B., Bath, B., Manning, C.D., Ng, A.Y.: Convolutional-recursive deep learning for 3d object classification. In: Advances in Neural Information Processing Systems, pp. 665–673 (2012)
16. Alexandre, L.A.: 3d object recognition using convolutional neural networks with transfer learning between input channels. In: Menegatti, E., Michael, N., Berns, K., Yamaguchi, H. (eds.) Intelligent Autonomous Systems 13, pp. 889–898. Springer, Switzerland (2016)
17. Höft, N., Schulz, H., Behnke, S.: Fast semantic segmentation of RGB-D scenes with GPU-accelerated deep neural networks. In: Lutz, C., Thielscher, M. (eds.) KI 2014. LNCS, vol. 8736, pp. 80–85. Springer, Heidelberg (2014)
18. Jia, Y., Shelhamer, E., Donahue, J., Karayev, S., Long, J., Girshick, R., Guadarrama, S., Darrell, T.: Caffe: convolutional architecture for fast feature embedding. In: Proceedings of the ACM International Conference on Multimedia, pp. 675–678. ACM (2014)
19. Hansen, L.K., Salamon, P.: Neural network ensembles. IEEE Trans. Pattern Anal. Mach. Intell. **10**, 993–1001 (1990)

Characterization of Multiresolution Models for Real-Time Rendering in GPU-Limited Environments

Francisco Ramos$^{(\boxtimes)}$, Joaquin Huerta, and Fernando Benitez

Institute of New Imaging Technologies, Universitat Jaume I,
Avenida de Sos Baynat s/n, Castellon, Spain
{francisco.ramos,huerta,benitezm}@uji.es

Abstract. Real-time visualization of 3D scenes is a very important feature of many computer graphics solutions. In applications such as computer-aided design, scientific visualization or even in the growing computer games market, the performance of visualization becomes essential. In addition, the complexity of the scenes is increasing and they now contain objects composed of thousands or even millions of polygons. Moreover, emergence of new standards and new supported functionalities in web or mobile environments enable us to efficiently render complex 3D scenes. However, in these environments GPU capabilities are partially supported. Therefore, it is necessary to resort to different techniques that allow us to maintain the quality and performance of 3D applications by managing that huge amount of geometry in such environments. Among the different solutions, many authors have concentrated on level-of-detail approaches. The main objective of this paper is to introduce studies on this topic, presenting the different solutions that currently exist in the field of real-time visualization of level-of-detail models that fits in GPU limited environments such as web or mobile platforms.

Keywords: Computer graphics · Multiresolution models · Level of detail · Triangle strip · Simplification

1 Introduction

Nowadays it is common to represent 3D scenes with a high degree of geometrical complexity as the latest technological advances have generated large databases of polygonal models. Many of the objects that are included in these scenes come from high-precision scanners, computer-aided design tools, digital terrain models or even from the tessellation of implicit surfaces. Thus, in general, the output objects are composed of millions of polygons that exceed by far the visualization capacities of present hardware, including the processor, memory, graphics

© Springer International Publishing Switzerland 2016
F.J. Perales and J. Kittler (Eds.): AMDO 2016, LNCS 9756, pp. 157–167, 2016.
DOI: 10.1007/978-3-319-41778-3_16

hardware, network bandwidth, etc. Applications such as computer games, distributed virtual environments or the creation of special effects for films make use of models generated by this sort of systems. In all these applications, a balance must be found between the accuracy with which a surface is modeled and the amount of time required to process it.

There are several important approaches that allow us to reduce the cost of representing a 3D scene, such as visibility algorithms, surface tessellation, mesh simplification or multiresolution models. The use of visibility algorithms allows us to prevent visual information from being lost when visualizing many objects, or parts of them. Surface approximation by means of triangle meshes is another technique to be taken into account. In general, it is assumed that the precision of the approximation is proportional to the number of triangles that form it. The aim is to produce the most simplified mesh that meets the requirements of the application. Nevertheless, simplification in runtime has a high temporal cost. The concept of level of detail or multiresolution modeling emerges with the purpose of supporting real-time simplification operations. This concept entails creating a model in a pre-process that stores several approximations (see Fig. 1) and that is capable of retrieving any of these approximations in an efficient way.

The aim of this paper is to present works on multiresolution modeling by focusing on web environments. It is possible to find in the literature different reviews [14, 36], but it was necessary to offer a more restricted revision centered on works which are subjected to be implemented in GPU limited environments such as web or mobile platforms [34] where only shader model 4 is supported.

2   Multiresolution Modeling

The techniques to control the level of detail of a surface in execution time are very important in real-time visualization systems. In any system, the capacity of the available hardware is essentially limited. Nevertheless, the complexity of a scene can vary substantially. Therefore, in order to keep a constant frame rate, the level of detail of the scene must not exceed the processing capacity of the graphics hardware.

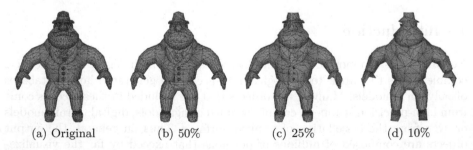

(a) Original   (b) 50%   (c) 25%   (d) 10%

Fig. 1. Approximations of the *Al Capone* model. The percentage corresponds to the number of vertices that compose the mesh in relation to the original one (3610 vertices).

Formally, a multiresolution model consists of a representation that stores a range of approximations of an object and that allows to obtain any of them as required. [6] The cost of extracting those approximations must be low as normally many of them will be needed in execution time. It is also important that the size of the multiresolution representation does not exceed to a high extent the size of the object in its most detailed approximation.

2.1   Discrete Multiresolution Models

The simplest method to create a multiresolution model is to generate a fixed set of approximations. In a given instant, the graphics application could select the approximation to visualize. In this case, a series of discrete levels of detail would be being used. This multiresolution model would consist of a set of levels of detail and some control parameters to change between them. The simplicity of this kind of models is its main characteristic. If good approximations of the original mesh can be produced, then a discrete multiresolution model can be generated and successfully applied. Free visualization systems like OSG and commercial ones like Renderman, [43] Open Inventor, [44] or IRIS performer, [20] include support for discrete levels of detail. Some 3D games engines such as Ogre3D, Fy3D or Nebula, also include this feature.

2.2   Continuous Multiresolution Models

Continuous multiresolution models are based on the same concept as discrete ones but, instead of creating individual levels of detail, this kind of models present a series of continuous approximations of an original object. The simplification method employed offers a continuous flow of simplification operations to progressively refine the original mesh.

The main advantage of these models is their better granularity, that is, the level of detail is specified exactly, and the number of visualized polygons is adapted to the requirements of the application. This granularity is usually of a few triangles, as the difference between contiguous levels of detail is usually of a vertex, an edge or a triangle. Moreover, the spatial cost is lower since the information is not duplicated. Obviously, the management of the level of detail in these models is an essential point, that is, the amount of time required to visualize a level of detail can never exceed the time required to visualize the object at its maximum resolution.

Characteristics and Classifications. It is possible to establish a characterization of continuous multiresolution models depending on the resolution they are capable of showing. Thus, multiresolution models can be divided into two groups. Uniform resolution models: they always visualize the same level of detail in all the geometry. Variable resolution models: they allow us to extract and visualize different resolutions throughout the surface of the object. They are also known as view-dependent models.

Uniform Resolution Models. Uniform resolution approaches are characterized by extracting and showing only one level of detail throughout the whole object. These models are very used in computer games as they are very fast and simpler to implement than variable resolution ones.

One of the first models to offer a neat solution to a continuous representation of polygonal meshes was Progressive Meshes. [17] From version 5.0, it has been included in Microsoft Corporation's DirectX graphics library. Later, its author [18] and other researchers [28,29,37] improved the original model.

Progressive Meshes simplifies a mesh $M = M^n$ in consecutive approximations M^i by applying a sequence of n edge collapses:

$$M^n \stackrel{Collapse_{n-1}}{\rightarrow} M^{n-1} \stackrel{Collapse_{n-2}}{\rightarrow} \ldots \stackrel{Collapse_0}{\rightarrow} M^0 \qquad (1)$$

The reverse operation can also be performed, recovering more detailed meshes from the simplest mesh M^0 by using a sequence of *vertex splits*:

$$M^0 \stackrel{Split_0}{\rightarrow} M^1 \stackrel{Split_1}{\rightarrow} \ldots \stackrel{Split_{n-1}}{\rightarrow} M^n = M \qquad (2)$$

A further improvement was the development of models based on primitives which implicitly store connectivity information. Thus, storing the meshes as triangle strips or fans considerably reduces the storage cost of a mesh, the amount of information sent to the graphics system and it also accelerates the visualization. [13]

One of the first models to use implicit connectivity primitives was MOMFan. [35] It employed triangle fans both in its data structure and in its visualization process. The main drawback lies in the high number of degenerate triangles produced in the representation, although they can be eliminated before the visualization. Another disadvantage of this model is that the average number of triangles that make up each triangle fan is small, losing the main advantage of using this kind of primitive.

At a later date the MTS model appeared. [2] This solution uses the primitive triangle strip both in the data structure and the rendering algorithm. Its core idea consists in using a collection of multiresolution triangle strips, each of them representing a triangle strip for each level of detail. All this is encoded as a graph, which involves a high storage cost. Moreover, the extraction of the level of detail is also a high time-consuming task.

As commented before, the evolution of graphics hardware has given rise to new techniques that allow us to accelerate multiresolution models. The use of techniques to create triangle strips that make maximum use of the cache of the GPU [1] and the new extensions of graphics libraries that allow the visualization of a whole mesh by means of a few instructions [16] are good examples of them.

Therefore, new papers designed to minimize the traffic between the CPU and the GPU appeared later on. These models try to make maximum use of the cache of vertices of the GPU, minimizing traffic as possible, [3,5,19] even reducing the pixel redrawing that does not contribute to the final scene. [26] The main idea is to organize the meshes in short and parallel strips, that is, linked along many edges that share as many vertices as possible. The work presented by Chow [5] allows different regions of a geometric model to be compressed with variable precision depending on the level of detail present at each region.

More recently, the LodStrips model was developed. [32] This continuous model is entirely based on optimized hardware primitives, triangle strips, and deal with the apparition of degenerate triangles applying pre-calculated filters. The authors improved the original model to include an adequate treatment of graphics hardware [33]. In Fig. 2, this model was applied to an animated mesh.

There are also several methods based on points as graphics primitives. [7,48] The latter proposes a method that converts a hierarchy of points and polygons into a linear list easily rendered by graphics hardware and with a minimum load for the CPU. The problem of this method is the impossibility of applying a hierarchical culling, given the nature of the data structure used.

Ji et al. [21] suggest a method to select and visualize several levels of detail by using the GPU. In particular, they encode the geometry in a quadtree based on a geometry atlas. In the first pass, the atlas is read as a texture in the GPU, where the level of detail is selected with a pixel shader that dumps the result into a buffer. Subsequently, that buffer is read in the CPU and the vertices selected are checked. Finally, another map with the vertices to be visualized is sent to the GPU, where all the vertices are encoded in a texture, avoiding sending them every time by the bus. The visualization primitive used in this solution is the triangle fan. The problem of this method is the process that the CPU must execute in every change of level of detail, testing the selection maps and creating the new map of vertices which is sent to the GPU. Moreover, if the mesh is too complex, the representation with quadtrees can be not very efficient and even the size of the video memory can be an important restriction.

Variable Resolution Models. As we have previously commented, the concept of variable resolution involves showing different levels of detail of the same object in a given moment.

HDS [24] and MT [8] were conceived as triangle-based multiresolution models, although they are both general schemes applicable in the creation of any multiresolution model. The first of them consists of a tree data structure that stores simplification sequences, and the second one of an acyclic graph. There are several models of this type [18,45].

Fig. 2. Uniform Resolution Model in triangle strips primitives applied to an animated mesh.

FastMesh [27] introduced a hierarchical framework which offered efficient algorithms and error metrics for both simplification and extraction. Nevertheless, the authors stress their interest on including triangle strips for faster rendering.

One of the first models to use triangle strips was VDPM [18]. In general, this model determines the triangles to be processed and then turns them into triangle strips to visualize them. This task consumes a considerable amount of time, but the final performance in the visualization improves because of the acceleration attained by using this sort of graphics primitive. Later on, Skip Strips [10] was the first model to store the triangle strips in its data structure. Triangle strips are initially calculated and, afterwards, simpler versions of them are rendered. Skip Strips also uses a series of filters in the visualization to eliminate degenerated triangles. This model presents also a high storage cost.

DStrips [39] is another model based on triangle strips. It calculates the triangle strips to be visualized in execution time, but it only processes the strips affected by the change of level of detail, without recalculating all the strips in the mesh. This mechanism reduces the time of extraction of the level of detail. Nevertheless, according to the results published, it is still a substantial time. Besides, its data structure is complex and it has a high spatial cost. Another approximation is Tunneling, [41] spread by Porcu. [25,30] Essentially, it involves using an algorithm that allows us to connect triangle strips that become more and more simplified and thus obtain strips with many triangles and reduce their total number. Its main problem is the time required to carry out these operations, which implies a high extraction cost of the levels of detail.

Massive Models. Present representations and extraction algorithms are not scalable for models made up of tens or hundreds of millions of polygons. The extraction cost is proportional to the size of the model, and it can be prohibitive for massive models.

Massive or *out-of-core* models are multiresolution approaches which have been specifically developed for meshes which exceed by far the capacities of present hardware. Therefore, only parts of the original mesh can be used for visualization. Given that these meshes surpass the capacity of the main memory, specific multiresolution techniques must be adopted for rendering in real-time this type of meshes. In general, these models create a simplification hierarchy in external memory that will be employed later for the online visualization of the required approximation of the original mesh.

The first paper directed at the visualization of massive models suggested the use of levels of detail in external memory. [11] This model generated in a preprocess a simplification hierarchy based on edge collapses that will be used later in the visualization. Afterwards works were presented, improving substantially the spatial cost by creating new formats of disk storage and the performance in visualization by using efficient data structures [9].

The model introduced by Erikson et al. [12] was developed to manage very large environments, and was later improved by Lakhia [23] to offer better results in dynamic scenarios. Hierarchical models are essentially discrete models and they suffer from *popping* artifacts when the scene changes in a fast pace. Lakhia tries to reduce these effects by means of certain heuristics that advance the load of levels of detail before they are visualized. Another problem of hierarchical models is that the quality of the simplifications diminishes as the simplification hierarchy becomes deeper.

More recent models are directed towards exploiting the graphics hardware with massive models. [38] In general, the previous models neither have a gradual transition between the different levels of detail nor support *texture mapping*. They are mainly based on updating the level of detail before the change is perceived. This model performs *geomorphing* in the GPU gradually, avoiding the typical *popping* effect. This model doubles the number of buffers used in the GPU when it performs geomorphing at coarser levels of detail, besides performing a great amount of rendering calls.

A model that incorporates simplification based on vertex hierarchy, *out-of-core* functions and occlusion culling is [46]. This model shows in its results a lower spatial cost than other models such as [9] or [18]. It is based on a cluster hierarchy of Progressive Meshes, where each cluster is made up of several nodes, and, in turn, each of these nodes contains a progressive representation of a portion of the original mesh. [17] This allows us to improve the performance through a hierarchical *culling*.

Kircher et al. [22] presented a multiresolution model for surfaces which become distorted in time, very used in films, games and certain scientific applications. This model allows rendering approximations at any level of detail for every frame of an animation. It also stores a simplification tree for each frame or deformed mesh, since, obviously, the simplification generated for a mesh is no good for another although it has been slightly modified. The model has a high spatial cost, but it is ideal for animation applications.

3   Characterization

In Table 1 we can observe a description of the multiresolution models for arbitrary polygonal meshes considered in this review. The description takes into account several aspects:

- Type: it indicates whether the model is discrete or continuous.
- Primitive: the sort of primitive the model uses in the visualization.
- Resolution: whether the model allows us to visualize various resolutions in the same mesh (variable) or it is only possible to see a level of detail throughout the approximation (uniform).
- Hierarchical: it indicates if the approch is hierarchical.
- GPU: it indicates if the model analyzed uses any of the latest capacities of present GPUs.
- Massive: whether the model is prepared for extremely big meshes.

Table 1. Characterization of the multiresolution models.

Model	Type	Primitive	Resolution	Hierarchical	GPU	Massive
Prog. Meshes [17]	Continuous	Triangles	Uniform	No	No	No
VDPM [18]	Continuous	Strips	Variable	No	No	No
HDS [24]	Continuous	Triangles	Variable	No	No	No
MT [8]	Continuous	Triangles	Variable	Yes	No	No
Skip Strips [10]	Continuous	Strips	Variable	No	No	No
MOMFan [35]	Continuous	Fans	Uniform	No	No	No
ExtVD [11]	Continuous	Triangles	Variable	No	No	Yes
MTS [2]	Continuous	Strips	Uniform	No	No	No
Tunneling [41]	Continuous	Strips	Variable	No	No	No
FastMesh [27]	Continuous	Triangles	Variable	Yes	No	No
HLods [12]	Discrete	Triangles	Variable	Yes	No	Yes
XFastMesh [9]	Continuous	Triangles	Variable	Yes	No	Yes
No tiene nombre [47]	Discrete	Strips	Uniform	Yes	No	No
DCLod [48]	Both	Points	Variable	No	No	No
CLodGPU [40]	Discrete	Triangles	Uniform	No	Geom.	No
DStrips [39]	Continuous	Strips	Variable	No	No	No
SequentialPoint [7]	Continuous	Points	Variable	No	No	No
EfficientHLod [23]	Discrete	Triangles	Variable	Yes	No	Yes
Prog. Buffers [38]	Discrete	Triangles	Variable	No	Geom.	Yes
Prog. Mult. Meshes [22]	Continuous	Triangles	Both	Yes	No	No
QuickVDR [46]	Continuous	Triangles	Variable	No	No	Yes
MeshGPU [4]	Discrete	Triangles	Variable	Yes	Text.	No
DynamicLOD [21]	Continuous	Fans	Variable	Yes	Text.	No
LodStrips [33]	Continuous	Strips	Uniform	No	No	No
SWPM [42]	Discrete	Triangles	Variable	Yes	Geom.	No
EfGPU [34]	Continuous	Triangles	Uniform	No	Yes	No
VDTes [31]	Continuous	Triangles	Variable	No	Yes	Yes

4   Conclusions

The use of a discrete or continuous multiresolution model in an application depends on its requirements. Discrete multiresolution models are a good alternative in applications which require few levels of detail in their objects. These models also offer a simple implementation and these levels of detail can be polished and improved considerably. Nevertheless, continuous models offer a high granularity, allowing us to adapt exactly the level of detail desired in each case. Furthermore, their evolution has allowed us to obtain very low level-of-detail extraction times and significant accelerations due to the irruption of the new and powerful GPUs.

Over the last years graphics hardware has undergone a real revolution: not only its computational power has been remarkably increased, but also its cost has decreased, thus facilitating its availability in any computer in the market. Both things, its easy availability and the high processing capacity reached during these years, have driven the developers to make the most of graphics hardware with new objectives, from the production of videogames and computer-generated films to computer-aided design and scientific visualization, or even to solve problems unrelated to computer graphics. [15] Apart from powerful and cheap, graphics hardware has also become flexible, that is, from being a simple memory device to being a configurable unit and, finally, to becoming a parallel processor totally programmable. However, more restrictive environments such as web or mobile ones, are not capable to exploit all the features in most recent GPUs as they only support partial functionality on those ones. Thus, it is necessary to classify and know the limitations of multiresolution works in order to be implemented in GPU limited platforms.

Acknowledgements. This work has been supported by the European Union, project H2020-MSCA-ITN-2014.

References

1. Beeson, C., Demer, J.: Nvstristrip library (2002)
2. Belmonte, O., Remolar, I., Ribelles, J., Chover, M., Rebollo, C., Fernandez, M.: Multiresolution triangle strips. In: VIIP, pp. 182–187 (2001)
3. Bogomjakov, A., Gotsman, C.: Universal rendering sequences for transparent vertex caching of progressive meshes. In: Graphics Interface, pp. 81–90 (1999)
4. Boubekeur, T., Schlick, C.: Generic mesh refinement on GPU. In: Graphics Hardware, pp. 99–104 (2005)
5. Chow, M.: Optimized geometry compression for real-time rendering. In: Visualization, pp. 347–354 (1997)
6. Clark, J.: Hierarchical geometric models for visible surface algorithms. CACM **10**(19), 547–554 (1976)
7. Dachsbacher, C., Vogelgsang, C., Stamminger, M.: Sequential point trees. ACM Trans. Graph. **22**(3), 657–662 (2003)
8. De Floriani, L., Magillo, P., Puppo, E.: Efficient implementation of multi-triangulations. IEEE Vis. **98**, 43–50 (1998)
9. Decoro, C., Pajarola, R.: Xfastmesh: Fast view-dependent meshing from external memory. In: IEEE Visualization, pp. 363–370 (2002)
10. El-Sana, J., Azanli, E., Varshney, A.: Skip strips: Maintaining triangle strips for view-dependent rendering. In: Visualization, pp. 131–137 (1999)
11. El-Sana, J., Chiang, Y.: External memory view-dependent simplification. Eurographics **3**, 139–150 (2000)
12. Erikson, C., Manocha, D., Baxter, W.: Hlods for faster display of large static and dynamic environments. In: Symposium on Interactive 3D Graphics, pp. 111–120 (2001)
13. Evans, F., Skiena, S., Varshney, A.: Optimizing triangle srips for fast rendering. In: IEEE Visualization, pp. 319–326 (1996)
14. Garland, M.: Multiresolution modeling: survey and future opportunities. In: Eurographics, pp. 111–131 (1999)

15. GPGPU: General-purpose computation using graphics hardware (2007). http://www.gpgpu.org
16. Silicon Graphics: Arb vertex buffer object specification (2003)
17. Hoppe, H.: Progressive meshes. In: SIGGRAPH, pp. 99–108 (1996)
18. Hoppe, H.: View-dependent refinement of progressive meshes. In: SIGGRPAH, pp. 189–198 (1997)
19. Hoppe, H.: Optimization of mesh locality for transparent caching. In: SIGGRAPH, pp. 269–276 (1999)
20. Rohlf, J., J.H.: Iris performer: a high performance multiprocessing toolkit for real-time 3D graphics. In: SIGGRAPH, pp. 381–394 (1994)
21. Ji, J., Wu, E., Li, S., Liu, X.: Dynamic LOD on GPU. In: CGI (2005)
22. Kircher, S., Garland, M.: Progressive multiresolution meshes for deforming surfaces. In: Eurographics, pp. 191–200 (2005)
23. Lakhia, A.: Efficient interactive rendering of detailed models with hierarchical levels of detail. In: International Symposium on 3D Data Processing, Visualization, and Transmission, pp. 275–282 (2004)
24. Luebke, D., Erikson, C.: View-dependent simplification of arbitrary polygonal environments. In: SIGGRAPH, pp. 199–208 (1997)
25. Porcu, M.B., Sanna, N., Scateni, R.: Efficiently keeping an optimal stripification over a CLOD mesh. In: WSCG 2005, vol. 2, pp. 73–80 (2005)
26. Nehab, D., Barczak, J., Sander, P.V.: Triangle order optimization for graphics hardware computation culling. In: Symposium on Interactive 3D Graphics and Games, pp. 207–211 (2006)
27. Pajarola, R.: Fastmesh: Efficient view-dependent meshing. In: PG 2001, Proceedings of the 9th Pacific Conference on Computer Graphics and Applications, p. 22. IEEE Computer Society, Washington, DC (2001)
28. Pajarola, R., Rossignac, J.: Compressed progressive meshes. Trans. Visual Comput. Graphics **6**(1), 79–93 (2000)
29. Popovic, J., Hoppe, H.: Progressive simplicial complexes. In: SIGGRAPH, pp. 217–224 (1997)
30. Porcu, M., Scateni, R.: An iterative stripification algorithm based on dual graph operations. In: Eurographics 2003, pp. 69–75 (2003)
31. Puig, A., Ramos, F., Ripolles, O., Chover, M., Sbert, M.: View-dependent tessellation and simulation of ocean surfaces. Sci. World J. **1**, 1–13 (2014)
32. Ramos, J.F., Chover, M.: LodStrips: level of detail strips. In: Bubak, M., van Albada, G.D., Sloot, P.M.A., Dongarra, J. (eds.) ICCS 2004. LNCS, vol. 3039, pp. 107–114. Springer, Heidelberg (2004)
33. Ramos, F., Chover, M., Ripolles, O., Granell, C.: Continuous level of detail on graphics hardware. In: Kuba, A., Nyúl, L.G., Palágyi, K. (eds.) DGCI 2006. LNCS, vol. 4245, pp. 460–469. Springer, Heidelberg (2006)
34. Ramos, F., Ripolles, O., Chover, M.: Efficient visualization of 3D models on hardware-limited portable devices. Multimedia Tools Appl. **73**(2), 961–976 (2014)
35. Ribelles, J., López, A., Remolar, I., Belmonte, O., Chover, M.: Multiresolution modelling of polygonal meshes using triangle fans. In: DGCI, pp. 431–442 (2000)
36. Ribelles, J., Lopez, A., Belmonte, O., Remolar, I., Chover, M.: Multiresolution modeling of arbitrary polygonal surfaces: a characterization. Comput. Graphics **26**(3), 449–462 (2002)
37. Sander, P., Snyder, J., Gortler, S., Hoppe, H.: Texture mapping progressive meshes. In: SIGGRAPH 2001, pp. 409–416 (2001)

38. Sander, P.V., Mitchell, J.L.: Progressive buffers: View-dependent geometry and texture for LOD rendering. In: Symposium on Geometry Processing, pp. 129–138 (2005)
39. Shafae, M., Pajarola, R.: Dstrips: Dynamic triangle strips for real-time mesh simplification and rendering. In: Pacific Graphics Conference, pp. 271–280 (2003)
40. Southern, R., Gain, J.: Creation and control of real-time continuous level of detail on programmable graphics hardware. Comput. Graph. Forum **22**(1), 35–48 (2003)
41. Stewart, J.: Tunneling for triangle strips in continuous level-of-detail meshes. In: Graphics Interface, pp. 91–100 (2001)
42. Turchyn, P.: Memory efficient sliding window progressive meshes. In: WSCG (2007)
43. Upstill, S.: The Renderman Companion. Addison Wesley, Reading (1990)
44. Wernecke, J.: The Inventor Mentor: Programming Object-Oriented 3D Graphics With Open Inventor, Release 2. Addison-Wesley, Reading (1994)
45. Xia, J.C., El-Sana, J., Varshney, A.: Adaptive real-time level-of-detail rendering for polygonal models. Trans. Visual Comput. Graphics **3**(2), 171–183 (1997)
46. Yoon, S., Salomon, B., Gayle, R.: Quick-VDR: interactive view-dependent rendering of massive models. IEEE Trans. Vis. Comput. Graph. **11**(4), 369–382 (2005)
47. Zach, C.: Integration of geomorphing into level of detail management for realtime rendering. In: SCCG 2002 (2002)
48. Zach, C., Mantler, S., Karner, K.: Time-critical rendering of discrete and continuous levels of detail. In: Eurographics 2002, pp. 1–8 (2002)

RGB-D Segmentation of Poultry Entrails

Mark Philip Philipsen[1(✉)], Anders Jørgensen[1,3],
Sergio Escalera[2], and Thomas B. Moeslund[1]

[1] Visual Analysis of People Laboratory, Aalborg University, Aalborg, Denmark
mpph@create.aau.dk
[2] University of Barcelona and Computer Vision Center, Barcelona, Spain
[3] IH Food, Copenhagen, Denmark

Abstract. This paper presents an approach for automatic visual inspection of chicken entrails in RGB-D data. The point cloud is first over-segmented into supervoxels based on color, spatial and geometric information. Color, position and texture features are extracted from each of the resulting supervoxels and passed to a Random Forest classifier, which classifies the supervoxels as either belonging to heart, lung, liver or misc. The dataset consists of 150 individual entrails, with 30 of these being reserved for evaluation. Segmentation performance is evaluated on a voxel-by-voxel basis, achieving an average Jaccard index of 61.5 % across the four classes of organs. This is a 5.9 % increase over the 58.1 % achieved with features derived purely from 2D.

1 Introduction

As part of the quality control in poultry processing plants, the entrails of the slaughtered chickens are visually inspected e.g. to ensure that the organ extraction was successful. The entrails are extracted via the abdomen when the chickens are hanging upside down. Hearts and livers are sold separately for human consumption and it is therefore important that these organs are extracted undamaged. The lungs are not fit for consumption, but difficult to extract because they are intertwined with the chicken's ribs. Incomplete removal of entrails is a quality issue for chickens that are sold whole.

Inspection of these three organs is currently done manually, which is incredibly strenuous for the operator and limits the throughput of the entire processing plant. Assessing the quality of a set of entrails, calls for a segmentation method for the organs of interest. Entrails are non-rigid bodies, without straight lines and sharp edges, that only satisfies a weak spatial arrangement. In recent work by [1], a modified auto-context algorithm was developed to segment pig organs in RGB images. The modified algorithm uses an atlas of iteratively updated organ positions.

Quality control of organic material has often been done with hyper spectral imaging (HSI). HSI makes it possible to capture nuances in color, that are normally not visible with RGB cameras [2,3,6,9,14]. [13] was able to detect splenomegaly in poultry carcasses using ultra violet (UV) and color imaging.

F.J. Perales and J. Kittler (Eds.): AMDO 2016, LNCS 9756, pp. 168–174, 2016.
DOI: 10.1007/978-3-319-41778-3_17

The use of UV aids in separating the spleen from the liver, which proved difficult in RGB images. [4] concluded that near infrared imaging can be used to access quality measures like tenderness and color of fresh beef. [7] discovered that two wavelengths, namely, 600 nm and 720 nm, were optimal for detecting gallbladders attached to chicken livers.

Shape and depth information have been applied to other segmentation domains with good results. With the recent advances in available depth sensors, like Intel's RealSense and Microsoft's Kinect, this type of data has become very accessible. In this paper we show that state of the art 3D segmentation algorithms can be used for segmentation of chicken entrails in RGB-D data.

2   Setup

The dataset was captured using the Intel RealSense F200 3D camera. The chicken entrails were viewed frontally, from a distance of 35 cm, while placed in a hanger similar to the ones used on the production line. The entrails were taken directly from the production line and placed in the hanger, while retaining the same orientation as on the line. Figure 1 shows the setup used for data collection and the 3D camera's frontal view of the target.

A total of 150 unique entrails were captured. The first 120 of these were reserved for training, while the remaining 30 were used in the evaluation. The calibration between RGB and D is given by the Intel RealSense SDK.

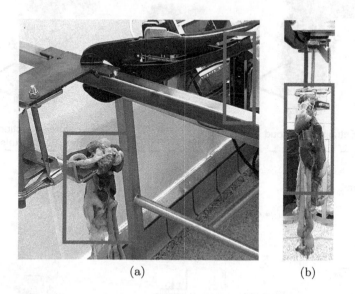

(a)   (b)

Fig. 1. (a) Hanger and 3D camera setup. (b) View from the camera. Red marks the target entrails and green marks the camera. (Color figure online)

3 Segmentation Approach

Most existing research in segmentation of 3D scenes is focused on scenes with man-made objects, which exhibit straight lines and sharp edges. Two widely used datasets with these types of objects are the NYU V1 [12] and V2 [8] datasets. [15] is an example of recent work that addresses this type of data. They segment the point cloud into supervoxels and use a Random Forest (RF) classifier to initialize the unary potentials of a densely interconnected Conditional Random Field (CRF). In this paper we apply a similar framework to objects with significantly different characteristics. Our system differs from [15], by not including the CRF that is used for refining the labeling and by omitting the features that are specific to man-made object, as well as the features that utilize the orientation of the room. Figure 2 gives an overview of the pipeline for segmenting entrails into heart, liver, lung and misc. Figure 3a shows a labeled set of entrails.

First the raw point cloud is cropped, leaving behind only the central region where the organs of interest are located. All of the points that remain in the point cloud are clustered into supervoxels based on spatial, color and geometric similarity. Color, position and texture features are extracted from each of the supervoxels and passed to a RF classifier, that labels each supervoxel as either heart, lung, liver or misc.

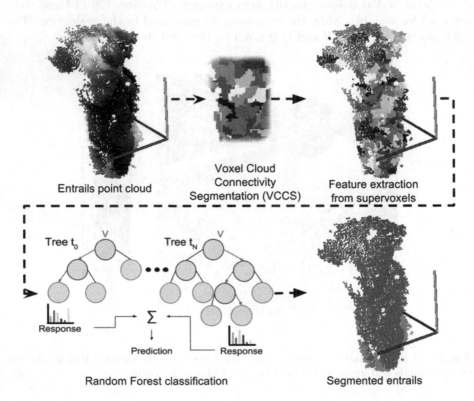

Entrails point cloud

Voxel Cloud
Connectivity
Segmentation (VCCS)

Feature extraction
from supervoxels

Tree t_0 Tree t_N

Response

Σ

Prediction   Response

Random Forest classification

Segmented entrails

Fig. 2. Overview of the segmentation pipeline.

Supervoxel Segmentation. The purpose of over-segmentation is to reduce the amount of data and limit noise while preserving organ borders. We use the Voxel Cloud Connectivity Segmentation (VCCS) [10] supervoxel segmentation algorithm. VCCS produces the supervoxels by seeding the point cloud geometrically even. An iterative clustering algorithm groups voxels within $\sqrt{3}R_{seed}$ of each seed in a 39 dimensional space, based on spatial, color and geometric similarity. The importance of each feature type can be adjusted using weights. The 39 dimensional feature vectors consists of the CIELab channels, 3D point coordinate and the Fast Point Feature Histograms [11] descriptor.

Random Forest. A label prediction for each supervoxel is given by a RF classifier. The RF consists of an ensemble of label distributions in the leaf nodes of the trees. The label distributions are created, during training, from the labels of training features that reaches particular leaf nodes when traversing through the RF. The dataset is skewed from the differences in organ sizes. Hence, priori probabilities that reflect the skewed distribution are assigned each class. Training is done, based on features extracted from supervoxels belonging to 120 sets of entrails. A feature vector and a label is passed for each supervoxel. Since the dataset is annotated on a voxel-by-voxel level, the label of a supervoxel is determined by majority vote on the voxel labels belonging to the given supervoxel. The feature vectors used for the RF consists of the mean and standard deviation of each CIELab channel and the supervoxel center coordinate, which brings the total of features to 9.

4   Evaluation

Since we have a manually annotated dataset we use a supervised evaluation approach, where the similarity between a labeled GT and the segmented output is quantified using the Jaccard Index. Figure 3(a) shows one example of a RGB 2D image that is used when annotating the entrails. Figure 3(b) shows the resulting annotation in 2D. Because of the uncertainty when annotating border regions, evaluation is done, using annotations with a "don't care" zone on the border of each class, as done in [5]. The annotation with the "don't care" zone can be seen in Fig. 3(c). Before the labels can be used for training and evaluation they are mapped onto the 3D point clouds, resulting in the labeled point cloud shown in Fig. 3(d).

The final evaluation based on the 30 entrails in the test set, is done on a voxel-by-voxel basis. Every point belonging to a given supervoxel, thus inherits the supervoxel's label. Finally, the quality of the segmentation can be evaluated by comparing the predicted labels in Fig. 4(b) to the GT Fig. 4(c).

4.1   Results

Table 1 shows the voxel-wise Jaccard index for segmentation of the four classes. For the exclusively 2D based results, the features that are related to 3D are

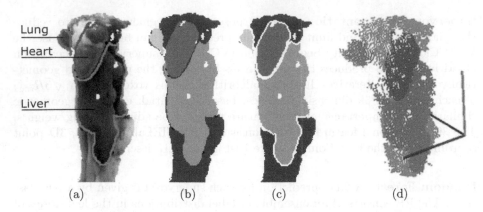

Fig. 3. (a) 2D RGB image of entrails, with labeled organs. (b) Annotation in 2D. (c) Annotation with one pixel wide "don't care" zone around each class. (d) Annotation mapped to 3D. (Color figure online)

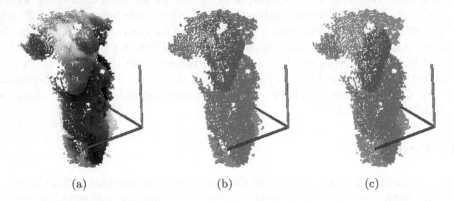

Fig. 4. (a) Original RGB point cloud. (b) Segmented point cloud. (c) GT point cloud with one voxel wide "don't care" zone around each class. Green is misc., red is heart, blue is liver and purple is lung. (Color figure online)

disabled. This is primarily impacting the clustering into supervoxel, as the geometric similarity is an important feature for that.

It is clear from Fig. 4 and Table 1 that the lung and heart are the most challenging organs to segment. The heart is small and much of it is covered by fat, which makes the color features much less effective. The lungs are also small and often occluded, therefore there is few voxels available for training and testing. Additionally, the lungs exhibit large variance in color, based on the amount of blood left in them. The segmentation example in Fig. 4 indicates that the miss-classification of the misc. class as either heart or lung is the main issue. This might be addressed by modifying the weights on each class during training or by looking into the impact of the different features. In this case, it is likely that the spatial feature is too significant in the upper part of the point cloud.

Table 1. Voxel-wise Jaccard index for the four classes.

	Misc	Heart	Liver	Lung	Avg.
2D	62.9 %	44.4 %	76.8 %	**48.4 %**	58.1 %
2D+3D	**66.1 %**	**53.1 %**	**79.2 %**	47.5 %	**61.5 %**

5 Conclusion

We presented an approach for automatic visual inspection of chicken entrails and show that a segmentation algorithm previously used on man-made objects is able to function on vastly different objects. We achieve an average Jaccard index of 61.5 % across the four organ classes. This is a 5.9 % increase over the 58.1 % achieved with features derived purely from 2D. Thus, the segmentation benefits from the additional information, that is available in RGB-D compared to RGB. Our use of 3D derived features is mainly limited to the segmentation into supervoxels. Therefore, improvements might lie in utilizing posterior optimizations as well as global and neighborhood features, many of which would be based on 3D.

Acknowledgments. Thanks to GUDP for financial support and to Danpo for providing access to their facilities. The work has been partially supported by Spanish project TIN2013-43478-P.

References

1. Amaral, T., Kyriazakis, I., Mckenna, S.J., Ploetz, T.: Weighted atlas auto-context with application to multiple organ segmentation. In: Proceedings of WACV (2016)
2. Chao, K., Yang, C.C., Kim, M.S., Chan, D.E.: High throughput spectral imaging system for wholesomeness inspection of chicken. Appl. Eng. Agric. **24**(4), 475–485 (2008)
3. Dey, B.P., Chen, Y.R., Hsieh, C., Chan, D.E.: Detection of septicemia in chicken livers by spectroscopy. Poult. Sci. **82**(2), 199–206 (2003)
4. Elmasry, G., Sun, D.W., Allen, P.: Near-infrared hyperspectral imaging for predicting colour, pH and tenderness of fresh beef. J. Food Eng. **110**(1), 127–140 (2012)
5. Everingham, M., Van Gool, L., Williams, C.K.I., Winn, J., Zisserman, A.: The PASCAL Visual Object Classes Challenge Results (VOC 2008) (2008)
6. Huang, H., Liu, L., Ngadi, M.O.: Recent developments in hyperspectral imaging for assessment of food quality and safety. Sensors **14**(4), 7248–7276 (2014)
7. Jørgensen, A., Moeslund, T.B., Jensen, E.M.: Detecting gallbladders in chicken livers using spectral analysis. In: Proceedings of the British Machine Vision Conference 2015. British Machine Vision Association (2015)
8. Silberman, N., Hoiem, D., Kohli, P., Fergus, R.: Indoor segmentation and support inference from RGBD images. In: Fitzgibbon, A., Lazebnik, S., Perona, P., Sato, Y., Schmid, C. (eds.) ECCV 2012, Part V. LNCS, vol. 7576, pp. 746–760. Springer, Heidelberg (2012)

9. Panagou, E.Z., Papadopoulou, O., Carstensen, J.M., Nychas, G.J.E.: Potential of multispectral imaging technology for rapid and non-destructive determination of the microbiological quality of beef filets during aerobic storage. Int. J. Food Microbiol. **174**, 1–11 (2014). http://dx.doi.org/10.1016/j.ijfoodmicro.2013.12.026
10. Papon, J., Abramov, A., Schoeler, M., Wtter, F.: Voxel cloud connectivity segmentation - supervoxels for point clouds. In: 2013 IEEE Conference on Computer Vision and Pattern Recognition (CVPR), pp. 2027–2034, June 2013
11. Rusu, R.B., Blodow, N., Beetz, M.: Fast point feature histograms (FPFH) for 3D registration. In: IEEE International Conference on Robotics and Automation (ICRA 2009), pp. 3212–3217, May 2009
12. Silberman, N., Fergus, R.: Indoor scene segmentation using a structured light sensor. In: Proceedings of the International Conference on Computer Vision - Workshop on 3D Representation and Recognition (2011)
13. Tao, Y., Shao, J., Skeeles, K., Chen, Y.R.: Detection of splenomegaly in poultry carcasses by UV and color imaging. Trans. ASAE **43**(2), 469–474 (2000)
14. Trinderup, C.H., Dahl, A.L., Michael, J., Jensen, K., Conradsen, K.: Utilization of multispectral images for meat color measurements, pp. 43–48 (2013)
15. Wolf, D., Prankl, J., Vincze, M.: Fast semantic segmentation of 3D point clouds using a dense CRF with learned parameters. In: 2015 IEEE International Conference on Robotics and Automation (ICRA), pp. 4867–4873, May 2015

Convolutional Neural Network Super Resolution for Face Recognition in Surveillance Monitoring

Pejman Rasti[1]($\boxtimes$), Tõnis Uiboupin[1], Sergio Escalera[2],
and Gholamreza Anbarjafari[1]

[1] iCV Research Group, Institute of Technology, University of Tartu,
Tartu, Estonia
{pejman.rasti,donuz,shb}@ut.ee
[2] Computer Vision Center and University of Barcelona,
Barcelona, Spain
sergio@maia.ub.es

Abstract. Due to the importance of security in society, monitoring activities and recognizing specific people through surveillance video cameras play an important role. One of the main issues in such activity arises from the fact that cameras do not meet the resolution requirement for many face recognition algorithms. In order to solve this issue, in this paper we are proposing a new system which super resolves the image using deep learning convolutional network followed by the Hidden Markov Model and Singular Value Decomposition based face recognition. The proposed system has been tested on many well-known face databases such as FERET, HeadPose, and Essex University databases as well as our recently introduced iCV Face Recognition database (iCV-F). The experimental results show that the recognition rate is improving considerably after apply the super resolution.

Keywords: Super resolution · Deep learning · Surveillance videos · Face recognition · Hidden markov model · Support vector machine

1 Introduction

Today, world security standards in crowded areas like airports, metro, shopping malls have been highly increased. One way for avoiding threats is to use video surveillance. Systems like CCTV have been around for quite a while, but has required a lot of manual work to check the live feed or saved data.

One way to make this more efficient is to deploy automated system to detect and recognize people from the video stream. This requires finding the face and applying face recognition on it. Such automation is complicated by multiple factors. One of the main problems is low image resolution, because of cameras often covering large areas to reduce cost. One way to reduce such an effect is to apply image super resolution (SR). In this paper we are testing the effect of enhancing face image resolution by applying SR to face recognition performance.

© Springer International Publishing Switzerland 2016
F.J. Perales and J. Kittler (Eds.): AMDO 2016, LNCS 9756, pp. 175–184, 2016.
DOI: 10.1007/978-3-319-41778-3_18

1.1 Super Resolution

Image super resolution (SR) techniques aim at enhancing the resolution of images acquired by low resolution (LR) sensors, while also minimizing added visual artifacts. Such techniques are expected to enable overcoming limitations of LR imaging such as surveillance cameras. There are theoretically two main approaches to SR: *multi* images SR and *single* image SR. In this work we have focused on second approach, since first hasn't proven to be very effective in this area. The field of single image SR has been shown considerable attention [1–4]. Interpolation has been widely adopted in many super resolution techniques [5–7]. In past five to ten years a wide range of new approaches have been suggested which improve conventional linear interpolators. The proposed method in [3] uses self-similarity of image patches within and across different scales in the same image in single image SR. Techniques in [1,2] are based on sparsely representing low and high resolution (LHR) patch-pairs in a dictionary pair, namely dictionary low (D_l) and dictionary high (D_h). The main idea behind this approach is that each LHR patch-pair is sparsely represented over the dictionaries where the resulting representations α_l, α_h have pre-specified correspondence. Sparse representation invariance [1,2] is a common assumption here. The idea is that patches in an LHR pair have the same sparse representation over the LHR dictionary pair ($\alpha_l = \alpha_h$). Joint learning of the dictionary pair is used to get meaningful recovery of the HR patch. The authors of [1,2] have suggested that for recovering the HR patches, first a dictionary D_l that best fits the LR patches should be learned, and then a dictionary D_h that works best with the resulting coefficients α_l.

In [4], an SR algorithm based on sparse representation of patch-pairs over a dictionary pair was introduced. However, no invariance assumption is made. Instead a parametric model which captures the statistical dependencies between the sparsity patterns of the LHR coefficients and between the corresponding nonzero coefficients is suggested. Prediction of α_l from α_h is done using the MMSE estimator, which arises directly from the model and has a closed form formula. This model does not require the dictionary pair to be strictly aligned or even to be of the same size. This removes any restrictions of the LR dictionary. Because of this, very small orthogonal dictionaries are used for the LR patches, which help to reduce the computational cost of the scale-up scheme.

Dong et al. [8] proposed a deep convolutional neural network (CNN) based single image super resolution method and showed that the traditional sparse-coding-based algorithm can also be seen as a kind of deep convolutional network. The end-to-end mapping between LR images and HR images was optimized in Dong's SR method, which achieves excellent reconstruction performance.

1.2 Face Recognition

As in the case of image super resolution, several face recognition methods have been proposed. Next we describe the most relevant ones. Principal components analysis (PCA), Linear discriminant analysis (LDA) [9–12], and probability distribution function based face recognition [13] are some well-known appearance-based techniques, although PCA suffers from sensitivity to illumination conditions.

Hidden Markov Models (HMM) based approaches have been widely used in recent years [14]. Samaria and Harter [15] suggested to model facial features from frontal images by a top-bottom HMM. Kohir and Desai [16] proposed using DCT coefficients as features in a top-down HMM, which increased face recognition performance. A pseudo 2D representation of the face by using a combination of left-right models arranged in an ordered sequence [17] were reported to achieve higher recognition rates. More recently HMM based face recognition methods, like Pseudo 2D HMM with DCT coefficients features [18], Singular Value Decomposition (SVD) coefficients [19], and with Wavelet coefficients features [20], have been proposed [21].

Singular Value Decomposition (SVD) can be used to represent algebraic properties of an image [22]. Singular values of a data matrix give information about the noise level, the entry, the rank of the matrix, etc. and reflect some features of the patterns of the matrix.

In this work, we investigate the importance of the state-of-the-art CNN SR algorithm of [8] in improving recognition accuracies of the state-of-the-art face recognition algorithm of [14] for working with LR surveillance camera. To the extent of our knowledge, face recognition in different resolutions has not been studied extensively, except in [23] in which optical ow based SR is used to enhance accuracies of face recognition. However, our proposed system is the first one in which SR algorithms have been employed for improving quality of LR input facial images before face recognition. We show in this paper that such SR algorithms produce HR details that are not necessarily recovered by simple upscaling algorithms, like bicubic interpolation. It is shown in this paper that results of the deep learning-based SR produces images that are of better quality compared to the input LR images. We show that employing such higher resolution images improves the recognition accuracy of a state-of-the-art face recognition algorithm.

The remainder of this paper is organized as follows. A detailed overview of the proposed method is presented in Sect. 2. Section 3 contains the outcome of experimental results. Finally, Sect. 4 concludes the paper.

2   The Proposed Method

In this work, a deep learning convolutional network SR [8] method is proposed in order to solve the challenge of face recognition in surveillance videos. Face recognition is done after SR by adopting HMM and SVD [14].

First, the Viola and Jones [24] algorithm was used to extract only faces from each image to reduce the effects of background and clothing to face recognition results. Also, all images are downsampled by factor of 4 in order to simulate the situation of taken images by using surveillance cameras.

For SR purposes the deep learning convolutional networks [8] method has been adopted. In order to find super resolved images, first a bicubic interpolation technique is used for upscaling the image to the desired size. The interpolated image is denoted as **Z**. Our goal is to recover from **Z** an image $F(\mathbf{Z})$ which is as similar as possible to the ground truth high resolution (HR) image **R**. We still call **Z** a LR image for the ease of presentation, although it has the same size as **R**. We wish to learn a mapping **F**, which conceptually consists of three operations:

1. **Patch extraction and representation:** this operation extracts (overlapping) patches from the LR image **Z** and represents each patch as a high dimensional vector. These vectors comprise a set of feature maps, of which the number equals the dimensionality of the vectors.
2. **Non-linear mapping:** this operation nonlinearly maps each high dimensional vector onto another high dimensional vector. Each mapped vector is conceptually the representation of a HR patch. These vectors comprise another set of feature maps.
3. **Reconstruction:** this operation aggregates the above HR patch-wise representations to generate the final HR image. This image is expected to be similar to the ground truth **R** (Fig. 1).

Each database used in our work has 10 poses per person. Five of each pose of persons are used to train HMM [14], and the remaining 5 are used for testing. Both training and test images go through the face recognition process which is divided into seven steps as will be explained in detail here. These steps are: filtering, generating observation vectors, feature extraction, feature selection, quantization, training and face recognition. In filtering, a 3×3 minimum filter is applied to the face image to remove unwanted artifacts, such as highlights in subjects' eyes due to flash, and salt noise. After the filtering is done, the face image is converted into a one dimensional sequence. This is done by sliding an **L** window from top to bottom of the image, which creates a sequence of overlapping blocks of width **W** and height **L** of each face image of width **W** and height **H**. Next, the features are extracted. Here, instead of using gray values of pixels in sampling windows, SVD coefficients are used as features. Once the features are extracted a subset of features that lead to smallest classification error and computational cost are extracted from SVD which contains three matrices ($\mathbf{U}$, $\mathbf{\Sigma}$ and $\mathbf{V}$) two first coefficients of $\mathbf{\Sigma}$ ($\mathbf{\Sigma_{11}}$ and $\mathbf{\Sigma_{22}}$) and first coefficient

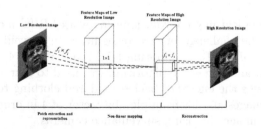

Fig. 1. The flowchart of the SR method.

of U (U_{11}) are used to associate each block. This decreases significantly the length of observation vectors and also computational complexity and sensitivity to noise, changes in illumination, shift and rotation. Since SVD coefficients have innately continuous values, which can lead to an infinite number of possible observation vectors that cannot be modeled by discrete HMM, the features need to be quantized. Considering vector $X = (x_1, x_2, \ldots, x_n)$ the quantized value of x_i is computed as below:

$$x_{i_{quantized}} = \left[\frac{x_i - x_i^{min}}{(x_i^{max} - x_i^{min})/D_i} \right] \tag{1}$$

x_i^{max} and x_i^{min} are the maximum and minimum that x_i can get in all possible observation vectors respectively and D_i is the number of distinct levels to quantize to. Here the first feature (Σ_{11}) is quantized into 10, second (Σ_{22}) into 7 and third (U_{11}) into 18 levels. After each face image is represented by observation vectors, they are modeled by seven-state HMM. The Baum-Welch algorithm [25] is used to train an HMM model for each person in the database. Finally, for each test image the probability of the observation vector (O) in respect to each HMM face model λ is calculated for classification. A person on a test image (m) is classified as person (d) if:

$$P\left(O^{(m)} \mid \lambda_d\right) = \max_n P\left(O^{(m)} \mid \lambda_n\right) \tag{2}$$

Figure 2 shows an overview of the proposed method.

3 Experimental Results

Four face databases are used in the experiments. These databases are the facial recognition technology (FERET) database [26,27], Essex Faces facial images collection [28], Head Pose Image database (HP) [29] and our recently introduced iCV Face Recognition database (iCV-F) [30].

3.1 Data

The iCV-F database consists of face images of 31 subjects of which each subject has 10 images. The database includes people wearing glasses or not and various

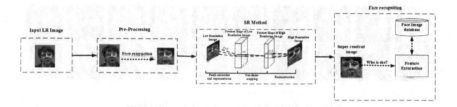

Fig. 2. The flowchart of the proposed system.

skin color. Models were asked to make different facial expressions while the photos were taken. Figure 3 shows some images of the iCV-F database.

The FERET program was sponsored by the Department of Defense's Counterdrug Technology Development Program through the Defense Advanced Research Products Agency (DARPA). It ran from 1993 through 1997 and its primary mission was to develop an automatic face detection system to assist security, intelligence and law enforcement. FERET database was collected to support testing and evaluation of face recognition algorithms. The photos were taken in a semi-controlled environment. The same physical setup was used in each photography session to maintain consistency in the whole database. There are some minor differences in images gathered on different dates due to reassembling the equipment for each session. The final corpus consists of 14051 eight-bit grayscale images with views of models' heads ranging from frontal to both left and right profiles. [26,27]. In 2003 a color version of the database was released by DARPA. It included 2413 HR, 24-bit color still facial images of 856 individuals. The selected subset of FERET images database consists of 500 color images.

The Essex Faces consists of 1500 images. The subjects of the database sat at fixed distance from the camera and were asked to speak during the photoshoot. Speaking is for introducing variations of facial expressions. Original images of the database are 180 by 200 pixels. The background of all photos is plain green. No head scale is used. There are very minor changes in head turn, tilt and slant and in position of face in image. No lighting variation in the photos. Also there is no individual hairstyle variation since the photos were taken in a single session [28].

The HP database consists of 2790 face images of 15 individuals with variations of pan and tilt angles from −90 to +90 degrees. It has 2 series of 93 images, all in different poses, for each person. The reason for having 2 series is to have known and unknown faces for training and algorithms. The database features people of various skin color and with or without glasses. The background of images is neutral and uncluttered for focusing on face operations [29]. The subset of the HP database used in this work includes 150 images. Faces in the selected subset are turned only in the horizontal direction.

Our own faces database (iCV-F) consists of 310 images. Photos were taken in 2 sessions in similar conditions. The database includes people wearing glasses or

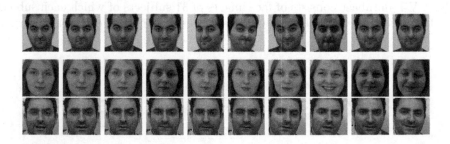

Fig. 3. Some samples of iCV-F database.

not and various skin color. Models were asked to make different facial expressions while the photos were taken.

3.2 Evaluation Protocol

The facial images first have been passed through the Viola-Jones face detector and the segmented faces are resized to 60×60 pixels. These images are then downsampled by a factor of 4 in order to achieve low resolution input images. Figure 4 shows the LR and super resolved images. The low resolution images have the size of 15×15 and super resolved images 60×60.

3.3 Results

In order to evaluate and verify the efficiency and reliability of the proposed SR method in terms of providing sufficiently illustrative information for face recognition under various experimentation scenarios, it is applied to numerous databases, where the recognition rates (RR) are obtained for three variants of the images, which are, namely, the original, LR and super-resolved ones. More clearly, the underlying notion is that the performance of the SR technique taken into account is implicitly represented by the capability of the face recognition algorithm in fulfilling its task properly, since it stands for its level of effectiveness in retrieving the data lost at the downsampling stage. The latter is denoted by the amount of improvement appearing in the face recognition rate using the super-resolved images as the subjects, while being compared against that of the LR ones. In other words, when recognizing the faces using the super-resolved images, a more powerful SR method leads to recognition rates closer to the case of considering the original ones.

The databases utilized in the context of the experiments conducted for the purpose of this study include Essex, HP, FERET and iCV-F. Separate recognition rates are reported by using the original, LR and super-resolved images. In order to evaluate the stressfulness of the proposed SR method in enhancing the recognition rate from the case of using the LR images towards the one achieved by taking advantage of the original images, it is shown by the metric compensation ratio (CR), which shows the percentage of the difference between the

Fig. 4. LR (15×15 at left) and SR (60×60 at right) version of images of different databases. The first row belongs to Essex database, the second row is for the FERET database, and the third and fourth rows belong to the HP and iCV-F databases respectively.

recognition rate achieved on the LR images and that of the original ones that is compensated by super-resolving the images, being mathematically expressed as follows:

$$CR = \frac{RR_{SR} - RR_{LR}}{RR_O - RR_{LR}} \tag{3}$$

where RR_O, RR_{LR} and RR_{SR} stand for the recognition rates accomplished using the original, LR and super resolved images, respectively. The results of the above procedure are shown in Table 1.

Table 1. The RR_O, RR_{LR}, RR_{SR} and CR values, in percent, achieved by applying the proposed SR method on the Essex, HP, FERET and iCV-F databases, which are sorted in the descending order of CR.

RR	RR_{LR}	RR_{SR}	RR_O	CR
Essex	75.82	86.8	99.20	46.96
HP	26.67	37.33	50.67	44.42
iCV-F	72.83	78.1	98.06	20.89
FERET	20	21.60	31.6	13.79

The fact that the CR has taken positive values in the case of all the databases utilized shows that the proposed SR method has always led to improvements in the face recognition rate, demonstrating its superiority. Using the Essex and HP databases, the latter enhancement is considerable, and takes values as high as **46.96 %** and **44.42 %**, respectively. Nevertheless, the recognition rate achieved by using the HP and FERET databases is essentially low, which is due to the lack of robustness in the HMM-based face recognition algorithm [14] against the pose changes, which is widely apparent in both of the foregoing databases. However, the efficiency of the proposed method is clearly shown by the improvements accomplished in recognizing the faces from the Essex and iCV-F databases. Although the recognition rates using the LR images from the foregoing databases are already relatively high, still applying the proposed method has resulted in considerably better recognition rates in both of the cases.

4   Conclusion

In this work, a deep learning convolutional network SR method is proposed in order to solve the challenge of face recognition in surveillance videos. Face recognition is done after super resolution by adopting HMM and SVD. The system has been tested on many well-known face databases such as FERET, HP, and Essex University databases as well as our own face database. The experimental results show that the recognition rate is increasing considerably after applying the SR by using facial and natural images dictionary.

Acknowledgment. This work is supported Estonian Research Council Grant (PUT638) and the Spanish Project TIN2013-43478-P.

References

1. Yang, J., Wright, J., Huang, T.S., Ma, Y.: Image super-resolution via sparse representation. IEEE Trans. Image Process. **19**(11), 2861–2873 (2010)
2. Zeyde, R., Elad, M., Protter, M.: On single image scale-up using sparse-representations. In: Boissonnat, J.-D., Chenin, P., Cohen, A., Gout, C., Lyche, T., Mazure, M.-L., Schumaker, L. (eds.) Curves and Surfaces 2011. LNCS, vol. 6920, pp. 711–730. Springer, Heidelberg (2012)
3. Yang, J., Lin, Z., Cohen, S.: Fast image super-resolution based on in-place example regression. In: 2013 IEEE Conference on Computer Vision and Pattern Recognition (CVPR), pp. 1059–1066. IEEE (2013)
4. Peleg, T., Elad, M.: A statistical prediction model based on sparse representations for single image super-resolution. IEEE Trans. Image Process. **23**(6), 2569–2582 (2014)
5. Rasti, P., Demirel, H., Anbarjafari, G.: Image resolution enhancement by using interpolation followed by iterative back projection. In: 2013 21st Signal Processing and Communications Applications Conference (SIU), pp. 1–4. IEEE (2013)
6. Rasti, P., Lusi, I., Sahakyan, A., Traumann, A., Bolotnikova, A., Daneshmand, M., Kiefer, R., Aabloo, A., Anbarjafar, G., Demirel, H., et al.: Modified back projection kernel based image super resolution. In: 2014 2nd International Conference on Artificial Intelligence, Modelling and Simulation (AIMS), pp. 161–165. IEEE (2014)
7. Wang, L., Xiang, S., Meng, G., Wu, H., Pan, C.: Edge-directed single-image super-resolution via adaptive gradient magnitude self-interpolation. IEEE Trans. Circuits Syst. Video Technol. **23**(8), 1289–1299 (2013)
8. Dong, C., Loy, C.C., He, K., Tang, X.: Image super-resolution using deep convolutional networks. IEEE Trans. Pattern Anal. Mach. Intell. **38**(2), 295–307 (2015)
9. Turk, M., Pentland, A.P., et al.: Face recognition using eigenfaces. In: IEEE Computer Society Conference on Computer Vision and Pattern Recognition (CVPR 1991), Proceedings, pp. 586–591 (1991)
10. Pentland, A., Moghaddam, B., Starner, T.: View-based and modular eigenspaces for face recognition. In: 1994 Computer Society Conference on Computer Vision and Pattern Recognition (CVPR 1994), Proceedings, pp. 84–91. IEEE (1994)
11. Belhumeur, P.N., Hespanha, J.P., Kriegman, D.J.: Eigenfaces vs. fisherfaces: recognition using class specific linear projection. IEEE Trans. Pattern Anal. Mach. Intell. **19**(7), 711–720 (1997)
12. Zhao, W., Chellappa, R., Nandhakumar, N.: Empirical performance analysis of linear discriminant classifiers. In: 1998 IEEE Computer Society Conference on Computer Vision and Pattern Recognition, Proceedings, pp. 164–169. IEEE (1998)
13. Demirel, H., Anbarjafari, G.: Data fusion boosted face recognition based on probability distribution functions in different colour channels. EURASIP J. Adv. Signal Process. **2009**, 25 (2009)
14. Miar-Naimi, H., Davari, P.: A new fast and efficient HMM based face recognition system using a 7-state HMM along with SVD coefficients (2008)
15. Samaria, F.S., Harter, A.C.: Parameterisation of a stochastic model for human face identification. In: Proceedings of the Second IEEE Workshop on Applications of Computer Vision, pp. 138–142. IEEE (1994)

16. Kohir, V.V., Desai, U.B.: Face recognition using a DCT-HMM approach. In: Fourth IEEE Workshop on Applications of Computer Vision (WACV 1998), Proceedings, pp. 226–231. IEEE (1998)

17. Samaria, F.S.: Face recognition using hidden markov models, Ph.D. dissertation, University of Cambridge (1994)

18. Eickeler, S., Müller, S., Rigoll, G.: Recognition of JPEG compressed face images based on statistical methods. Image Vis. Comput. 18(4), 279–287 (2000)

19. Anand, C., Lawrance, R.: Algorithm for face recognition using HMM and SVD coefficients. Artif. Intell. Syst. Mach. Learn. 5(3), 125–130 (2013)

20. Bicego, M., Castellani, U., Murino, V.: Using hidden markov models and wavelets for face recognition. In: 12th International Conference on Image Analysis and Processing, Proceedings, pp. 52–56. IEEE (2003)

21. Bobulski, J.: 2DHMM-based face recognition method. In: Choraś, R.S. (ed.) Image Processing and Communications Challenges 7. Advances in Intelligent Systems and Computing, vol. 389, pp. 11–18. Springer, Heidelberg (2016)

22. Klema, V.C., Laub, A.J.: The singular value decomposition: its computation and some applications. IEEE Trans. Autom. Control 25(2), 164–176 (1980)

23. Lin, F., Fookes, C., Chandran, V., Sridharan, S.: Super-resolved faces for improved face recognition from surveillance video. In: Lee, S.-W., Li, S.Z. (eds.) ICB 2007. LNCS, vol. 4642, pp. 1–10. Springer, Heidelberg (2007)

24. Viola, P., Jones, M.J.: Robust real-time face detection. Int. J. Comput. Vis. 57(2), 137–154 (2004)

25. Rabiner, L.R.: A tutorial on hidden Markov models and selected applications in speech recognition. Proc. IEEE 77(2), 257–286 (1989)

26. Phillips, P.J., Wechsler, H., Huang, J., Rauss, P.J.: The FERET database and evaluation procedure for face-recognition algorithms. Image Vis. Comput. 16(5), 295–306 (1998)

27. Phillips, P.J., Moon, H., Rizvi, S., Rauss, P.J., et al.: The FERET evaluation methodology for face-recognition algorithms. IEEE Trans. Pattern Anal. Mach. Intell. 22(10), 1090–1104 (2000)

28. Collection of facial images Faces94. http://cswww.essex.ac.uk/mv/allfaces/faces94.html

29. Head pose image database. http://www-prima.inrialpes.fr/perso/Gourier/Faces/HPDatabase.html

30. Collection of facial images. http://icv.tuit.ut.ee/databases.html

3D Morphable Face Models and Their Applications

Josef Kittler[1(✉)], Patrik Huber[1], Zhen-Hua Feng[1],
Guosheng Hu[2], and William Christmas[1]

[1] Centre for Vision, Speech and Signal Processing, University of Surrey,
Guildford, UK
{j.kittler,p.huber,z.feng,w.christmas}@surrey.ac.uk
[2] LEAR Team, Inria Grenoble Rhone-Alpes, Grenoble, France
guosheng.hu@inria.fr

Abstract. 3D Morphable Face Models (3DMM) have been used in face recognition for some time now. They can be applied in their own right as a basis for 3D face recognition and analysis involving 3D face data. However their prevalent use over the last decade has been as a versatile tool in 2D face recognition to normalise pose, illumination and expression of 2D face images. A 3DMM has the generative capacity to augment the training and test databases for various 2D face processing related tasks. It can be used to expand the gallery set for pose-invariant face matching. For any 2D face image it can furnish complementary information, in terms of its 3D face shape and texture. It can also aid multiple frame fusion by providing the means of registering a set of 2D images. A key enabling technology for this versatility is 3D face model to 2D face image fitting. In this paper recent developments in 3D face modelling and model fitting will be overviewed, and their merits in the context of diverse applications illustrated on several examples, including pose and illumination invariant face recognition, and 3D face reconstruction from video.

Keywords: 3D Morphable Model · 3D face reconstruction · Face model fitting · Applications

1 Introduction

3D face models are a powerful tool used for a variety of applications in computer vision, face analysis, and face recognition, as well as in computer graphics and animation. They typically depict a face using a 3D polygonal mesh. Depending on the type of 3D sensor used for the acquisition of 3D face data, the mesh may simply represent the shape, or additionally associate with each vertex the face surface texture by augmenting the captured geometry with RGB data. Consistency of the face representation over different faces is achieved by registering a deformable generic 3D face mesh to the input data.

© Springer International Publishing Switzerland 2016
F.J. Perales and J. Kittler (Eds.): AMDO 2016, LNCS 9756, pp. 185–206, 2016.
DOI: 10.1007/978-3-319-41778-3_19

The term "model" is somewhat ambiguous. It can signify a mesh of shape and texture values for a specific face. It can relate to a generic mesh with its capability to deform to a particular 3D face image. It is also used as a representation of a collection of 3D faces in terms of its statistical distribution of shape and texture values. In this paper the use of the term "model" primarily refers to this latter notion.

Statistical models of classes of objects are very important in pattern recognition. They are the basis of statistical decision rules and as such have been used extensively also in 3D face analysis and recognition [40]. Principal Component Analysis (PCA) methods are popular as they provide a concise form for any distribution of highly correlated variables [63] as well as scope for dimensionality reduction. The advantage of statistical 3D face models over their 2D counterparts [6,12,34] is their ability to model the intrinsic surface properties of faces, rather than their appearance, which are a function of pose and illumination.

Blanz and Vetter in 1999 [4] were the first to recognise the generative capacity of Principal Component Analysis (PCA) methods, and proposed 3D Morphable Model (3DMM) to capture variations of 3D faces, as well as to synthesise new faces. Their work inspired subsequent research which focused on reconstructing the 3D model parameters from a single 2D image using an analysis-by-synthesis approach that models how a particular face is generated in terms of shape, texture, pose and light. In 2006, Paysan et al. [41] made their model available to academic institutions. In 2016, Huber et al. [28] published the Surrey Face Model, including a real-time shape fitting algorithm.

One of the main topics of research in the area of 3D Morphable Models is analysis-by-synthesis, which involves fitting the 3D model to a 2D image. By virtue of the fitting process, the 3D parameters (including pose, texture and light) of the input image can be reconstructed so that the model-synthesised 2D face image is as close as possible to the original image. Numerous papers have focused on this problem [2,16,25,27,38,47,50,52,69], with significant progress reported in the last few years. Recently, Schönborn et al. [53] took on the challenge of fitting 3DMM to images in-the-wild, accomplishing that with an Markov Chain Monte Carlo based fitting method, but achieving far from real-time speeds.

The model's ability to generate faces with distinct properties, as well as to modify them in existing subjects (for example expressions, or attributes like gender), enables the conduct of studies in the psychology of human face perception [37,57–59]. The model can also be used to generate arbitrary samples from the statistical distribution for use as training data in 2D- or 3D-based algorithms.

Once the 3D model is fitted to a 2D image, it can be used for pose correction in 2D face recognition [11,25,56]. Recent work has also used 3D face models for tracking in, and for 3D face reconstruction from, monocular videos (e.g. [30]). Most of the methods reconstruct face shape in great detail, but are suitable only for controlled, frontal conditions, e.g. [8], while others require tedious subject-specific pre-training (e.g. [20,29]). The strength of a 3DMM is that it can be used as a prior in learning algorithms, benefiting from prior knowledge about faces. In contrast to model-free tracking, which can result in implausible faces, a face model restricts the search space to produce plausible results.

Building a 3D Morphable Model is a time-consuming exercise, involving 3D data collection and a chain of processes, starting from 3D data annotation [33] of key 3D facial features, which are required by a registration algorithm that maps the raw face data onto a standard 3D mesh [5,21,32,47,50,51]. Once the 3D face images available for training are registered, the PCA analysis is performed to find the subspace spanned by the shape and texture data. The two sets of bases obtained by PCA then constitute the 3DMM model. Instances of the statistical model are defined by shape and texture parameters which are the coefficients (coordinates) associated with the bases.

The aim of this paper is to discuss the merits of 3D morphable face models and to present examples of their use cases. After describing the model and the model synthesis pipeline in Sect. 2, we present an application of using model-generated 3D face data to improve the performance of a 2D landmark detection algorithm (Sect. 3). In Sect. 4, we discuss an analysis-by-synthesis approach for fitting the 3D model and parameters to a single 2D image. We then present results for real-time model fitting on videos achieved by introducing acceleration steps incorporated in the fitting algorithms in Sect. 5.

2   3D Morphable Face Models

The visual appearance of 3D objects and scenes is a function of their shape and surface texture properties, referred to as albedo. There are many approaches to modelling 3D objects and 3D environments, but from the appearance point of view, apart from the albedo, the pertinent characteristic of 3D objects is their surface shape, and a common way to represent it is in terms of a 3D surface mesh of vertices and their 3D coordinates. Given a set of vertices we can then associate with each vertex not only its geometric information (3D coordinates) but also its albedo, expressed in terms of a triplet of RGB values.

The 3D mesh can be considered as a surface sampling scheme, which could be dense and regular. However, for the sake of efficiency, the common strategy is to sample the object surface nonuniformly, more densely in the parts of the surface where the shape is changing rapidly, and more sparsely in slowly varying areas.

Each physical object model could have its own object specific mesh. However when dealing with an object class, such as faces, it is convenient to adopt a common mesh, defined by a fixed number of vertices, n, for all instances of the class. From the point of view of any subsequent analysis, it may also be convenient if each vertex has a specific identity, in other words representing semantically the same point on all instances of the object class. For example, in the case of the human face, particular vertices will represent the tip of the nose, the corner of the left eye, etc. In this paper, as we are concerned with modelling 3D faces, this consistency of face surface representation in terms of vertices of corresponding identity is of paramount importance. It can be achieved by a process of registration [5,47], which maps a canonical mesh template onto each raw 3D face image. Once 3D faces are registered, we can then build a statistical model representing the whole 3D face population, as follows.

Let the ith vertex v_i of a registered face be located at (x_i, y_i, z_i), and have the RGB colour values (r_i, g_i, b_i). A registered face can be represented in terms of shape and texture as a pair of vectors:

$$\mathbf{s} = (x_1, y_1, z_1, ..., x_n, y_n, z_n)^T$$
$$\mathbf{t} = (r_1, g_1, b_1, ..., r_n, g_n, b_n)^T \tag{1}$$

where n is the number of vertices

As the samples of a face surface conveyed by its vertices are correlated, we may construct more concise statistical models by transforming the registered 3D face data into another coordinate system. A common approach is to remove redundancy by means of PCA. Let $\mathbf{S}$ and $\mathbf{T}$ denote the matrices of shape and texture principal components of dimensionality $3n \times n_s$ and $3n \times n_t$ respectively. By decorrelating the data, the number of bases (columns) of these matrices can be significantly smaller than the number of vertices n. A sample from a 3D face distribution then can be represented as

$$\mathbf{s} = \mathbf{s}_0 + \mathbf{S}\boldsymbol{\alpha} \tag{2}$$

and

$$\mathbf{t} = \mathbf{t}_0 + \mathbf{T}\boldsymbol{\beta} \tag{3}$$

where $\mathbf{s}_0$ and $\mathbf{t}_0$ are the mean shape and the mean texture respectively. $\boldsymbol{\alpha} = (\alpha_1, ..., \alpha_{n_s})^T$ is a vector of shape coefficients and $\boldsymbol{\beta} = (\beta_1, ..., \beta_{n_t})^T$ is a vector of texture coefficients. As a byproduct of the PCA analysis, these coefficients are uncorrelated. Their standard deviations, estimated from training data, define the range of 3D faces that can be expressed by the 3D face model. Figure 1 shows how the shape and texture vary as the first three model parameters of a trained 3DMM vary.

By changing $\boldsymbol{\alpha}$ and $\boldsymbol{\beta}$ we can generate, or morph, new faces. This gives the model its name as the 3D Morphable face Model (3DMM). The constant part of the 3DMM consists of four components: the shape and texture bases $\mathbf{S}$ and $\mathbf{T}$, and the mean face shape $\mathbf{s}_0$ and mean face texture $\mathbf{t}_0$. The coefficients $\boldsymbol{\alpha}$ and $\boldsymbol{\beta}$ afford a low-dimensional *coding* of a 3D face. From (2) and (3) we can see that the coding of the mean face is $\boldsymbol{\alpha} = \mathbf{0}$, $\boldsymbol{\beta} = \mathbf{0}$. We assume the coefficients are distributed normally:

$$p(\boldsymbol{\alpha}) \sim \mathcal{N}(0, \boldsymbol{\sigma}_s) \tag{4}$$
$$p(\boldsymbol{\beta}) \sim \mathcal{N}(0, \boldsymbol{\sigma}_t) \tag{5}$$

The human face is a deformable object. The shape changes dynamically with expression or when the subject is talking. In principle, the shape model bases could capture these shape variations. However, to construct such a model would require a huge training set of 3D face images containing all the shape variations

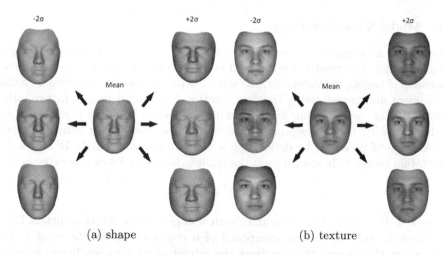

| | (a) shape | | (b) texture |

Fig. 1. The mean and varied faces in shape and texture of the high-resolution Surrey Face Model. The figures show how the shape and texture of the faces vary from the mean as the first three PCA coefficients vary between -2 and +2 standard deviations.

Fig. 2. The figure illustrates how expression can be removed from or added to a face. *(left)*: Input frame. *(middle)*: Expression-neutralised 3D model. *(right)*: Face with artificially added smile expression.

of interest. A more efficient solution is to accommodate expression variations as a separate mode of variation of a subset of vertices from their locations in the neutral expression face. This extension models the face shape as

$$\mathbf{s} = \mathbf{s}_0 + \mathbf{S}\boldsymbol{\alpha} + \mathbf{E}\boldsymbol{\psi} \qquad (6)$$

where $\mathbf{E}$ is a matrix of n_e expression basis vectors (blend shapes) and $\boldsymbol{\psi} = (\psi_1, ..., \psi_{n_e})^T$ is a vector of the associated expression coefficients. In Fig. 2, we fit the 3D model to a person exhibiting expressions. We can then render the face with just the identity and without expressions by setting the blendshape coefficients to zero, or synthesise novel expressions by modifying the blendshape coefficients accordingly.

2.1   Model View Rendering

Given a 3D face image (1), we can render 2D views by projecting it using a camera model. The rendered image will be a function of the camera view point. Instead of changing the viewpoint, the same 2D image could be obtained by fixing the camera and transforming the coordinates of the input image. In the latter formulation of the rendering problem, which we adopt here, the transformation of the input 3D face corresponds to changing the pose of the subject's head. The change of pose will be defined by a (3×3) rotation matrix $\mathbf{R}$ and a $3D$ translation vector τ. In matrix form the transformed shape $\tilde{\mathbf{s}}$ can be expressed as

$$\tilde{\mathbf{s}} = \mathbf{U}^T \mathbf{s} + \tilde{\tau} \tag{7}$$

where $\mathbf{U}$ is the block diagonal matrix with n copies of the rotation matrix $\mathbf{R}$ on its diagonal, and $\tilde{\tau}$ is a vector composed of n copies of the displacement τ. For each vertex the camera then projects the triplet of its 3D coordinates into $2D$ pixel location in the camera image plane as

$$\mathbf{s}' = \mathbf{Q}\tilde{\mathbf{s}} + \mathbf{O} \tag{8}$$

where $\mathbf{Q}$ is a block diagonal matrix of size $(2n \times 3n)$ with the projection matrices P_i, $i = 1, ...n$

$$P_i = \begin{bmatrix} \frac{f}{z_i} & 0 & 0 \\ 0 & -\frac{f}{z_i} & 0 \end{bmatrix} \tag{9}$$

defined in terms of the camera focal length f on its diagonal, and the $2n$-dimensional vector $\mathbf{O}$ is a stack of n copies of the $2D$ coordinates of the optical axis in the image plane. The resulting vector $\mathbf{s}'$ contains the pairs of 2D coordinates (x_i', y_i') of the projected mesh of 3D vertices $(\tilde{x}_i, \tilde{y}_i, \tilde{z}_i)$. Note that each P_i is a function of the depth coordinate $\tilde{z}_i$. For faces at a distance exceeding $10\times$ the radius of subject's head, the z coordinate is relatively constant; in this case we can use an affine projection (in which $P_i = P_j, \forall i, j$) instead, without incurring any significant approximation errors.

The pixel value at locations $\mathbf{s}'$ will depend on the albedo $\mathbf{t}$ and the scene illumination. Different illumination models can be adopted for lighting the face, but we shall adopt the Phong model. Accordingly, the rendered $2D$ image, represented by a $2n$-dimensional vector $\mathbf{a}^M$, is generated by the interplay of face albedo $\mathbf{t}$ and incident light, assumed to be the sum of contributions from ambient, diffuse and specular lights:

$$\mathbf{a}^M = \underbrace{\mathbf{l}_a * \mathbf{t}}_{\text{ambient}} + \underbrace{(\mathbf{l}_d * \mathbf{t}) * (\mathbf{N}\mathbf{d})}_{\text{diffuse}} + \underbrace{\mathbf{l}_d * \mathbf{e}}_{\text{specular}} \tag{10}$$

where the ambient light $\mathbf{l}_a$ is a $3n$-dimensional vector, composed of n copies of triplet $(l_a^r, l_a^g, l_a^b)^T$ of ambient light intensities in the red, green and blue spectrum channels

$$\mathbf{l}_a = (l_a^r, l_a^g, l_a^b, ...l_a^r, l_a^g, l_a^b)^T \in \mathbb{R}^{3n} \tag{11}$$

Similarly, $\mathbf{l}_d$ is a $3n$ dimensional vector, composed of n copies of triplet $(l_d^r, l_d^g, l_d^b)^T$ of directed light strengths in RGB channels

$$\mathbf{l}_d = (l_d^r, l_d^g, l_d^b, ..., l_d^r, l_d^g, l_d^b)^T \in \mathbb{R}^{3n} \tag{12}$$

and $*$ denotes the element-wise multiplication operation. The matrix $\mathbf{N} = (\mathbf{N}^T, \mathbf{N}^T, \mathbf{N}^T)^T$, where $\mathbf{N} \in \mathbb{R}^{n \times 3}$ is a stack of the surface normals $\mathbf{N}_i \in \mathbb{R}^3$ at vertices $i = 1, ..., n$; $\mathbf{d} \in \mathbb{R}^3$ is the light direction; vector $\mathbf{e} \in \mathbb{R}^{3n}$ is a stack of the specular reflectance e_i of vertex $i = 1, ..., n$ (which could be different for the three channels), i.e.,

$$e_i = k_s \langle \mathbf{v}_i, \mathbf{r}_i \rangle^\gamma \tag{13}$$

where $\mathbf{v}_i$ is the viewing direction of the ith vertex. Since the camera is located at the origin, the value of $\mathbf{v}_i$ is equal to the position $(\tilde{x}_i, \tilde{y}_i, \tilde{z}_i)^T$ of this vertex. $\mathbf{r}_i$ denotes the reflection direction of the ith vertex: $\mathbf{r}_i = 2\langle \mathbf{N}_i, \mathbf{d}\rangle \mathbf{N}_i - \mathbf{d}$. k_s and γ are two constants of the specular reflectance and shininess respectively [47]. Note that k_s and γ are determined by the facial skin reflectance property, which is similar for different people. They are assumed constant over the whole facial region. For the sake of simplicity, here we also assume that k_s and γ are the same for the three colour channels. Thus each component e_i is repeated three times in constructing vector $\mathbf{e}$. In this work, k_s and γ are set to values 0.175 and 30 respectively following [47].

To summarise the face image rendering options, let ρ denote the set of parameters

$$\rho = \{\mathbf{R}, \tau, f\} \tag{14}$$

1. Given a 3D face image we can render its projection in:
   (a) different poses using parameter set ρ,
   (b) different poses under different lighting using parameters $\rho, \mathbf{l}_a, \mathbf{l}_d, \mathbf{d}, k_s, \gamma$.
2. We can generate a 3D image using the 3D face model using parameters $\boldsymbol{\alpha}, \boldsymbol{\beta}, \boldsymbol{\psi}$ and render its 2D projection in different poses and under different illumination by choosing parameters $\rho, \mathbf{l}_a, \mathbf{l}_d, \mathbf{d}, k_s, \gamma$.
3. We can fit a 3D face shape model $\boldsymbol{\alpha}, \boldsymbol{\psi}$ to a 2D input face image and then relight it and remap it to other poses.
4. We can fit a full 3D face model to a 2D input face image to obtain $\boldsymbol{\alpha}, \boldsymbol{\beta}, \boldsymbol{\psi}$, and then render other 2D poses of the reconstructed 3D face under new illumination using parameters $\rho, \mathbf{l}_a, \mathbf{l}_d, \mathbf{d}, k_s, \gamma$.

In all cases it is important to check all vertices for visibility so that parts of the self-occluded face do not contribute to the rendered pixel values.

In the following sections we will illustrate various applications of the 3D face model and its generative capacity, as well as its rendering and face image manipulation capability.

3   Using Generative 3DMM for Data Augmentation

One practical application of 3D models is data augmentation for 2D methods in computer vision and image understanding, in particular for learning-based

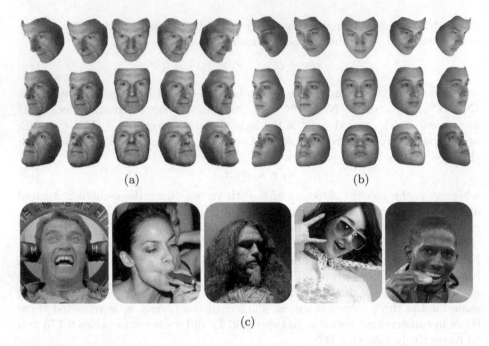

(a)   (b)

(c)

Fig. 3. A comparison of rendered faces from: (a) a real 3D face scan from our dataset; (b) a 3D face synthesised by manipulating the control parameters of our 3D morphable face model; and (c) real 2D face images.

methods that require a large amount of training data for successful model training [17, 42, 43, 46]. For example, Rätsch et al. [46] used 3DMM-generated data to improve the accuracy of a 2D pose predictor with support vector regression. Pishchulin et al. [43] proposed the synthesis of realistic human body images with random backgrounds using a 3D shape model, and demonstrated superior performance in the tasks of people detection and human pose estimation. Pepik et al. [42] generated a set of virtual images with a 3D CAD model for fine-grained object detection and pose estimation using deformable part models constrained by 3D geometric information. We proposed the Cascaded Collaborative Regression (CCR) algorithm that used 3DMM to generate a massive dataset of annotated training face images [17]. In this section, we provide a brief overview of the CCR algorithm for 2D Facial Landmark Detection (FLD), which is trained on a mixture of synthetic and real faces.

3.1   Facial Landmark Detection of 2D Faces

Given a 2D face image, the task of FLD is to obtain the coordinates of a set of pre-defined key points, also known as face shape or landmarks. A 2D face shape is a vector that consists of the coordinates of a set of pre-defined landmarks $\mathbf{c} = [x_1, y_1, \cdots, x_L, y_L]^T$, where L is the number of landmarks and

$[x_l, y_l]^T$ are the coordinates of the lth landmark. The landmarks of a face are important for many practical applications, such as face alignment, face tracking, face recognition and 3D face reconstruction from 2D images. Popular facial landmark detection algorithms include Active Shape Model (ASM) [13], Active Appearance Model (AAM) [12,19], Constrained Local Model (CLM) [14] and cascaded-regression-based methods [15,18]. In recent years, cascaded-regression-based methods have become very popular because they can provide accurate landmarks for unconstrained faces in the wild [9,17,18,62].

With the initial shape estimation $\mathbf{c}$ of a 2D face image $\mathbf{I}$, a 2D FLD algorithm finds a mapping function,

$$\mathbf{\Phi} : \mathbf{f} \mapsto \delta\mathbf{c}, \tag{15}$$
$$s.t. \ \|\mathbf{c} + \delta\mathbf{c} - \mathbf{c}^*\|_2^2 = 0,$$

where $\delta\mathbf{c}$ is the shape update to the initial shape estimate, $\mathbf{c}^*$ is the ground truth shape of the input image, $\mathbf{f} = f(\mathbf{I}, \mathbf{c}) \in \mathbb{R}^{N_f}$ is the extracted shape-related face texture features from the input image $\mathbf{I}$ with the current shape estimate $\mathbf{c}$, $f(\mathbf{I}, \mathbf{c})$ is a feature extraction function and N_f is the dimentionality of the extracted feature vector. In general, we extract local features around each landmark, for example HOG features, and then concatenate the extracted local features around all landmarks to form a single vector. To obtain such a projection, we can use any regression method such as linear regression, random forests and even deep neural networks. However, for faces in the wild, it is very difficult to obtain accurate landmarks if we only use a single regressor because of various changes of the appearance of a human face in pose, expression, illumination and occlusion. To deal with this challenge, cascaded regression has recently gained popularity.

In cascaded regression, the mapping function $\mathbf{\Phi}$ is a strong regressor formed by a sequence of weak regressors in cascade:

$$\mathbf{\Phi} = \phi_1 \circ \cdots \circ \phi_M, \tag{16}$$

where ϕ_m is the mth weak regressor. In CCR [17], linear regression is used for each weak regressor hence the mth weak regressor is $\phi_m = \{\mathbf{A}_m, \mathbf{b}_m\}$, where $\mathbf{A}_m \in \mathbb{R}^{2L \times N_f}$ is the projection matrix, and $\mathbf{b}_m \in \mathbb{R}^{2L}$ is the offset.

The training of a cascaded regressor $\mathbf{\Phi}$, in essence, is learning-based and data-driven. A large number of annotated faces are required for successful model training. However, the collection of training data is often time-consuming and involves a considerable amount of tedious manual work. To deal with this issue, our CCR uses 3D faces to render 2D faces with arbitrary pose variations for a cascaded-regression-based FLD training [17].

In practice, either a real 3D face scan or a generated 3D face from a 3DMM can be used to render 2D face images. As discussed in the previous section, a 3D morphable face model can generate arbitrary 3D faces by adjusting its shape and texture model parameters. Figure 3 demonstrates a set of rendered 2D faces, from either real 3D face scans (Fig. 3a) or generated 3D faces using 3DMM (Fig. 3b). However, as indicated in [17], a facial landmark detector trained merely from rendered faces often fails to adapt to real faces. The main reason is that the synthesised faces rendered from 3D face scans and real faces belong to different domains. Furthermore, the synthesised faces lack realistic variations in appearance, such as lighting, make-up, skin colour, occlusion and sophisticated background, as shown in Fig. 3c.

To tackle this problem, the CCR method in [17] efficiently exploits synthesised and real faces in a compound training scheme with a dynamic mixture weighting schedule. An important innovation of CCR is to progressively adapt the relative contributions of synthesised and natural images. At the beginning of CCR training, the synthetic data dominates the training; the impact of the synthetic data is then progressively reduced as the training proceeds. Thus CCR is first trained on a mixed dataset with a large number of synthesised images to improve the generalisation capacity followed by adaptation using a small number of real faces.

3.2   Cascaded Collaborative Regression with a Mixture of Real and Synthetic Faces

Given a mixed training dataset with N_v synthesised images $\{\tilde{\mathbf{I}}^{(1)}, \cdots, \tilde{\mathbf{I}}^{(N_v)}\}$, N_r real images $\{\mathbf{I}^{(1)}, \cdots, \mathbf{I}^{(N_r)}\}$, and the corresponding ground truth shapes $\{\tilde{\mathbf{c}}^{*(1)}, \cdots, \tilde{\mathbf{c}}^{*(N_v)}\}, \{\mathbf{c}^{*(1)}, \cdots, \mathbf{c}^{*(N_r)}\}$, CCR first generates the initial shape estimates $\{\tilde{\mathbf{c}}^{(1)}, \cdots, \tilde{\mathbf{c}}^{(N_v)}\}$ and $\{\mathbf{c}^{(1)}, \cdots, \mathbf{c}^{(N_r)}\}$ for model training, by putting a reference shape in the detected face bounding box [17, 62, 64].

Then CCR recursively learns the weak regressors from $m = 1$ to M. In the training phase, the initial shape estimates $\mathbf{c}$ are used to obtain the first weak regressor $\phi_1 = \{\mathbf{A}_1, \mathbf{b}_1\}$, and then it applies this trained weak regressor to update all initial shapes to train the next weak regressor, until all the weak regressors in $\mathbf{\Phi} = \{\phi_1, \cdots, \phi_M\}$ are obtained. To be more specific, the cost function of learning the mth weak regressor $\phi_m = \{\mathbf{A}_m, \mathbf{b}_m\}$ by CCR is:

$$\mathbf{J}(\mathbf{A}_m, \mathbf{b}_m) = \frac{\omega(m)\mathbf{J}_v + (1 - \omega(m))\mathbf{J}_r}{2N} + \lambda\|\mathbf{A}_m\|_F^2, \tag{17}$$
$$0 \leq \omega(m) \leq 1,$$

where $\omega(m)$ is a dynamic mixing parameter, $N = N_v + N_r$ is the total number of the training samples, λ is the weight of the regularisation term and $\|\cdot\|_F$ is the Frobenius norm. $\mathbf{J}_v$ is the cost function calculated from the synthesised training samples:

$$\mathbf{J}_v = \sum_{n=1}^{N_v} \|\mathbf{A}_m\tilde{\mathbf{f}}^{(n)} + \mathbf{b}_m - \delta\tilde{\mathbf{c}}^{(n)}\|_2^2, \tag{18}$$

and $\mathbf{J}_r$ is the cost function calculated from the real training samples:

$$\mathbf{J}_r = \sum_{n=1}^{N_r} \|\mathbf{A}_m\mathbf{f}^{(n)} + \mathbf{b}_m - \delta\mathbf{c}^{(n)}\|_2^2, \tag{19}$$

where $\mathbf{f}^{(n)} = f(\mathbf{I}^{(n)}, \mathbf{c}^{(n)}) \in \mathbb{R}^{N_f}$ is the extracted shape-indexed local feature for the nth training example, $\mathbf{A}_m \in \mathbb{R}^{2L \times N_f}$ is the projection matrix of the mth weak regressor, $\mathbf{b}_m \in \mathbb{R}^{2L}$ is the offset of the mth weak regressor, $\delta\mathbf{c}^{(n)} = \mathbf{c}^{*(n)} - \mathbf{c}^{(n)}$ is the shape difference between the ground truth shape $\mathbf{c}^*$ and the current shape estimate $\mathbf{c}^{(n)}$.

The dynamic weighting parameter $\omega(m)$ is set to be a decreasing function:

$$\omega(m) = \frac{1}{1 + e^{K(m-1)}}, \tag{20}$$

where K is a shrinking rate. By design, the mixed training data dominates the training of the first few weak regressors in the cascaded strong regressor, which enables the landmark detector to accommodate pose variations. The smaller set of real faces dominates the training of the last few weak regressors, which enhances the accuracy of the final shape estimates.

For the first weak regressor training, the current shape estimate is the initial shape estimate. For the remaining weak regressors, i.e. $m > 1$, the current shape estimate $\mathbf{c}^{(n)}$ is obtained by applying the previous $m - 1$ weak regressors to the initial shape estimate $\mathbf{c}^{(n)}$,

$$\mathbf{c}^{(n)} \leftarrow \mathbf{c}^{(n)} + \mathbf{A}_k \mathbf{f}^{(n)} + \mathbf{b}_k, \tag{21}$$

for $k = 1, \cdots, m - 1$. Note that the extracted shape-related features $\mathbf{f}^{(n)}$ is changed after each shape update. Once the CCR is trained, given an input face image and the initial shape estimate, we recursively apply all the weak regressors to the initial shape estimate and obtain the predicted face shape of the input image. For more details of the CCR algorithm, the reader is referred to [17].

We have evaluated our CCR method both on synthetic face datasets and real face datasets with human faces in the wild, and obtained superior performance in terms of accuracy and speed, compared to state-of-the-art methods [17]. It is particularly notable that the use of the synthesised faces generated by the 3DMM improves the generalisation capability of CCR. Some examples of 2D facial landmarks that it generated for the Caltech Occluded Faces in the Wild (COFW) dataset [7] are shown in Fig. 4; these landmarks are robust to appearance variations in expression, occlusion, pose and illumination.

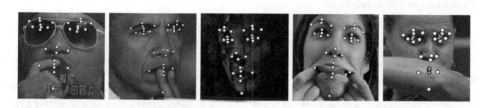

Fig. 4. Some 2D FLD examples from the Caltech Occluded Faces in the Wild (COFW) dataset [7], landmarked by the CCR algorithm.

4   3D-assisted 2D Face Recognition

Unconstrained 2D face recognition is a very challenging problem as the appearance of human face is dramatically affected by many factors, including the subject's pose, expression and illumination. Although the last decade has recorded significant advances in 2D face recognition technology, to a great extent they are limited to faces constrained to near frontal pose and subject to neutral illumination. In principle, it would be possible to build face recognition systems for unconstrained scenarios, but this would require a huge amount of training data which captures all the modes of variation of the face appearance. Another prerequisite would be to extend the notion of face registration, which for frontal faces is quite simple, but for which in the case of arbitrary poses, many additional complexities are introduced.

In this section we explore the possibility of using the 3D face model discussed in Sect. 2 as a tool for 3D-assisted 2D face recognition. The first step is to fit a 3D face model to the input 2D image. A number of options are then opened [1, 3, 36, 39, 44, 65, 68]:

- The estimated pose and illumination can be used to remap a frontal face gallery image into the same pose and illumination conditions of the unknown input image to perform the matching [39, 44, 68].
- The estimated pose and illumination can be used to remap the input image to the frontal pose with canonical illumination. After the remapping a standard 2D face recognition engine can be used for matching based on local features, such as Gabor features [65], Local Binary Pattern [39, 68], Local Gabor Binary Pattern [67], and Local Phase Quantisation [24].
- The estimated shape and skin texture parameters of the reconstructed 3D face model of the input image can be used directly for matching in 3D in a holistic fashion [2, 5, 49, 50].

4.1   3D Model to 2D Face Image Fitting

The key enabling step of these options is the process of fitting a 3D face model to a 2D image. Let us assume that the input image is landmarked. The methods discussed in Sect. 3 can be used for that purpose. Let us lump together all illumination parameters as

$$\mu = (\mathbf{l}_a, \mathbf{l}_d, \mathbf{d}, k_s, \gamma)^T \tag{22}$$

Fitting the 3D face involves looking for pose, shape texture and illumination parameters ρ, α, β, μ so that the model reconstructed image

$$\mathbf{a}^M = (r_1^M, g_1^M, b_1^M, \ldots\ldots, r_n^M, g_n^M, b_n^M)^T \tag{23}$$

is as close as possible to the input image. Recall that the reconstructed image is defined on the 2D mesh of projected vertices, $\mathbf{s}'$. This mesh samples the input

2D image. Stacking the RGB values of the corresponding samples into a vector $\mathbf{a}^I$

$$\mathbf{a}^I = (r_1^I, g_1^I, b_1^I, \ldots\ldots, r_n^I, g_n^I, b_n^I)^T \tag{24}$$

we can then compare the synthesised and input images by measuring the error $||\mathbf{a}^I - \mathbf{a}^M||$. Noting that the samples picked from the input image by the mesh are a function of ρ, α, the objective of the fitting process is to solve the optimisation problem

$$\min_{\alpha,\beta,\rho,\mu} \|\mathbf{a}^I(\rho,\alpha) - \mathbf{a}^M(\rho,\alpha,\beta,\mu)\|^2 + \lambda_1\|\alpha \div \sigma_s\|^2 + \lambda_2\|\beta \div \sigma_t\|^2 \tag{25}$$

where the last two terms induce regularisation of the estimated parameters. The symbol $\div$ denotes element-wise division.

The problem formulated in (25) is very challenging because of its nonlinearity and its ill-posed nature [26,45]. The conventional approach to optimisation is to apply the Levenberg-Marquardt algorithm using Stochastic Newton Optimisation involving the sampling of random subsets of mesh vertices to achieve computational efficiency [4,5]. The Multi-Feature Fitting (MFF) variant [50], which uses many complementary features from the input image, such as edge and specularity highlights, is known to achieve the best fitting performance. The inverse compositional algorithm of [48] enhances efficiency by modifying the cost function so that its Jacobian can be regarded as constant to avoid updates. However, it cannot deal with illumination effects. A number of algorithms attempt to gain speed by linearising some stages of the optimisation problem. However the required assumptions limit the applicability of these solutions. For instance [49] requires the direction of lighting as input. In Zhang et al. algorithm [66], improved in [60], the camera model is optimised by the Levenberg-Marquardt method, and shape parameters are estimated by a closed-form solution using only facial feature landmarks. However, these approaches cannot recover specular reflection and are limited to affine projection. The work in [2] also uses an affine camera to accelerate the process of fitting.

Fig. 5. Albedo 3DMM construction. Left to right: RGB and preprocessed texture map, shape, and registered face.

In the approach exemplified here, we accelerate the fitting process by omitting the illumination estimation. We call this Albedo 3DMM (AB3DMM). This is achieved by building the 3DMM model using photometrically normalised texture images, as proposed in [25]. This is illustrated in Fig. 5. Accordingly, the grey-level texture is defined as

$$t = (i_1, ..., i_n)^T \tag{26}$$

where i_j is the image intensity at the jth vertex. Before fitting the AB3DMM, the input image must first be photometrically normalised. We found that the reconstructions using preprocessing by the single scale retinex method [31] and Large and Small Features Normalisation [61] (example image shown in Fig. 6) gave the best results.

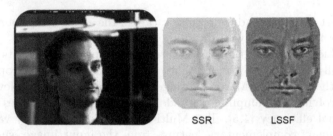

Fig. 6. An example face image reconstructed by different AB3DMMs. From left to right: Original image; Single Scale Retinex [31]; Large and Small Features Normalisation [61]

The impact of eliminating the task of illumination estimation is significant. The update of a^M no longer involves the surface normal and becomes independent of not only μ but also of α and ρ. Hence the optimisation problem simplifies to

$$\min_{\alpha,\beta,\rho} \|a^I(\rho,\alpha) - a^M(\beta)\|^2 + \lambda_1\|\alpha \div \sigma_s\|^2 + \lambda_2\|\beta \div \sigma_t\|^2 \tag{27}$$

resulting in a considerable speedup.

4.2 Experiments

Databases and Protocols. To ensure reproducibility of the experiments and comparability with other methods, we tested our approach on the well-known CMU-PIE [55] and MultiPIE [22] face databases.

A subset of the CMU-PIE database covering both illumination and pose variations is used for evaluation. It is divided into a gallery set containing 68 frontal images of 68 subjects under neutral light, and probe set containing 2,856 images of the same subjects with frontal and side poses under 21 different light directions. The results are summarised by averaging the rank 1 recognition rates under different light directions.

We also experimented with a subset of the MultiPIE database in the first session consisting of 249 subjects with 7 poses, from left 45° and right 45° yaw in steps

Table 1. Mean recognition rates of all 68 subjects of the CMU-PIE databases averaged over 22 illumination conditions per pose using a single frontal-pose gallery image.

	front	side	mean
MFF [50]	98.90	96.10	97.50
Z&S [66]	96.50	94.60	95.50
3DMM [2]	99.50	95.10	97.30
3DMM [49]	97.00	91.00	94.00
LPQ + LSSF	**100.00**	99.26	99.62
LPQ + SSR	**100.00**	**99.39**	**99.69**
LPQ + RAW	98.59	96.14	97.34

of $15°$, and 20 illuminations. The 249 frontal images under neutral illumination are the gallery set and the remaining 34,611 images are the probe set.

Face Recognition Engine. Face matching is performed using a 2D face recognition engine [10] employing a multi resolution local phase quantisation descriptor. By virtue of the model fitting process, the shape, texture and camera parameters α, β, ρ are estimated. We normalise the pose of the input image by transforming it to a frontal view. The pixel values of the occluded part are reconstructed by the estimated β, and those of the visible part are extracted from the illumination-normalised input image.

Experimental Set-up. Before AB3DMM fitting, each test image is first illumination-normalised. The reconstructed image is extracted and scaled to a size of 142×120 (rows $\times$ columns). The reconstructed images of different illumination normalisations are shown in Fig. 6. The LPQ operator is then applied. The normalised image is divided into 7×7 non-overlapping regions and the LPQ codes from each region are summarised in the form of a histogram. The histograms from all the regions are concatenated to form a face descriptor. The matching is accomplished using the chi-square distance between the histograms computed for the probe and each gallery image.

Results on CMU-PIE. The results, reported in Table 1, show that the illumination and pose normalisation using AB3DMM improve performance. The matching approach using the 2D face recognition engine on the normalised images are better than those obtained using the 3D model parameters [2,49]. LPQ-based face recognition is very good even on the raw images, but with illumination normalisation the recognition rate reaches 99.69 % rank-1 recognition rate, which is around 2 % better than the best state-of-the art method [50].

Results on MultiPIE. In this experiment, we measure the performance of our LPQ systems on the larger, MultiPIE data set. The results, summarised in Fig. 7, report the average recognition rates over all illumination conditions on 6 different poses. Note that the performance of all systems, including the state-of-

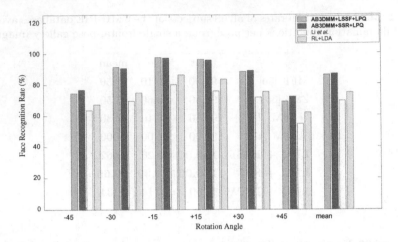

Fig. 7. Results for pose variations averaging over all the illuminations, compared with Li et al. [35] and RL+LDA [70]. (Color figure online)

the-art methods, degrades under illumination changes. Our system achieves the highest recognition rate, regardless of which of the two preprocessing stages are used. Although the best of the state-of-the-art systems [70], RL+LDA, achieves 98.4 % under only pose changes, it drops by around 23 % to 74.7 % under both pose and illumination changes. In contrast, our best system, SSR+LPQ drops by 13 % to 86.76 %. This demonstrates that, with a limited amount of data available for training, deep learning approaches do not necessarily offer competitive solutions. The use of prior knowledge conveyed by the 3D model in conjunction with conventional face recognition engine provides a better solution to the pose- and illumination-invariant face recognition problem.

5   Real-Time Fitting on Videos

The demand has also increased in recent years to track and reconstruct 3D objects from monocular video sequences and live streams in real time. Reconstructing a 3D face from 2D is still an inherently challenging problem, even when multiple frames are available. When the object to be reconstructed is known, as in our case a face, a 3D Morphable Face Model can be of great help to aid the reconstruction in the form of a face prior. However, most of the current 3DMM fitting methods require of the order of minutes to fit to an image, and are thus not suitable for application on videos. Here we present an approach that makes using a 3DMM on video feasible by introducing several simplifications to the traditional analysis-by-synthesis fitting method.

In this particular application of reconstructing a 3D face from a monocular video, we are mainly interested in recovering the original texture, and thus do not fit a colour and light model, which is a time-consuming task since it involves analysis-by-synthesis. Instead, we fit the shape and a camera model, both with

Fig. 8. View visibility information (including regions of self-occlusions) from the 3D face model. *(left)*: Input frame. *(right)*: red = 0° (facing the camera), blue = 90° or facing away. JET colourmap.

Fig. 9. *From left to right*: Frame from the original video; reconstructed face texture using our real-time method; ground-truth face texture; and rendering with novel pose and neutral expression.

closed-form solutions, and then obtain a complete reconstruction by extracting and fusing the face texture from the original frames.

Pose and Shape Fitting. First, we simplify the camera model to an affine projection, and solve it with the closed-form solution derived by Hartley and Zisserman [23]. In applications where the video is not a face close-up (e.g. from a mobile camera), the approximation of the affine camera model works well. Second, given the estimated camera, the 3D shape model is fitted to a sparse set of 2D landmarks to produce a 3D shape estimate. We find the most likely vector of PCA shape coefficients α by minimising a cost function based on the 2D landmarks and the corresponding 3D model vertices. This can be achieved via a closed-form solution; details to the algorithm can be found in [2,28].

Expression Modelling. Since videos and live streams contain in-the-wild scenarios where people are talking and show expressions, we use a set of 6 linear expression blendshapes to model expressions, as described in Sect. 2. The expression coefficients ψ are fitted using the same closed-form solution as for the shape coefficients fitting, with the identity shape coefficients fixed. These two algorithms are alternated until convergence, which usually takes around 5 to 8 iterations. Using this approach, the model's shape can be fitted in under

50 ms. When including the time for texture remapping, the run time is approximately 100 ms per frame on an Intel Core i7-4700MQ.

Texture Fusion. To obtain a holistic view on the subject from all view angles, we remap the texture to a common reference, fusing the texture from multiple frames. For this we use a weighting that is dependent on the 3D pose of the fitted model so that we can leverage the full power of the 3D model. For each vertex, we can calculate its visibility w.r.t. pose and self-occlusion, and its view angle towards the camera, assuming that vertices facing the camera provide better texture information than those facing away. Figure 8 shows an example frame from a video and the corresponding visibility map, with red vertices facing the camera and blue vertices facing away or being occluded. Using this weighting, we compute a weighted average of each pixel in the texture map, where dense correspondence has already been established between frames through the 3D model fitting.

The tracking is run with 68 landmarks detected by a landmark regressor as presented in Sect. 3, and the whole pipeline evaluated on the 300-videos-in-the-wild (300-VW, [54]) database. Figure 9 shows a frame of one of these videos, the reconstructed face texture using our real-time method, a hand-crafted ground-truth for comparison, and a 3D model rendering with neutral expression.

6   Conclusions and Future Work

Since their conception more than two decades ago, 3D morphable face models have attracted considerable interest because of their ability to model intrinsic properties of 3D faces, such as shape and skin texture, rather than their appearance. The latter is dramatically affected by the sensing device, subject's pose, expression and illumination conditions. In this paper we focused on the use of 3DMM in 2D face analysis and recognition. We overviewed some recent developments in fitting 3D face model to 2D images, and discussed a number of applications of 3DMM to illustrate its versatility. These included facial landmarking of 2D face images exploiting the generative capacity of 3DMM to augment the training set for cascaded regression, pose and illumination invariant face recognition, and 3D face reconstruction from video.

References

1. Abiantun, R., Prabhu, U., Savvides, M.: Sparse feature extraction for pose-tolerant face recognition. IEEE Trans. Pattern Anal. Mach. Intell. **36**(10), 2061–2073 (2014)
2. Aldrian, O., Smith, W.A.P.: Inverse rendering of faces with a 3D morphable model. IEEE Trans. Pattern Anal. Mach. Intell. **35**(5), 1080–1093 (2013)
3. Asthana, A., Marks, T.K., Jones, M.J., Tieu, K.H., Rohith, M.: Fully automatic pose-invariant face recognition via 3D pose normalization. In: IEEE International Conference on Computer Vision, (ICCV), pp. 937–944. IEEE (2011)
4. Blanz, V., Vetter, T.: A morphable model for the synthesis of 3D faces. In: the 26th Annual Conference on Computer Graphics and Interactive Techniques, (SIG-GRAPH), pp. 187–194. ACM Press/Addison-Wesley Publishing Co. (1999)

5. Blanz, V., Vetter, T.: Face recognition based on fitting a 3D morphable model. IEEE Trans. Pattern Anal. Mach. Intell. **25**(9), 1063–1074 (2003)
6. Boom, B.J., Spreeuwers, L.J., Veldhuis, R.N.J.: Subspace-based holistic registration for low-resolution facial images. EURASIP J. Adv. Signal Process. **2010**, 1–14 (2010)
7. Burgos-Artizzu, X., Perona, P., Dollár, P.: Robust face landmark estimation under occlusion. In: IEEE International Conference on Computer Vision, (ICCV), pp. 1513–1520 (2013)
8. Cao, C., Bradley, D., Zhou, K., Beeler, T.: Real-time high-fidelity facial performance capture. ACM Trans. Graph. **34**(4), 46:1–46:9 (2015)
9. Cao, X., Wei, Y., Wen, F., Sun, J.: Face alignment by explicit shape regression. Int. J. Comput. Vis. **107**(2), 177–190 (2014)
10. Chan, C., Tahir, M.A., Kittler, J., Pietikäinen, M.: Multiscale local phase quantization for robust component-based face recognition using kernel fusion of multiple descriptors. IEEE Trans. Pattern Anal. Mach. Intell. **35**(5), 1164–1177 (2013)
11. Chu, B., Romdhani, S., Chen, L.: 3D-aided face recognition robust to expression and pose variations. In: IEEE Conference on Computer Vision and Pattern Recognition, (CVPR), pp. 1907–1914 (2014)
12. Cootes, T.F., Edwards, G.J., Taylor, C.J.: Active appearance models. IEEE Trans. Pattern Anal. Mach. Intell. **23**(6), 681–685 (2001)
13. Cootes, T.F., Taylor, C.J., Cooper, D.H., Graham, J.: Active shape models-their training and application. Comput. Vis. Image Underst. **61**(1), 38–59 (1995)
14. Cristinacce, D., Cootes, T.F.: Feature detection and tracking with constrained local models. In: British Machine Vision Conference, (BMVC), pp. 929–938 (2006)
15. Dollár, P., Welinder, P., Perona, P.: Cascaded pose regression. In: IEEE Conference on Computer Vision and Pattern Recognition, (CVPR), pp. 1078–1085 (2010)
16. Egger, B., Schönborn, S., Forster, A., Vetter, T.: Pose normalization for eye gaze estimation and facial attribute description from still images. In: Jiang, X., Hornegger, J., Koch, R. (eds.) GCPR 2014. LNCS, vol. 8753, pp. 317–327. Springer, Heidelberg (2014)
17. Feng, Z.H., Hu, G., Kittler, J., Christmas, W., Wu, X.J.: Cascaded collaborative regression for robust facial landmark detection trained using a mixture of synthetic and real images with dynamic weighting. IEEE Trans. Image Process. **24**(11), 3425–3440 (2015)
18. Feng, Z.H., Huber, P., Kittler, J., Christmas, W., Wu, X.J.: Random cascaded-regression copse for robust facial landmark detection. IEEE Signal Process. Lett. **22**(1), 76–80 (2015)
19. Feng, Z.H., Kittler, J., Christmas, W., Wu, X.J., Pfeiffer, S.: Automatic face annotation by multilinear AAM with missing values. In: IEEE International Conference on Pattern Recognition, (ICPR), pp. 2586–2589. IEEE (2012)
20. Garrido, P., Valgaert, L., Wu, C., Theobalt, C.: Reconstructing detailed dynamic face geometry from monocular video. ACM Trans. Graph. **32**(6), 158:1–158:10 (2013)
21. Gökberk, B., Akarun, L.: Comparative analysis of decision-level fusion algorithms for 3D face recognition. In: IAPR International Conference on Pattern Recognition, (ICPR), pp. 1018–1021 (2006)
22. Gross, R., Matthews, I., Cohn, J., Kanade, T., Baker, S.: Multi-pie. Image Vis. Comput. **28**(5), 807–813 (2010)
23. Hartley, R.I., Zisserman, A.: Multiple View Geometry in Computer Vision, 2nd edn. Cambridge University Press, Cambridge (2004)

24. Hu, G., Chan, C.H., Kittler, J., Christmas, W.: Resolution-aware 3D morphable model. In: British Machine Vision Conference, (BMVC), pp. 1–10 (2012)
25. Hu, G., Chan, C., Yan, F., Christmas, W.J., Kittler, J.: Robust face recognition by an albedo based 3D morphable model. In: IEEE International Joint Conference on Biometrics, (IJCB), pp. 1–8 (2014)
26. Hu, G., Mortazavian, P., Kittler, J., Christmas, W.J.: A facial symmetry prior for improved illumination fitting of 3D morphable model. In: International Conference on Biometrics, (ICB), pp. 1–6 (2013)
27. Huber, P., Feng, Z., Christmas, W., Kittler, J., Rätsch, M.: Fitting 3D morphable models using local features. In: IEEE International Conference on Image Processing, (ICIP) (2015). http://dx.doi.org/10.1109/ICIP.2015.7350989
28. Huber, P., Hu, G., Tena, R., Mortazavian, P., Koppen, W.P., Christmas, W., Rätsch, M., Kittler, J.: A multiresolution 3D morphable face model and fitting framework. In: International Conference on Computer Vision Theory and Applications (VISAPP) (2016). http://dx.doi.org/10.5220/0005669500790086
29. Ichim, A.E., Bouaziz, S., Pauly, M.: Dynamic 3D avatar creation from hand-held video input. ACM Trans. Graph. **34**(4), 45:1–45:14 (2015)
30. Jeni, L., Cohn, J., Kanade, T.: Dense 3D face alignment from 2D videos in real-time. In: 2015 11th IEEE International Conference and Workshops on Automatic Face and Gesture Recognition, (FG), vol. 1, pp. 1–8 (2015)
31. Jobson, D.J., Rahman, Z.U., Woodell, G.A.: Properties and performance of a center/surround retinex. IEEE Trans. Image Process. **6**(3), 451–462 (1997)
32. Kakadiaris, I.A., Passalis, G., Toderici, G., Murtuza, M.N., Lu, Y., Karampatziakis, N., Theoharis, T.: Three-dimensional face recognition in the presence of facial expressions: an annotated deformable model approach. IEEE Trans. Pattern Anal. Mach. Intell. **29**(4), 640–649 (2007)
33. Koppen, W.P., Chan, C., Christmas, W.J., Kittler, J.: An intrinsic coordinate system for 3D face registration. In: IAPR International Conference on Pattern Recognition, (ICPR), pp. 2740–2743 (2012)
34. Lanitis, A., Taylor, C.J., Cootes, T.F.: Automatic interpretation and coding of face images using flexible models. IEEE Trans. Pattern Anal. Mach. Intell. **19**(7), 743–756 (1997)
35. Li, A., Shan, S., Gao, W.: Coupled bias-variance tradeoff for cross-pose face recognition. IEEE Trans. Image Process. **21**(1), 305–315 (2012)
36. Li, S., Liu, X., Chai, X., Zhang, H., Lao, S., Shan, S.: Morphable displacement field based image matching for face recognition across pose. In: Fitzgibbon, A., Lazebnik, S., Perona, P., Sato, Y., Schmid, C. (eds.) ECCV 2012, Part I. LNCS, vol. 7572, pp. 102–115. Springer, Heidelberg (2012)
37. Little, A., Hancock, P., DeBruine, L., Jones, B.: Adaptation to antifaces and the perception of correct famous identity in an average face. Frontiers Psychol. **3**, 1–9 (2012)
38. Mortazavian, P., Kittler, J., Christmas, W.: 3D morphable model fitting for low-resolution facial images. In: 5th IAPR International Conference on Biometrics, (ICB), pp. 132–138. IEEE (2012)
39. Niinuma, K., Han, H., Jain, A.: Automatic multi-view face recognition via 3D model based pose regularization. In: BTAS, pp. 1–8 (2013)
40. Pan, G., Han, S., Wu, Z., Wang, Y.: 3D face recognition using mapped depth images. In: IEEE Conference on Computer Vision and Pattern Recognition Workshops, (CVPRW), p. 175 (2005)

41. Paysan, P., Knothe, R., Amberg, B., Romdhani, S., Vetter, T.: A 3D face model for pose and illumination invariant face recognition. In: IEEE International Conference on Advanced Video and Signal based Surveillance (AVSS) (2009)
42. Pepik, B., Stark, M., Gehler, P., Schiele, B.: Teaching 3D geometry to deformable part models. In: IEEE Conference on Computer Vision and Pattern Recognition, (CVPR), pp. 3362–3369 (2012)
43. Pishchulin, L., Jain, A., Andriluka, M., Thormahlen, T., Schiele, B.: Articulated people detection and pose estimation: Reshaping the future. In: IEEE Conference on Computer Vision and Pattern Recognition, (CVPR), pp. 3178–3185 (2012)
44. Prabhu, U., Heo, J., Savvides, M.: Unconstrained pose-invariant face recognition using 3D generic elastic models. IEEE Trans. Pattern Anal. Mach. Intell. **33**(10), 1952–1961 (2011)
45. Ramamoorthi, R., Hanrahan, P.: A signal-processing framework for reflection. ACM Trans. Graph. **23**(4), 1004–1042 (2004)
46. Rätsch, M., Huber, P., Quick, P., Frank, T., Vetter, T.: Wavelet reduced support vector regression for efficient and robust head pose estimation. In: IEEE Ninth Conference on Computer and Robot Vision (CRV), pp. 260–267 (2012). http://dx.doi.org/10.1109/CRV.2012.41
47. Rodriguez, J.T.: 3D Face Modelling for 2D+3D Face Recognition. Ph.D. thesis, Surrey University, Guildford, UK (2007)
48. Romdhani, S., Vetter, T.: Efficient, robust and accurate fitting of a 3D morphable model. In: IEEE International Conference on Computer Vision, (ICCV), pp. 59–66. IEEE (2003)
49. Romdhani, S., Blanz, V., Vetter, T.: Face identification by fitting a 3D morphable model using linear shape and texture error functions. In: Heyden, A., Sparr, G., Nielsen, M., Johansen, P. (eds.) ECCV 2002, Part IV. LNCS, vol. 2353, pp. 3–19. Springer, Heidelberg (2002)
50. Romdhani, S., Vetter, T.: Estimating 3D shape and texture using pixel intensity, edges, specular highlights, texture constraints and a prior. In: IEEE Conference on Computer Vision and Pattern Recognition, (CVPR), vol. 2, pp. 986–993. IEEE (2005)
51. Salah, A.A., Akarun, L.: 3D facial feature localization for registration. In: Gunsel, B., Jain, A.K., Tekalp, A.M., Sankur, B. (eds.) MRCS 2006. LNCS, vol. 4105, pp. 338–345. Springer, Heidelberg (2006)
52. Sánchez-Escobedo, D., Castelán, M., Smith, W.A.P.: Statistical 3D face shape estimation from occluding contours. Comput. Vis. Image Underst. **142**, 111–124 (2016)
53. Schönborn, S., Forster, A., Egger, B., Vetter, T.: A Monte Carlo strategy to integrate detection and model-based face analysis. In: Weickert, J., Hein, M., Schiele, B. (eds.) GCPR 2013. LNCS, vol. 8142, pp. 101–110. Springer, Heidelberg (2013)
54. Shen, J., Zafeiriou, S., Chrysos, G.G., Kossaifi, J., Tzimiropoulos, G., Pantic, M.: The first facial landmark tracking in-the-wild challenge: benchmark and results. In: IEEE International Conference on Computer Vision Workshop, (ICCVW), pp. 1003–1011 (2015)
55. Sim, T., Baker, S., Bsat, M.: The CMU pose, illumination, and expression database. IEEE Trans. Pattern Anal. Mach. Intell. **25**, 1615–1618 (2003)
56. Tena, J.R., Smith, R.S., Hamouz, M., Kittler, J., Hilton, A., Illingworth, J.: 2D face pose normalisation using a 3D morphable model. In: IEEE Conference on Advanced Video and Signal Based Surveillance (AVSS), pp. 51–56, September 2007

57. Walker, M., Jiang, F., Vetter, T., Sczesny, S.: Universals and cultural differences in forming personality trait judgments from faces. Soc. Psychol. Pers. Sci. **2**, 609–617 (2011)
58. Walker, M., Vetter, T.: Portraits made to measure: manipulating social judgments about individuals with a statistical face model. J. Vis. **9**, 1–13 (2009)
59. Walker, M., Vetter, T.: Changing the personality of a face: perceived big two and big five personality factors modeled in real photographs. J. Pers. Soc. Psychol. **110**, 609–624 (2015). http://dx.doi.org/10.1037/pspp0000064
60. Wang, Y., Liu, Z., Hua, G., Wen, Z., Zhang, Z., Samaras, D.: Face re-lighting from a single image under harsh lighting conditions. In: IEEE Conference on Computer Vision and Pattern Recognition, (CVPR), pp. 1–8. IEEE (2007)
61. Xie, X., Zheng, W.S., Lai, J., Yuen, P.C., Suen, C.Y.: Normalization of face illumination based on large-and small-scale features. IEEE Trans. Image Process. **20**(7), 1807–1821 (2011)
62. Xiong, X., De la Torre, F.: Supervised descent method and its applications to face alignment. In: IEEE Conference on Computer Vision and Pattern Recognition, (CVPR), pp. 532–539 (2013)
63. Xu, C., Wang, Y., Tan, T., Quan, L.: Automatic 3D face recognition combining global geometric features with local shape variation information. In: IAPR International Conference on Pattern Recognition, (ICPR), pp. 308–313 (2004)
64. Yan, J., Lei, Z., Yi, D., Li, S.Z.: Learn to combine multiple hypotheses for accurate face alignment. In: IEEE International Conference on Computer Vision Workshops, (ICCVW), pp. 392–396, December 2013
65. Yi, D., Lei, Z., Li, S.Z.: Towards pose robust face recognition. In: IEEE Conference on Computer Vision and Pattern Recognition, (CVPR), pp. 3539–3545 (2013)
66. Zhang, L., Samaras, D.: Face recognition from a single training image under arbitrary unknown lighting using spherical harmonics. IEEE Trans. Pattern Anal. Mach. Intell. **28**(3), 351–363 (2006)
67. Zhang, W., Shan, S., Gao, W., Chen, X., Zhang, H.: Local gabor binary pattern histogram sequence (lgbphs): a novel non-statistical model for face representation and recognition. In: IEEE Conference on Computer Vision and Pattern Recognition, (CVPR). vol. 1, pp. 786–791 (2005)
68. Zhang, X., Gao, Y., Leung, M.K.H.: Recognizing rotated faces from frontal and side views: An approach toward effective use of mugshot databases. IEEE Trans. Inf. Forensics Secur. **3**(4), 684–697 (2008)
69. Zhu, X., Yan, J., Yi, D., Lei, Z., Li, S.Z.: Discriminative 3D morphable model fitting. In: International Conference on Automatic Face and Gesture Recognition (FG) (2015)
70. Zhu, Z., Luo, P., Wang, X., Tang, X.: Deep learning identity preserving face space. In: International Conference on Computer Vision, (ICCV), vol. 1, p. 2 (2013)

CUDA Achievements
and GPU Challenges Ahead

Manuel Ujaldón[✉]

Computer Architecture Department, University of Málaga, Málaga, Spain
ujaldon@uma.es

Abstract. The computational power and memory bandwidth of graphics processing units (GPUs) have turned them into attractive platforms for general-purpose applications at significant speed gains versus their CPU counterparts [1]. In addition, an increasing number of today's state-of-the-art supercomputers [2] include commodity GPUs to bring us unprecedented levels of high performance and low cost. In this paper, we describe CUDA as the software and hardware paradigm behind those achievements. We summarize its evolution over the past decade, explain its major features and provide insights about future trends for this emerging trend to continue as flagship within high performance computing.

Keywords: GPGPU · CUDA · High performance computing

1 Introduction

High-performance computing is undergoing a period of rapid change. Once multi-core processors were established as the most popular CPU architecture, there was a steady transition to many-core systems. Disruptive technologies such as heterogeneous multicores and many-core GPUs offered excellent performance/cost ratios for scientific applications, and an increasing number of developers learnt to program these processors to take full advantage of that emerging power. Since then, GPUs have moved closer to CPUs in terms of functionality and programmability, and CPUs have also acquired features that are GPU alike.

Last decade ended with the hardware industry moving towards a stronger CPU-GPU coupling. Two good exponents representing this trend were the Fusion project led by AMD to integrate a CPU and GPU on a single chip, and the Larrabee project led by Intel to develop a many-core hybrid platform using x86 CPUs. The Intel movement continued with Knights Ferry (2010), Knights Corner (2011) and Knights Landing (2013) to establish the MIC (Many Integrated Core) Architecture [3] and finally release the Xeon Phi family of accelerators [4]. In 2016, the last generation of Xeon Phi was released to include memory controllers for 3D DRAM, allowing programmers to use the x86 instruction set architecture and choose where they allocate DRAM memory, either using typical DDR modules or novel 3D cubes [5].

© Springer International Publishing Switzerland 2016
F.J. Perales and J. Kittler (Eds.): AMDO 2016, LNCS 9756, pp. 207–217, 2016.
DOI: 10.1007/978-3-319-41778-3_20

In parallel with the CPU evolution, the GPU started its own way towards high performance computing fifteen years ago. Graphics programming experienced a revolution with the advent of shaders, methods to program vertex and pixel processors to leverage creativity in visual effects. First, HLSL (High Level Shading Language, 2001) led by Microsoft for its Direct3D pipeline and then GLSL (OpenGL Shading Language, 2002), the OpenGL counterpart, became popular at that time, soon followed by Cg (C for Graphics, 2003). Cg was developed by Nvidia in collaboration with Microsoft, and it is based on the C programming language incorporating vector data types to enable parallel processing on GPUs. The Cg compiler outputs DirectX or OpenGL shader programs and may be seen as a superset of those early movements. In 2005, Nvidia unified vertex and pixel shaders leading to a more versatile core design called streaming processor. That provided the atom of the many-core architecture, and in November, 2006, CUDA (Compute Unified Device Architecture) [7] was announced.

CUDA is a programming interface and set of supported hardware to enable general purpose computation on Nvidia GPUs. The CUDA driver transforms a typical graphics pipeline into a many-core architecture. With a set of directives on top of a CPU programming language like C or Fortran, CUDA enables heterogeneous computing and parallel programming for the GPU to accelerate as kernels those procedures that are computationally expensive on CPUs.

The rest of this paper focuses on CUDA C and Nvidia GPUs. Nevertheless, a CUDA source code can also be compiled for other target platforms like AMD GPUs or x86_64 CPUs using cross-compilers and compilation environments like the PGI CUDA compiler, Ocelot and MCUDA. And CUDA has also third party wrappers available for Python, Perl, Java, Fortran, Ruby, Lua, Haskell, MatLab and IDL, among many others.

1.1   GPU Advantages

GPUs gather a number of attractive features as high performance platforms. At user level, we may cite the following two:

- **Popularity and low cost.** GPUs are manufactured as commodity processors, which means wide availability at an affordable budget. This has confirmed GPUs as popular platforms among universities and students to run computationally expensive codes even on their own personal computers [1].
- **Easier than ever to be programmed.** Either using CUDA or OpenCL, the GPU is no longer that challenging architecture where programming was seen as a daunting task. This situation improves with an increasing number of supporting tools like libraries and code availability, debuggers and profiles for faster and more efficient development, cross-compilers and back-ends for enhancing portability, ...

At hardware level, we highlight two other important features:

- **Raw computational power.** Pascal, the latest generation of Nvidia's GPUs, exceeds 10 TFLOPS of peak performance in single-precision, whereas counterpart CPUs arguably reach 1 TFLOPS. That is an order of magnitude ahead (the CPU can claim that the peak processing power is harder to reach on the GPU to relax this difference in practice).

- **Memory bandwidth.** GPUs using GDDR5 video memory delivers 336 GB/s. (see Table 4 using Titan X as example), whereas a typical CPU operating on a 4 channel motherboard hardly reaches 64 GB/s. (see also Table 4 using an Intel Broadwell CPU). That is a 5x factor (in this case, the CPU die counts on larger caches to shorten the theoretical gap).

1.2 Code Programming

Multicore systems can be programmed using task-level parallelism, either relying on the scheduler of the operating system or programming explicitly via *POSIX threads*. On many-cores, a different programming method based on data parallelism has to be adpoted for better scalability. The SIMD paradigm (Single Instruction Multiple Data) re-emerges in this context as a viable solution with a simple idea: We run the same program in all cores, but each thread instantiates on a different data subset for each core to work effectively in parallel. The key for success on massive parallelism is **data partitioning**. Straightforward decompositions are usually derived from 1D, 2D and 3D matrices as input data sets, overall on regular access patterns, but the goal turns more difficult in the presence of irregular accesses or dynamic structures and/or pointers.

2 The CUDA Evolution

Almost reaching its tenth anniversary, the evolution of CUDA has been impressive. Table 1 enumerates major achievements according to Nvidia and the NSF.

Tables 2 and 3 summarize all the essential parameters for each GPU generation since CUDA was born. We show the information decomposed into five logical blocks: GPU generation characterization, computational resources, cache, DRAM memory and finally programming constraints.

The first generation was named Tesla, and had two different architectures, the original G80 and the subsequent GT200. The second generation, Fermi, introduced caches and double precision for floating-point arithmetic. The third generation, Kepler, incorporated additional support for irregular computing, like Hyper-Q and dynamic parallelism. The fourth generation, Maxwell, reorganized cores to optimize energy and introduced unified memory. The fifth generation, Pascal, consolidates unified memory and introduces 3D DRAM.

3 CUDA C

CUDA C extends ANSI C with several keywords and constructs which derive into a set of C language library functions as a specific compiler generates the executable code for the GPU in conjunction with the counterpart version running on the CPU acting as a host.

Table 1. The impressive evolution of CUDA over the last eight years.

Year	2008	2016
Number of GPUs accepting CUDA	> 100.000.000	> 600.000.000
CUDA downloads	> 150.000	> 3.000.000
CUDA-enabled supercomputers within Top500 list	1	104
Aggregate performance for those supercomputers	77 TFLOPS	54 PFLOPS
University courses teaching CUDA	60	> 800
Scientific papers published using CUDA	4.000	> 60.000

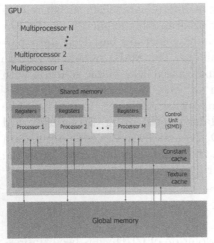

(a) CUDA hardware resources.

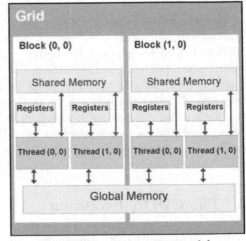

(b) CUDA programming model.

Fig. 1. The CUDA paradigm. On the hardware side (left), it consists of a number of twin multiprocessors, which are fed from CUDA blocks declared by the programmer.

Since CUDA is particularly designed for generic computing, it can leverage special hardware features not visible to more traditional graphics-based GPU programming, such as small cache memories, explicit massive parallelism and lightweight context switch among threads.

3.1   Hardware Platforms

All the latest Nvidia developments on graphics hardware are CUDA-enabled processors: For low-end users and gamers, we have the GeForce series starting from its 8th generation; for high-end users and professionals, the Quadro series; for general-purpose computing, the Tesla boards; finally, for low-power devices, the Tegra family. Overall, it is estimated to exist more than six hundred million CUDA-enabled GPUs at the end of 2015.

Table 2. The evolution of CUDA hardware and programming constraints over the first two generations, Tesla (with two representative models, the inaugural G80 and its sequel, GT200), and Fermi. We take as flagship for each generation what we consider the most popular GPU, together with a representative video memory in graphics cards at that time. All graphics cards share a similar cost, around $400 at launching date.

GPU architecture	G80	GT 200	Fermi
GeForce model	8800 GTX	GTX 280	GTX 480
Year	2006	2008	2010
Millions of transistors	680	1400	3000
Multiprocessors (SMs)	16	30	15
Cores/Multiprocesor	8	8	32
Total number of cores	128	240	480
Cores frequency	1.35 GHz	1.30 GHz	1.40 GHz
Shared memory/SM	16 KB	16 KB	48 KB
L2 cache/GPU	none	none	768 KB
Memory clock	2 × 900 MHz	2 × 1107 MHz	4 × 924 MHz
Bus memory width	384 bits	512 bits	384 bits
Memory bandwidth	86.4 GB/s	141.7 GB/s	177.4 GB/s
CUDA compute capability	1.0, 1.1	1.2, 1.3	2.0, 2.1
Active blocks/SM	8	8	8
Threads/block	512	512	1024
Threads/SM	768	1024	1536
32-bit registers/SM	8192	16384	32768

3.2   Execution Model

CUDA architectures are organized into multiprocessors, each having a number of cores. As technology evolves, future architectures from Nvidia will support the same CUDA executables, but they will be run faster for including more multiprocessors per die, and/or more cores, registers or shared memory per multiprocessor (see Tables 2 and 3).

For example, the Pascal parallel architecture is a SIMD (Single Instruction Multiple Data) processor endowed with 2560 cores in the GeForce GTX 1080 GPU. Cores are organized into 40 multiprocessors, each having a large set of 65536 registers, 64 KB shared memory very close to registers in speed (both 32 bits wide), and constants and texture caches of a few kilobytes. Each multiprocessor can run a variable number of threads, and the local resources are divided among them. In any given cycle, each core in a multiprocessor executes the same instruction on different data based on its `threadId`, and communication between multiprocessors is performed through global memory.

The CUDA programming model guides the programmer to expose fine-grained parallelism as required by massively multi-threaded GPUs, while at the

Table 3. The evolution of CUDA hardware and programming constraints for the last three generations: Kepler, Maxwell and Pascal. Again, we take as flagship of each generation what we consider the most popular GPU up to date, together with a representative video memory.

GPU architecture	Kepler	Maxwell	Pascal
GeForce model	GTX 680	GTX 980	GTX 1080
Year	2012	2014	2016
Millions of transistors	7100	5200	7200
Multiprocessors (SMs)	8	16	40
Cores/Multiprocesor	192	128	64
Total number of cores	1536	2048	2560
Cores frequency	1 GHz	1.12–1.21 GHz	1.60–1.73 GHz
L2 cache/GPU	1536 KB	3072 KB	4096 KB
Shared memory/SM	48 KB	64 KB	64 KB
Memory clock	2×3 GHz	2×3.5 GHz	4×2.5 GHz
Bus memory width	256 bits	256 bits	256 bits
Memory bandwidth	192.2 GB/s	224 GB/s	320 GB/s
CUDA compute capability	3.0	5.0	6.0
Active blocks/SM	16	32	32
Threads/block	1024	1024	1024
Threads/SM	2048	2048	2048
32-bit registers/SM	65536	65536	65536

same time providing scalability across the broad spectrum of physical parallelism available in the range of GPU devices.

Another key design goal of CUDA is to guarantee a smooth learning curve for most of programmers. To do so, it aims to extend a popular sequential programing language like C/C++ with a minimalist set of abstractions for expressing parallelism. This lets the programmer focus on the important issues of parallelism rather than grappling with the mechanics of an unfamiliar and cumbersome language.

3.3   Memory Spaces

The CPU host and the GPU device maintain their own DRAM and address space, referred to as *host memory* and *device memory* (on-board memory). The latter can be of three different types. From inner to outer, we have *constant memory*, *texture memory* and *global memory*. They all can be read from or written to by the host and are persistent through the life of the application. Texture memory is the more versatile one, offering different addressing modes as well as data filtering for some specific data formats. Global memory is the actual on-board video memory, usually exceeding 1 GB. of capacity and embracing GDDR3/GDDR5 technology. Constant memory has regular size of 64 KB and latency time close to a register set. Texture memory is cached to a few kilobytes.

Multiprocessors have on-chip memory that can be of two types: *registers* and *shared memory* (see Fig. 1b). Each processor has its own set of local 32-bit read-write *registers*, whereas a parallel data cache of *shared memory* is shared by all the processors within the same multiprocessor. The local and global memory spaces are implemented as read-write regions of device memory and were not cached until the Fermi architecture was born.

The fifth generation, Maxwell, introduced unified memory, and since then, programmer may choose to allocate memory together for the CPU and GPU spaces. The driver is responsible for migrating pages back and forth between main and video memory according to access patterns to maximize likelihood for a given processor to find its data inside its closer DRAM memory.

Finally, Pascal will provide hardware support for a joint access to unified memory, either from CPU or GPU. This will be possible once those models including 3D memory be introduced in 2017.

3.4   Programming Elements

There are some important elements involved in the conception of a CUDA program which are key for understanding the programming model as well as potential optimizations. Figure 1b summarizes their relations and we describe them below.

- A program is decomposed into **blocks** running in parallel. Assembled by the developer, a block is a group of threads that is mapped to a single multiprocessor, where they can share the so-called shared memory. All the threads in blocks concurrently assigned to a single multiprocessor divide the multiprocessor's resources equally amongst themselves. The data is also divided amongst all of the threads in SIMD fashion explicitly managed by the developer.
- A **warp** is a collection of 32 threads that can physically run concurrently on all of the multiprocessors. The size of the warp is less than the total number of cores due to memory access limitations. The developer has the freedom to determine the number of threads to be executed, but if there are more threads than the warp size, they are time-shared on the actual hardware resources. This can be advantageous, since time-sharing the ALU resources amongst multiple threads can overlap the memory latencies when fetching ALU operands.
- A **kernel** is a code function compiled to the instruction set of the device, downloaded on it and executed by all of its threads. Threads run on different processors of the multiprocessors sharing the same executable and global address space, though they may not follow exactly the same path of execution, since conditional execution of different operations on each multiprocessor can

be achieved based on a unique thread ID. Threads also work independently on different data according to the SIMD model. A kernel is organized into a **grid** as a set of **thread blocks**.

– A **grid** is a collection of all blocks in a single execution, explicitly defined by the application developer, that is assigned to a multiprocessor. The parameters invoking a kernel function call define the sizes and dimensions of the thread blocks in the grid thus generated, and the way hardware groups threads in warps affects performance, so it must be accounted for.

– A **thread block** is a batch of threads executed on a single multiprocessor. They can cooperate together by efficiently sharing data through its shared memory, and synchronize their execution to coordinate memory accesses using the __syncthreads() primitive. Synchronization across thread blocks can only be safely accomplished by terminating a kernel. Each thread block has its own *thread identifier*, which is the number of the thread within a 1D, 2D or 3D array of arbitrary size. The use of multidimensional identifiers helps to simplify memory addressing when processing multidimensional data. Threads placed in different blocks from the same grid cannot communicate, and threads belonging to the same block must all share registers and shared memory on a given multiprocessor. This tradeoff between parallelism and thread resources must be wisely solved by the programmer to maximize execution efficiency on a certain architecture given its limitations. These limitations are listed in the lower rows of Tables 2 and 3 for each hardware generation given different examples of CUDA Compute Capabilities (CCC).

At the highest level, a program is decomposed into kernels mapped to the hardware by a grid composed of blocks of threads scheduled in warps. No inter-block communication or specific schedule-ordering mechanism for blocks or threads is provided, which guarantees each thread block to run on any multiprocessor, even from different devices, at any time.

The number of threads in a thread block is limited to 1024 from the second generation on. Therefore, blocks of equal dimension and size that execute the same kernel can be batched together into a grid of thread blocks. This comes at the expense of reduced thread cooperation, but in contrast, this model allows thread blocks of the same kernel grid to run on any multiprocessor, even from different devices, at any time. Again, each block is identified by its *block identifier*, which is the number of the block within a one- or two-dimensional array of arbitrary size for the sake of a simpler addressing to memory.

Kernel threads are extremely lightweight, i.e. creation overhead is negligible and context switching between threads and/or kernels is essentially free.

Each source file containing these extensions must be compiled with the CUDA nvcc compiler [9]. Besides, CUDA comes with a runtime library, split into a host component, a device component and a common component, that supports built-in vector data types and texture types, and provides a number of mathematical functions, type conversion and casting functions, thread synchronization functions, and device and memory management functions.

Table 4. The incoming memory HBM for GPUs compared to existing video memory (GDDR5) and typical main memory on CPUs (DDR3).

Memory technology	DDR3	GDDR5	HBM1	HBM2
Adopted by	Intel CPU motherboards	Existing GPU boards	AMD GPUs in 2015/16	Nvidia GPUs in 2017
Pins for data	8/chip	32/chip	2 × 128/layer	2 × 128/layer
Prefetching	8/pin	8/pin	2/pin	2/pin
Access granularity	8 bytes/chip	32 bytes/chip	64 bytes/layer	64 bytes/layer
Bandwidth	2 GB/s/chip (2 Gbps/pin)	28 GB/s/chip (7 Gbps/pin)	32 GB/s/layer (1 Gbps/pin)	64 GB/s /layer (2 Gbps/pin)
Chips or layers	8 chips/module	12 chips/card	4 layers/cube	4, 8 layers/cube
Cubes per GPU	does not apply	does not apply	4	4
Bandwidth example	Broadwell CPU 2 GB/s x 8 chips x 4 channels = 64 GB/s	Maxwell Titan X 28 GB/s x 12 chips = 336 GB/s	AMD Fiji GPU 32 GB/s x 4 layers x 4 cubes = 512 GB/s	Pascal 64 GB/s x 4, 8 layers x 4 cubes = 1, 2 TB/s

Finally the CUDA environment also includes a number of higher-level mathematical libraries in constant evolution. Good examples are cuDDN for deep neural networks, cuBLAS and MAGMA for linear algebra cuSPARSE for handling sparse matrices and cuFFT for dealing with Fast Fourier Transforms [10].

4   A Look to the Future

The GPU is a platform in constant improvement, with a new generation coming every couple of years. Given the evolution over the past decade and taking a look into future generations we can identify three basic trends:

– **2007–2013. Raw processing power.** Nvidia first focused on throughput and GFLOPS by developing GPUs with an increasing number of cores, and programmers enjoyed a swift transition phase from 128 to 3072 cores during this short period of time. The pace was relaxed when manufacturing process in Nvidia products, led by TSMC, stabilized in 28 nm transistors during four consecutive years. The number of computational units will continue to grow in the future, possibly expanding the warp size to 64 for vector processing to be more rewarded. But none of these features represents a challenge for the CUDA programming model, where scalability is guaranteed. Developers adopting fine-grained parallelism when launching CUDA kernels will enjoy this higher number of cores without additional effort.
– **2014–2016. Low power.** GPUs were famous in the past for its extraordinary power consumption, easily exceeding 200 W. But these days they have conquered the Green500 list, the official ranking for the most power efficient supercomputers on earth. Nvidia learnt to design low power GPUs, basically keeping frequencies low and minimizing energy spent on communications via optimal wire routing and functional units layout. Multiprocessors in Maxwell are the best example of a well organized architecture where you even sacrifice

throughput (from 192 cores in Kepler down to 128) to deploy extraordinary ratios of GFLOPS/watt. On the programming side, the abolition of speculative techniques also favoured the power budget, a trend that we expect to continue in the future. Smaller 16 nm FinFET transistors and the new memory hierarchy will also help to optimize energy without additional programming effort.

- **2017–2020. Memory enhancements.** After more than 30 years fighting against the memory wall with caches, a new memory hierarchy rises in the horizon with the advent of 3D memory, also called Stacked DRAM or memory cubes. This technology provides data bandwidth over 1 TB/s. at lower latencies, 2.5x higher sizes and four times more energy efficient infrastructure. Nvidia has already announced that Pascal models for 2017 will be equipped with HBM2 (High Bandwidth Memory, gen. 2) developed by Samsung. Table 4 summarizes major HBM features compared to typical main memory for CPUs (DDR3) and existing video memory for GPUs (GDDR5, the so-called global memory in CUDA).

5   Concluding Remarks

We have described the evolution of the CUDA programming model and hardware architecture to enable GPUs as general-purpose processors. This emerging platform provides high performance, great scalability and low cost, and may be multiplied on a cluster of GPUs to even enhance parallelism in high performance computing. On a more modest alternative, we may think of a CPU-GPU hybrid system where an application can be decomposed into two parts to take advantage of the benefits of a bi-processor platform.

The GPU will continue to adapt to the usage patterns of both graphics and general-purpose programmers, with a focus on GFLOPS and memory access to become a solid alternative for high performance computing and low power devices. On the programming side, CUDA must evolve to include heterogeneous many-core systems including both CPUs and GPUs in a more integrated manner, inline with what we have recently seen with the advent of unified memory.

Acknowledgment. We thank Nvidia for hardware donation and travelling support under CUDA Teaching Center 2011–2016, CUDA Research Center 2012–2016 and CUDA Fellow 2012–2016 Awards.

References

1. General-Purpose Computation on Graphics Hardware. http://www.gpgpu.org
2. The Top 500 Supercomputers List. http://www.top500.org
3. Intel. Intel Delivers New Architecture for Discovery with Intel XeonPhi Coprocessors. https://newsroom.intel.com/news-releases/intel-delivers-newarchitecture-for-discovery-with-intel-xeon-phi-coprocessors

4. Jeffers, J., Reinders, J.: Intel Xeon Phi Coprocessor High-Performance Programming. Morgan-Kaufmann, San Francisco (2013)
5. The Hybrid Memory Cube Consortium Homepage. www.hybridmemorycube.org
6. Fernando, R., Kilgard, M.J.: The Cg Tutorial. The Definitive Guide to Programmable Real-Time Graphics. Addison-Wesley Professional, Boston (2005)
7. CUDA Zone. https://developer.nvidia.com/cuda-zone
8. The CUDA C Programming Guide. http://docs.nvidia.com/cuda/cuda-c-programmingguide
9. CUDA Toolkit for Nvidia developer. https://developer.nvidia.com/cuda-toolkit
10. GPU-Accelerated Libraries. https://developer.nvidia.com/gpu-acceleratedlibraries

Author Index